Classic Aircraft

Fighters

Classic Aircraft
Fighters
Bill Gunston

Grosset & Dunlap
A Filmways Company
Publishers·New York
in association with The Hamlyn Publishing Group, Ltd.

Contents

Front endpapers: *Ah, Spitfires! Well, they were, but now they are not. These, from the batch NX879 to PA129, are unique. Built as Spitfire VBs, they were rebuilt by Air Service Training Ltd as Seafire IB naval fighters, and renumbered. This photograph was passed for publication on 3 September 1943, fourth anniversary of the start of the Second World War.*

Opposite: *The F–86D 'Sabre Dogship' was the world's first all-weather, radar-equipped interceptor to be handled by one man. He was assisted by a formidable mass of electronics, which gave terrible trouble and ran about nine months later than production of airframes. Just ahead of the retracted mainwheels can be seen the large rectangular box containing the 24 Mighty Mouse missiles.*

Title pages: *Taken in late 1940, this photograph shows three Focke-Wulf Fw 190A–0 pre-production machines, probably the first time three had run their engines simultaneously. That on the left is one of the original small-wing (16 square metre) aircraft, with no outer-wing guns and less-raked landing gear.*

Back endpapers: *A bronzed ground crewman checks over Cdr Mitchell's cockpit during a spell at a shore NAS (Naval Air Station) for fighter squadron VF–96, one of the most famous US Navy units. This F–4J Phantom II was one of the new Navy ace MiG-killers in the South-East Asia theatre.*

Acknowledgments

The publishers are grateful to the following individuals and organisations for providing the illustrations in this book: Michael O'Leary, John Batchelor Ltd, Aeroplane Monthly, Chaz Bowyer, Philip Jarrett, Camera Press, Novosty Press Agency (A.P.N.), Chris Ellis, Flight International, Michael Turner, Pilot Press Ltd, Phoebus Publishing Co., and Anglia Aeropics. The cutaway drawing on page 26 is from the jacket of *Fighters*, Macdonald and Janes.

Copyright © 1978 by the Hamlyn Publishing Group Limited
London · New York · Sydney · Toronto
This Edition published 1978 by Grosset & Dunlap, Inc.
Library of Congress Catalog Card Number: 78-54627
ISBN: 0-448-16172-9

Published simultaneously in Canada

Printed and bound in Great Britain by Hazell, Watson & Viney Limited, Aylesbury, Buckinghamshire
Filmset by Keyspools Limited, Golborne, Lancashire.

Introduction

Picking the twenty-one greatest fighters is, of course, an impossible task. Some people would judge greatness solely on the numbers of a type built or of enemy aircraft downed by them, or on the number of famous aces who proclaimed their particular machine to be the greatest. I would give at least some weight to aircraft that made major advances in technology, doing things that previously were impossible or at least greatly in advance of the capability of earlier designs. In the case of this book the choice was slightly influenced by the availability of cutaway drawings, which it was desired to include.

While on the subject of which aircraft types to choose, probably most fighter enthusiasts would wish to pick at least one type that was not really significant or important but had, nevertheless, some indefinable appeal. In my case the odd-man-out is the Boeing P–26, the 'Peashooter'. Not many were built, it was not really an outstanding design (unlike almost all the other aircraft from that company) and, except in a few brief and rather unsuccessful moments over the Philippines in December 1941, never saw action. Yet it is one of the most famous of fighters – so famous one has to drop the British terminology of fighter and revert to the exciting old American term of 'pursuit', which was just as accurate in describing the role of the P–26. Why was the P–26 so famous? I have not got the faintest idea, except that these brightly-coloured snarling bundles of wire and aluminium were capable of

bringing out our latent youthful enthusiasm.

Heaven knows, the other types in this book were deadly serious. Upon them depended, not only the survival of their individual pilots, but to an increasing degree the survival of nations. This is seen most clearly in the Battle of Britain, but it was also true over the Russian front in 1941–45, in the invasions of German airspace in the Second World War by the courageous Americans, and more recently in a distressing number of 'limited' wars around the world, some of which have simmered for years and involved sophisticated modern aircraft. Contrary to the wording of a British government document in 1957, today's nations have either to convince themselves that they are of absolutely no economic, political or geographic importance whatsoever or they need manned fighters. More than 100 air forces today have fighters. Some have them for show; most use them as part of a credible defence system.

Designing a good fighter is one of the most difficult things men can attempt. In 1943, one of the top Soviet designers, Yakovlev, commented on how foolish it was to produce big warplanes as was being done increasingly; the victory – he said – went always to small, lightweight, nimble dogfighters like his Yaks, and the enemy Fw 190. Today the wheel, if there ever was one, has turned full circle. The 'light' fighters in the 1950s may have been discredited and ignored, but today's air forces are getting excited about fighters which, though heavy monsters by comparison with those of the Second World War, are still judged to be small and light compared with other modern tactical machines. To some degree this is making a virtue out of necessity; inflation is simply pricing the big ones out of practical consideration for most countries. But maybe one should think again. In 1940 the Americans carefully studied the fighting in Europe, tore up their plans for 1200 hp fighters, and set about building vast armadas of the most powerful fighters the world had seen – most of them with 2000–2500 horsepower Double Wasp engines, and some of them, such as the P–61 Black Widow and F7F Tigercat, with two! Nobody has publicly suggested this policy was mistaken, and the record shows a massive weight of evidence in favour of the big, long-range, heavily armed juggernauts. Of course, today's interceptors, with vast radars and 100-mile-range missiles, can be almost any size they like provided the money to make them is available. The problem comes in designing a fighter for close combat.

As I write this, there are emerging tantalizingly sparse details of a new Soviet fighter. All we know is that it is very good indeed. The Soviet designers have the great advantage that, secure in the knowledge that nobody will stand up and demand a cut in the defence budget, they can plan on the basis of future possibilities and future politico-military alliances around the world. The West can do little except try to counter each new Soviet weapon. Thus, the F–15 was designed to answer the Foxbat, and though in this case they turned out to be as alike as chalk and cheese, the point is that they differed by almost ten years in their timing. Politicians and even generals in the West are getting into the habit of regarding projected fighters as answers to the latest Soviet aircraft when the latter has reached the stage of appearing in the popular press. This is the recipe for disaster. Think what would have happened in 1939 if, seeing pictures of the Bf 109 in the papers, Britain had said it would build the Spitfire! No fighter can possibly hope for success unless it appears in service earlier than basically similar machines of potential enemies.

With each year, the production of a fighter becomes a bigger, longer-term programme. Some of the most famous fighters in history lasted as an effective force only for weeks, whereas today a successful type is almost assured of twenty years if not thirty before being replaced. Today's fighters are built almost like a battleship, and they need to be to survive thirty years of blasting off desert or arctic strips, flying through hailstorms at over Mach 1, and making arrested landings in small areas. When we visit collections of veteran planes and their replicas – unbelievably flimsy by contrast – and imagine them as front line aircraft in the First World War, we can see the amazing distance that fighter design has travelled in less than a human lifetime.

Fokker E-Types

One of the disappointments of aviation literature is that one of the greatest pioneer planemakers, Anthony Fokker, should have written an autobiography totally discredited as an historical document. The chapter entitled 'I invent the synchronized machine gun' has been especially criticised, because Fokker did no such thing. Indeed one of the true inventors was a Swiss-German, Franz Schneider, of the LVG aircraft company – but as usual a prophet is without honour in his own country, and Schneider was ignored. So were others who gave practical thought to the idea, such as Raymond Saulnier, of the French Morane-Saulnier company, and the Edwards Brothers in England, who submitted a detailed report on the subject to the War Office six months before the start of the First World War and merely received a polite acknowledgement. In Russia Lt Poplavko did manage to get his gear tested on the Sikorsky S–16, but got no further; on a lieutenant's pay he could never have bribed the Czarist officials effectively enough to progress further.

However, before condemning the officials in all these countries it is worth remembering that until well into the Second World War the accepted view of those in authority was that there was unlikely to be any role for flying machines in warfare, except possibly for reconnaissance. This belief never progressed to the apparently obvious conclusion, which was that if aerial reconnaissance was useful, both sides would fly reconnaissance aircraft, and inevitably try to prevent each other from accomplishing their mission. Why not use other specially equipped aircraft for this? In passing, it should be said that combat aircraft had in fact been in existence since 1911, in both reconnaissance and bombing roles, and used in actual warfare in Tripolitania and the Balkans.

Nobody knew, of course, how best an aviator could interfere with a hostile machine, far less how he could destroy it. In August 1910 a US Army officer, Lt Jake Fickel of the 29th Infantry, had persuaded pilot Glenn Curtiss to let him try pot-shots with a rifle at a ground target, much to

Curtiss's surprise because most passengers needed both hands to hold on with. A year after that machine guns had been mounted on aeroplanes, a Hotchkiss in France and a Benet-Mercier (basically the same gun) in the USA, but not with any really serious intent. In 1912 Maj Robert Brooke-Popham, CO of No 3 Squadron, RFC, tried firing a Lee-Enfield rifle from an aircraft at kites, but this was dangerous to the interested fellow-officers standing below on Salisbury Plain. A year later official tests were held in Britain to see which was the best machine gun for aircraft, and the new American/Belgian Lewis was selected; but no guns were bought.

Some people with a little foresight thought that more could be done, and a few even built what today we would call fighters. Geoffrey de Havilland designed the F.E.1 at the Royal Aircraft Factory at Farnborough, and from this prototype of 1910 derived the extremely important F.E.2 series of two-seat pusher fighters and the somewhat similar Airco D.H.1. Professor Challenger at Vickers designed a 'Destroyer', exhibited at Olympia in 1913, which matured as the F.B.5 Gunbus, another tandem-seat pusher with a machine gun in the front cockpit. De Havilland then built the single-seat D.H.2 with a Lewis gun aimed by the pilot. Not unnaturally the pilot found it difficult to hold the control column, throttle lever, depress the gun trigger

8

An early E.I, seen taking off. Fuselage attitude is almost level, and with both pilot and gun the climb-rate was modest. The dark object looking like a large rear-view mirror is a headrest (see photo p. 11).

and change the magazines all at once. Soon it was discovered that if the gun was bolted to the aircraft it could be aimed by aiming the whole aircraft at the enemy and some front-engined machines even had machine guns fixed on outriggers so that the bullets would clear the tips of their tractor propellers.

Two manufacturers who had never gone in for pushers were Morane-Saulnier in France and Fokker in Germany. The young Dutchman, obviously influenced by Morane-Saulnier and other French designers, concentrated on aerobatic monoplanes. After August 1914 he manufactured single-seaters for the German Army and Navy, though he could not keep pace with demand. Designated M.5, they reached 80 mph on an 80 hp Oberursel (Gnome-type) rotary engine, though they could not carry a gun other than the pilot's 'broomhandle' Mauser pistol. At the end of March 1915 Fokker was intrigued to learn of a Frenchman, Roland Garros, flying a Morane Type L, who could shoot down Germans with a machine gun firing ahead, in

between the revolving propeller blades. Five fell before his gun in the first half of April; then the Frenchman was forced to land in German territory and was captured before he could burn his aircraft.

Even if he had burned it, the secret would not have been difficult to discover in the remains. The Morane-Saulnier's famous pilot from the pre-war years had merely fixed steel deflecting wedges behind the propeller blades. Fokker, who was instantly summoned to Berlin whence the Morane had been taken, thought this crude. So it was, but it was still the result of months of experiments, and exhaustive tests at the Chauvière propeller factory. Saulnier and Garros had only reluctantly adopted the deflectors because the French officials had for three years shown no interest in progressing with Saulnier's properly-designed interrupter gear.

Before he left Berlin on a Tuesday young Fokker was given a Parabellum '08 ('Spandau') machine gun, and 100-round clips of ammunition. He immediately took the train back to his

Possibly the best of the Eindecker replicas at present flying, the Appleby E.III 'Nr 417/15' is based in the United States. It has certainly logged more flight time than most of the real E.IIIs.

A remarkable and authentic air-to-air photograph of the first pilot to destroy an enemy aircraft with an Eindecker – Leutnant Kurt Wintgens – on patrol in his E.I. In those days cameras were clumsy, and film-speed abysmal.

factory at Schwerin, carrying the gun and ammunition openly! By the Friday he was back in Berlin, but instead of copying the French deflectors he had designed, built and tested a proper interrupter gear. But the conception and fabrication was that of his engineers, and the principles were not original, though perhaps Fokker did not realise this at the time. His gear itself was primitive, a cam being added behind the rotating crankcase to actuate a push-rod. This operated the gun trigger mechanism at the appropriate time when the propeller blades were out of the line of fire. Incidentally, contrary to popular belief, 1915 machine guns did not fire once for every revolution of the propeller. In Fokker's case he timed the gun to fire once while the engine and propeller made two revolutions; thus, between each pair of successive bullets, the propeller blades passed through the line of fire four times. At first the gun had insisted on firing two rounds each time the cam and push-rod operated. It took 24 hours of non-stop work to make it fire only one round. Fokker had fixed a plywood disc to the propeller to see, at different engine speeds, where the bullets were going, and eventually managed to get them all in a group, roughly mid-way between the blades.

The air staff in Berlin were half incredulous and half delighted at the results of Fokker's work. The designer had fixed one of his short-span M.5K monoplanes to his 80 hp Peugeot car and towed it to the military field at Staaken for his demonstration. The resulting air-to-ground firing demonstration was, to put it mildly, a sensation, and the almost unbelievable decision by the sober general staff officers was that their young Flying Dutchman had to go to the Western Front and shoot down an Allied flyer. Near Verdun, Fokker demonstrated his gun again before the Crown Prince, saying 'It's like a boy throwing stones between the blades of a Dutch windmill'.

Fokker did go to the front, dressed as a German leutnant, but just as he was about to pump lead into a lumbering Allied Farman he felt, he says, a feeling of revulsion. It was too one-sided, and as a Dutchman, not his war, anyway. So the job of trying out the little Eindecker (monoplane) was assigned to a true leutnant, Oswald Boelcke. The rest is history. Boelcke brought down an enemy on his third mission. Fokker became the centre of German military aviation, with priority in getting his armament into large-scale production. Within a week

A real E.III, Nr 422/15, with single Parabellum 08 gun.
It is obviously at a front-line base.

An exceptionally clear photograph of an early E.I, one of only a handful built. This machine had the braced headrest to help the pilot sight his gun accurately (so did that of Wintgens, page 9, possibly the same machine).

another leutnant, Max Immelmann, had begun to score. Soon their victories had become news, and a new word had been coined: an 'ace'. At first an ace was a pilot who had shot down eight of the enemy, but as air fighting progressed the number rose to 16. By the end of the Second World War, the Luftwaffe was not especially impressed by a pilot who was still only in double figures.

Boelcke and Immelmann must be numbered among the very greatest aces. Admittedly their opposition was seldom dangerous, and with the Fokker E-series (E for Eindecker) they enjoyed an advantage of superior equipment which few fighter pilots would ever have again, but even so they had to work out from scratch how to plan a combat, how to attack, how to shoot with correct deflection, and what to do to counter each desperate attempt by the enemy to escape. The little Fokker monoplane was the aircraft in which all this happened, but it was in no sense a great fighter design.

The first production E.I fighters were delivered in June 1915, quickly followed by the much snappier E.II with a 100 hp Oberursel engine and with smaller wings which were not a success. The most important model was the E.III, of which about 350 were built, which had wings of even greater span than the E.I.

Though still basically a primitive little sporting machine, with lateral control by wing-warping, the E.III was absolutely deadly to the enemy. Its manoeuvrability was excellent, it could be aimed with precision, and a single machine gun was quite enough in mid-1915. A few pilots, following what seemed to be logical reasoning, fitted two guns, but the loss in aircraft performance outweighed the gain in firepower. Immelmann even gained a few victories in a remarkable E.IV, the last of the Eindeckers and which had a 160 hp two-row Oberursel, and to which he fitted three guns. But the majority had one Spandau, and the ability to nip in, point it accurately at the enemy pilot, and break away, was enough to give the Imperial German Military Aviation Service command of the air – the first time this phrase had had a real meaning. Newspapers reported on 'The Fokker Scourge' and described the stream of replacement pilots for the decimated RFC squadrons as 'Fokker fodder'. It was true. Flying the stable B.E.2cs they simply could not manoeuvre out of the line of fire, and the loss rate at last jolted the myopic Staff into the understanding that air warfare was not only possible but had already arrived.

Nieuport XVII

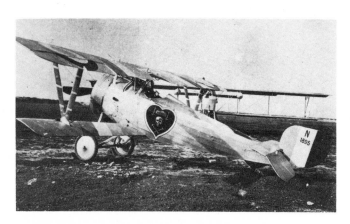

N1894, the Nieuport XVII (17) flown by Lt Charles Nungesser, No 3 French ace with 45 victories. Note his lucky symbols of a skull and crossbones, candles and coffin.

B1566 was a Nieuport 17 flown by the officer with it, Capt W. A. 'Billy' Bishop, VC, DSO, MC, later Air Marshal Sir William Bishop, top-scoring Canadian.

In 1911 a civilian Nieuport exceeded 100 mph, and, with the rival Deperdussin, the *marque* was universally accepted by aviators as the fastest in the sky. All these French racers were monoplanes, of outstandingly robust construction, and with so many fine examples around it is hard to comprehend the official ban on monoplanes imposed by the British government in 1912 – a ban which endured through the First World War. In fact, it faded so slowly that as late as 1934 the directors of Vickers Ltd argued that they would have no chance of getting anywhere officially if they built a monoplane, as was proposed by one of their engineers, a certain Barnes Wallis.

However, Nieuport happened by a quirk of fate to switch to biplanes in 1914. Their new designer, Gustave Delage, who joined the company in January 1914, noticed that the rules for the 1914 Gordon-Bennett air race which they wanted to enter stipulated the ability to fly extremely slowly. This was difficult on monoplanes, and Delage thought up a biplane with a novel feature. He made the lower wing, which was small, with variable incidence. It was a kind of groping search for extra lift combined with drag that today we get with slots and flaps.

To achieve what was wanted, the Nieuport X had a single spar in the lower wing, fastened to pivots on the bottom fuselage longerons. The

interplane struts took the form of a V, picking up on the same spar. Structure was entirely of wood, with fabric covering. The usual engine was an 80 hp Le Rhône or Anzani, and the speed nudged 90 mph. But on 4 August the Second World War began, and the race for which it was designed was cancelled. What was needed were aircraft for the Front, and the neat little Nieuport swiftly became a two-seat scout. Then, in 1915, many were converted to single-seat fighting scouts, with the front controls removed and front cockpit covered with fabric. A Lewis gun fired over the upper wing, aimed by the pilot to miss the propeller. Large numbers of several early Nieuport designs served with many of the Allies, and firmly established the company's name in the very front rank of air warfare.

Delage's next design, the XI, was possibly the smallest and lightest true combat aircraft in history. Often called the Bébé, it was even more a sesquiplane than the X, because the lower plane had only half the area of the upper so that, some have suggested, both the pro-monoplane and pro-biplane factions were satisfied. Whatever the reasoning, the layout resulted in an excellent view for the pilot and marvellous manoeuvrability. A Lewis was carried on the upper wing and there was petrol for 2½ hours. Though the engine was still only of 80 hp, the Bébé was much faster than the Fokker monoplanes, and the rate of

A Nieuport XI 'Bébé' armed with eight Le Prieur rockets for destroying kite balloons (one rocket has lost its head).

climb was markedly superior. It was mainly on these tiny fighting scouts that the outstanding pilots of the French Aviation Militaire began to even the score with the dreaded Eindecker, partly with the help of Capitaine Tricornot de Rose, who laid down the basis for aerial fighting and proved each theory in actual combat.

In 1916 the Nie. XVI (16) entered service with almost the same airframe as the Bébé but powered by the 120 hp Le Rhône 9JB, in a more rounded cowling. This could easily exceed 100 mph, and it also offered the pilot a choice of armament: the high-mounted Lewis gun, a synchronized Vickers, or eight Le Prieur rockets on the V-struts and used for destroying Hun observation balloons. It was more comfortable to fly, because it introduced a padded headrest for the pilot. Charles Guynemer, who went on to become the French No 2 ace with 54 confirmed victories, rose to eminence with a XVI, and this aircraft was the first to bear the famous name *Le Vieux Charles*.

But the best of the Nieuports was the XVII (17). This was almost the same as a Bébé XI, but the wings were larger; whereas the baby was often called the '13' (13 square metres) the XVII was the '15', which shows how confusing numbers can be. Most early 17s in mid-1916 had a Lewis gun over the upper wing, but before long the synchronized Vickers was almost standard.

The Allies were slow to adopt the kind of armament that the Eindecker had shown to be superior – mainly, it appears, because of indecision. The French had the Alkan interrupter mechanism, the Royal Naval Air Service the Scarff-Dibovski and the Royal Flying Corps a scheme developed by Vickers for their own gun, but the excellent Foster mount for a Lewis on the upper wing was a contributory factor in delaying the acceptance of the others. This mount enabled the gun to be fired at a shallow angle with accurate sighting, though the pilot had to pull the trigger almost at arm's length, and then to pull the whole gun down on curved tracks so that the ammunition drum could be changed.

Late in 1916, a Romanian mining engineer, Georges Constantinesco, and Major Colley of the Royal Artillery, devised the CC Gear which swept away all rival schemes used in most air forces and remained standard in the RAF until well into the Second World War. It worked hydraulically, the impulses being transmitted along oil pipes to the gun trigger motor, and thus could quickly be adapted to any type of engine, gun or aircraft. However, most Nie. 17s used the Vickers gear.

The trim Nieuport was surely everyone's idea of what a First World War fighting scout should be like. It was so small and simple that the pilot almost put it on, rather than climbed aboard, and his own weight made a significant difference to flight performance. With a light pilot it 'climbed like a witch' according to Commander Samson of the RNAS. Manoeuvrability was possibly better than that of any other scout of the day, though of course there are no actual data to go by because such comparisons were not usually measured in those days, or if they were the paperwork is lost. However, surely the proof of the matter lies in the fact that the leading Allied aces tended to choose a Nieuport when they could, almost without question, have had any mount they wished.

A mixture of Nieuport scouts of No 1 Sqn, RFC, at Bailleul, on 27 December 1917. Aircraft H is a 27, and M a 24bis. The censor obliterated the serial numbers.

Nungesser, Guynemer, De Rose, Boyeau, Canada's 'Billy' Bishop and Britain's Albert Ball all selected the XVII.

In the great air battles over the grim Somme offensive in the late summer of 1916, Allied pilots, mainly flying the Nieuport, finally nailed the Fokker scourge and established for the first time a fair measure of supremacy over the enemy. Over this one small sector of the Front the Germans lost over 50 aircraft in the first eight weeks of the battle. Seven were Roland scouts shot down by Ball, who liked to formate directly below and fire up at almost 90° with his Lewis gun on its Foster mount. By late September he had 30 confirmed and 19 possible victories. Guynemer bagged nine in the first two weeks, and scored 23 by November 1916. The Nie. 17 '15' served with every Allied air force.

Important though it was, the success of the Nieuport fighters was short-lived. Successful action breeds reaction and this is especially the case with weapons in wartime. The German commanders reacted swiftly to their sudden loss of command in the sky during the Somme

campaign. Part of their trouble seemed to be their organization, or lack of it, so Boelcke was recalled from the Russian Front, where he was giving morale-boosting talks, to reorganise the Imperial fighter squadrons or Jagdstaffeln, a name usually shortened to Jastas. Previously German aircraft had been loosely assigned to various kinds of field unit which often varied greatly in strength and equipment. Boelcke, who had become the most influential pilot in the world and spokesman for all German fighter tacticians, argued that each Jasta should have only one type of aircraft,

Seen alongside a D.H.4 at Serny on 17 February 1918, this Nie.27 appears to be having its engine pulled through prior to starting up to serve as escort.

should train as a unit, and even learn to fight in close partnership with other Jastas on the same or neighbouring sectors of the Front. Previously, Allied airmen had fallen before the guns of Eindeckers that worked in pairs. The formations or Escadrilles of Nieuports had made the pendulum swing back against the Germans, and the lesson was applied quickly. Before long one of the pilots brought back from the Russian front by Boelcke, a young nobleman, Manfred Freiherr von Richthofen, was to take the strategy and tactics of aerial fighting to undreamed-of heights with one of the most famous military units since The Light Brigade.

Whereas the Eindeckers had vanquished their opponents rather like a farmer shooting rabbits, the emergence of the Nieuports, backed up by a few lesser 'fighters' such as the Fee (F.E.2b), D.H.2 and Gunbus, ensured that from mid-1916 onwards the combat would not be entirely one-sided. Now Germany needed new aircraft to carry out Boelcke's theories. Fokker strove to improve the Eindecker, but to little avail. More power and more guns could not reasonably be accommodated, and when the bright young Dutchman started afresh, designing the biplanes Boelcke had suggested, he seemed to lose his magic touch and produced indifferent aircraft that could not hold their own with the Nieuport. In those days there were not many real experts on aircraft design, and fewer still in positions of authority. Should fighters be monoplanes or biplanes? How could Germany beat the nimble, fast-climbing Nieuports? The uninspired answer that emerged was to try to copy it.

During the summer of 1916 several German designers had produced fighting scouts of formidable potential, the best being the Albatros D.I designed by Robert Thelen which, though bigger, heavier and slightly more ponderous than the Eindeckers and Nieuports, carried two synchronized guns and had superior all-round performance. In general, it is indisputable that good aircraft emerge from good original design and not from slavish copying of features in other good designs. Yet in 1916 this was not understood. The Nieuports had a big upper wing and a small single-spar lower wing, and they could turn on the proverbial sixpence. So Thelen and the other German designers were told to adopt the same idea. One of the results was Thelen's Albatros D.III, which reached the Front at the beginning of 1917. It appeared to be better than the D.I and D.II with their equal-size wings, and became one of the greatest fighters of the Second

World War and a major cause of the pendulum swinging back in favour of Germany. Yet this was not because of any inherent superiority of the sesquiplane configuration. Indeed, even the Nieuports were good little fighters that happened to be sesquiplanes and not, as the Idflieg staff officers supposed, good because they were sesquiplanes. When Thelen copied the arrangement on his excellent D.III he left out the feature that had been Delage's reason for the single-spar lower wing in the first place: variable incidence. The lower planes of the Albatros were fixed, and could not pivot. Thelen, bothered by thought of possible weakness in a single spar, added a rear spar, but did not join it to the fuselage!

However, his thinking was basically right because the single-spar lower plane proved to be the Achilles heel of the Albatros scouts. By 1917, dogfighting was a life-and-death matter in which, if he was to survive, a pilot had to fly his steed round the sky with firm force, and wring out every last iota of manoeuvrability. When this was done with the D.III the poor torsional rigidity of the lower wing sometimes caused the whole plane to collapse, with catastrophic results. Thelen tried to cure this by adding small diagonal bracing struts between the V interplane struts and the lower leading edge. It is, incidentally, true to say that weakness of the single-spar lower wings was also the only real fault in the Nieuports.

One that didn't make it: Nie.XVII bis N3204, flown by Lt F. P. Reeves of 6(N) Sqn RFC, was shot down on 6 June 1917 by Vzfw Riesinger of Jasta 12.

Spad VII and XIII

In very general terms, the Nieuports were the greatest French fighters of the first half of the First World War and the Spads were the greatest of the second half. But the Spad company produced many fighters over a long period, and the last saw active service with the Armée de l'Air up to the Second World War. Founded in 1910, the company's name derived from Société des Productions Armand Deperdussin, but in 1915 it changed it to Société Anonyme Pour l'Aviation et ses Dérivés, keeping the same initials. In 1915 the name had acquired little fame. Its chief product in that year was a handful of Spad A2 fighters which, along with a few prototypes by others, had a layout that can truly be called unique. The A2 was a tractor biplane with an observer/gunner's nacelle added immediately in front of the propeller. The nacelle pivoted on the landing gear and could be hinged forward for access to the 110 hp Le Rhône 9J. When in position it was

latched by steel tubes to the upper wing and to a ball race running on a shaft at the front of the propeller. Anything more certain to be unpopular with either member of the crew would be hard to find, but it was one designer's attempt to get over the lack of a gun interrupter gear.

The only pilots and observers who used the A2 in quantity were Russians as with the Czar's forces anything was better than nothing, but the A2 and its variations were unacceptable to the French, who only had a total of 42 and used them for less than three months. Technical director of SPAD, Louis Bécherau, knew he had to do better, and the wisest decision he made was one that may not have been obvious in 1915, though today we can see it clearly: the rotary engine used in the Spad was obsolescent. So he turned to the Hispano-Suiza company, where the Swiss, Marc Birkigt, had just created two classic innovations that were to go on developing for the next half-

A Spad VII of the Royal Flying Corps, almost certainly built in Britain by the Air Navigation Co (British Blériot and Spad Co) of Addlestone.
Others were built by Mann, Egerton for the RNAS.

A Spad XIII, apparently of the second production series with the supercharged 8 Be engine and less-rounded wing tips.

century, a 20 mm cannon and a water-cooled vee-type engine. The engine had eight cylinders, in two cast-aluminium blocks, and though Birkigt promised 150 hp there was every hope of realizing considerably more with further development. This seemed just what Bécherau wanted, and in November 1915 he completed the prototype Spad V, from which stemmed the VII that flew in April 1916.

Compared with a typical Nieuport, the Spad VII was bigger and tougher and, instead of being a featherlight mount, behaved as a veritable battleship. Of course, to modern eyes it still seems small and flimsy, but to the Aviation Militaire pilots the contrast was tremendous. At first the new Spad was criticised for being less manoeuvrable than the little Nieuports, but the French Staff had taken a fancy to Bécherau's design and production swelled each week until, by 1917, eight factories were building it at a rate faster than any other aircraft in the world. And the choice was right. In a sky filled with

lumbering pushers, fighters with inadequate armament and hordes of vulnerable 'Fokker Fodder', the Spad VII was the toughest weapon imaginable. It weighed about 50 per cent more than most small single-seat scouts, but it had a performance that seemed incredible. The prototype had reached 122 mph, and climbed to 3000 m (9843 ft) in 15 minutes and to twice this height in an hour. The Nieuport could not even reach 6000 m.

Deliveries of the Spad VII began in September 1916. The usual armament was a single Vickers, offset to the right, with a Hispano (Birkigt) synchronization gear. On deeper acquaintance the former Bébé pilots clearly saw the merit of the new fighter, though they behaved as countless fighter pilots have done ever since : they tended to love the devil they knew. The whole history of fighters has been linked with the story of pilots getting used to a machine or an idea and trying to cling to it after it had been outmoded. The fact their lives depended on their aircraft and guns

John Batchelor's drawing of a Fokker E.III is both technically and aesthetically satisfying (it shows the twin-gun armament usually judged not worth while, because of loss of flight performance).

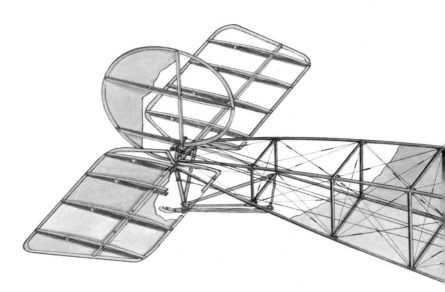

N3363G shows only faintly, as intended, on this near-perfect reproduction Fokker E.III, with pseudo Idflieg number '417/15', the last two digits being the supposed year of contract date. Purists insist that the term 'replica' be reserved for aircraft built by the original manufacturer.

SPECIFICATIONS

Types E.I, E.II, E.III and E.IV
Engine: E.I, one 80 hp Oberursel U.O. seven-cylinder rotary. E.II and E.III, 100 hp Oberursel U.I; E.IV, 160 hp Oberursel 14-cylinder two-row rotary.
Dimensions: span (E.I) 28 ft (8·53 m); (E.II) 26 ft 2¾ in (8·00 m); (E.III) 31 ft 2¾ in (9·52 m); length (E.I) 22 ft 2 in (6·75 m); (E.II) 23 ft 2 in (7·1 m); (E.III) 23 ft 11½ in (7·3 m); height (E.I) 9 ft 6 in (3·12 m); (E.II) 7 ft 10 in (2·6 m); (EIII) 9 ft 1¾ in (2·79 m).
Weights: empty (all types), about 1 100 lb (500 kg); loaded (E.I) 1 239 lb (562 kg); (E.II) 1 340 lb (609 kg); (E.III) 1 400 lb (635 kg).
Performance: maximum speed (E.I) 82 mph (132 km/h); (E.II) 87 mph (140 km/h); (E.III) 83 mph (134 km/h); service ceiling (E.I) 10 170 ft (3 100 m); (E.II) 12 000 ft (3 650 m); (E.III) 11 500 ft (3 500 m); endurance (E.III) 2 hr 45 min.

A famous fighter that rivalled anything the Germans achieved in the way of vivid colouring. Though it belonged to the 94th 'Hat in Ring' Aero Squadron it was not the mount of Capt Eddie Rickenbacker, who ended the war as the squadron's commander with 26 confirmed victories.

was irrelevant; to some degree it was a case of skill with the old and hamfistedness with the new, but in some instances the reactionary outlook of fighter pilots – whom the layman might expect to be the most progressive people in the world – has been extraordinary.

But the reputation of the Spad was quickly made and news of it travelled fast, especially on the Western Front in the winter of 1916–17. Times were hard. The Germans had used their solid, straight-six water-cooled engines of 160 to 220 horsepower to create a range of fighters that were extremely formidable. Halberstadts, Rolands, Pfalzes, two-seat Hannovers and, above all, the Albatros D.III were establishing supremacy once again for the Iron Cross, and April 1917 was to be remembered with a shudder by the RFC as 'Bloody April'. Now the Spad VII was here to be used against them. It had arrived none too soon.

Eventually no fewer than 5600 were delivered. They equipped dozens of squadrons of nearly all the Allies, including of course the French S 3 *Les Cicognes*, probably the most famous fighter outfit in history apart from the Red Baron's circus. Two companies in Britain built 200 Spads for the RFC – half were to have gone to the RNAS if they had not taken the Sopwith Triplane instead – and the Spad VII was one of the foremost fighters in Italy's war against Austro-Hungary and also

important in Belgium and Russia. In December 1917, it became the first important fighter to serve with the US Army's American Expeditionary Force.

There was nothing unconventional about the Spad VII; indeed its very lack of odd features helped sweep away belief that such features – a very small lower wing for instance – possessed some magical power. It was just a very strong, serviceable airframe fitted with a great engine.

As Birkigt had expected, his vee-8 engine proved capable of development to run at higher crankshaft speeds (with a reduction gear to the propeller) and increased cylinder pressures. By the end of 1916 the 8Bc had been cleared for production at 200 hp, closely followed by the 8Be and 8Bec of 220 hp. With this power the Spad could carry heavier armament, so Bécherau produced an improved fighter carrying two Vickers guns, and this materialised as the Spad XIII, first flown in April 1917. It had an airframe with slightly greater dimensions than the VII and numerous other small changes such as a variation in the shape of the wings and tail, but the main change was in the additional gun and in performance improved to the point where few if any First World War aircraft could equal it. The level speed of about 138 mph was around 30 mph faster than other fighters of 1917 and 20 mph faster than such types as the Fokker D.VII, the

Sopwith Snipe and the S.E.5a of 1918.

Thanks to the qualities of the Hispano engine, which I suppose could be called the 'Merlin of the First World War', the Spad VII and XIII were built in far greater numbers than any other fighter aircraft of the pre-1939 era. Total production of the XIII, by nine French companies, is believed to have been 8472, making a total with the VII of around 14400. To this must be added 300 of a third type, the XII, which at Guynemer's suggestion, was fitted with a 37 mm Hotchkiss cannon. Birkigt had from the start designed his engine so that a cannon, such as his own 20 mm, could be mounted directly on the crankcase between the cylinder blocks. A geared drive raised the propeller shaft into line with the barrel of the gun, which actually passed through the shaft and propeller hub, emerging about an inch in front of it. The XII, which incorporated many of the airframe changes of the XIII, had technical problems and did not fly until July 1917, by which time hundreds of the Spad XIII had flown. Guynemer used the prototype to destroy four enemy aircraft, and René Fonck obtained 11 of his 75 kills with a later aircraft. In 1917 a single hit with a 37 mm cannon shell was almost sure to prove lethal, but the size, weight and recoil of the big gun and the choking cordite fumes it produced were serious drawbacks that prevented the Spad XII from becoming the standard type.

More than any other type, the Spad XIII was the leading fighter on the Allied side in terms of numbers used and diversity of user in the final 18 months of the war. The only country that did not adopt it as standard was Britain, which had good fighters of its own, the only unit to fly it being RFC/RAF 23 Squadron. The French Aviation Militaire had made the XIII almost its only front-line fighter by 1918, and the United States adopted it and built it in unheard-of numbers, though many were cancelled and left uncompleted at the Armistice. Had the full American contracts gone through the number of Spads by 1920 would easily have exceeded 25000, and such a quantity would have rendered other Allied fighters superfluous. In fact, the use of the Spad XIII and its various developments might have been even more widespread than it was, because in Britain the whole 1919 fighter programme was thrown into chaos by the complete failure of the engine the new aircraft were to use, the ABC Dragonfly. Had the Armistice not been agreed in November 1918, and had Germany been in a position to keep fighting, the Spad might, by 1919, have equipped the RFC fighter squadrons.

Possibly the most famous Spad of all : the XIII Vieux Charles *of Capt Georges Guynemer, France's No 2 with 54 victories. Like many of the greatest aces, Guynemer disappeared in unknown circumstances during a dogfight.*

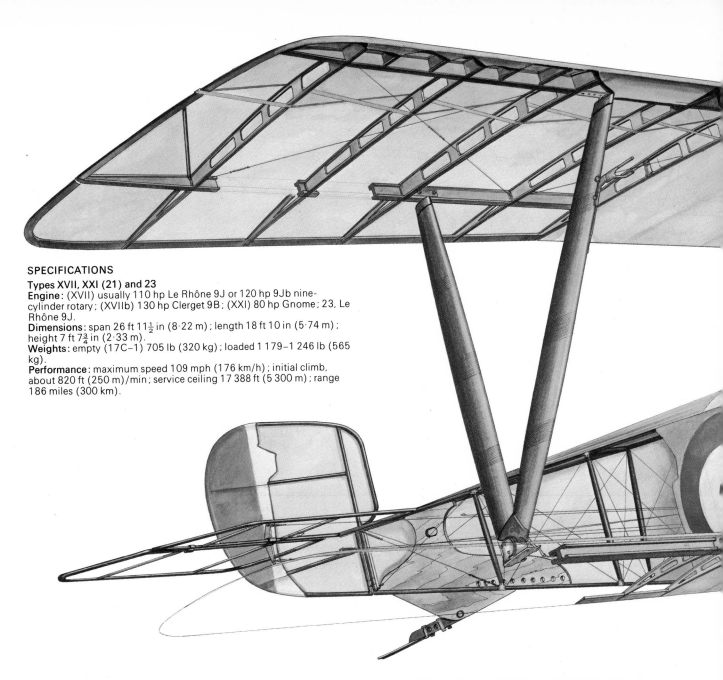

SPECIFICATIONS

Types XVII, XXI (21) and 23

Engine: (XVII) usually 110 hp Le Rhône 9J or 120 hp 9Jb nine-cylinder rotary; (XVIIb) 130 hp Clerget 9B; (XXI) 80 hp Gnome; 23, Le Rhône 9J.

Dimensions: span 26 ft 11½ in (8·22 m); length 18 ft 10 in (5·74 m); height 7 ft 7¾ in (2·33 m).

Weights: empty (17C–1) 705 lb (320 kg); loaded 1 179–1 246 lb (565 kg).

Performance: maximum speed 109 mph (176 km/h); initial climb, about 820 ft (250 m)/min; service ceiling 17 388 ft (5 300 m); range 186 miles (300 km).

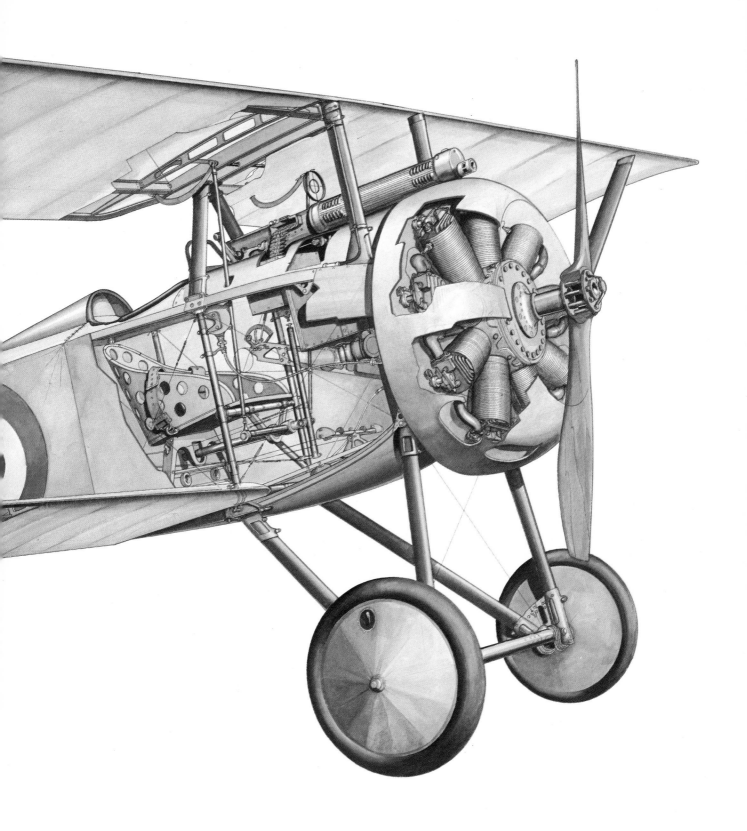

One of the most successful fighters of the First World War, the Nieuport XVII (17) was the personal choice of several aces. John Batchelor's cutaway, never before published in colour, gives a perfect impression of the simple yet tough structure. The ailerons, on the upper wing, were worked by vertical rods driving torsion tubes behind the rear spar.

Quite unlike its predecessors, the Nieuport 28 was an important scout of 1918, but only because the Americans wanted a modern fighter quickly. Almost unused by France, hundreds went to the AEF, where Lt Doug Campbell became the first US ace. A greater ace, Raoul Lufbery, was killed in a Nie.28. This is a modern reproduction.

Sopwith Camel

Though this chapter is ostensibly about the Camel one cannot treat this famed warplane in a vacuum. It grew out of experience with other famous combat aircraft and it led directly to others, merely happening to be the member of the family that matured at the height of the First World War, so that it could be put into vast quantity production and set a great record in air combat. In fact not least of the Camel's claims to fame is that it shot down more enemy aircraft than any other type of aircraft in the war. This is especially noteworthy when the number of Camels made is compared with the total number of Spads.

T. O. M. Sopwith was one of the great pioneers of winged flight and, as Sir Thomas Sopwith, he is still keeping an eye on things in his 90th year. He gained British Aviator's Certificate No 31 in 1910, and promptly began winning major prizes in flying events until, when an Army officer named Trenchard wanted to learn to fly, Sopwith was the man he picked as his instructor. Trenchard was the man who commanded the Royal Flying Corps in France, formed and commanded the Independent Air Force in 1918 and can fairly be called the father of the RAF. He was also to become a very important customer of young Sopwith's in a quite different way. Sopwith founded his own company in 1912 and, helped by his Australian mechanic Fred Sigrist – who had been hired originally to look after Sopwith's yacht – started designing aircraft. In a disused skating rink at Canbury Park Road, Kingston-on-Thames, Sopwith quickly showed considerable potential, first with the Bat Boat, an outstanding flying boat, and then with the Tabloid.

On 29 November 1913 the Tabloid, which had been built in secret, was flown from Brooklands to Farnborough where its performance astonished everyone. Though conventional in structure, with a wire-braced wooden framework covered with fabric, it was notable on several counts. It was the simplest and neatest machine anyone had seen, and also one of the smallest. It had only one pair of interplane struts on each side

– it was what is called a single-bay biplane – and all previous machines had two or three pairs. Looking back now, it showed the way design was going to settle down, and was, in fact, just like a smaller edition of a First World War fighter, designed years before most of them had even been thought of and at a time when many designers were still building things more like a Wright Flyer. For the record, the Tabloid had an 80 hp Gnome engine but was timed at 92 mph and reached 1200 ft in one minute from takeoff.

This baby biplane did much to convince the monoplane enthusiasts that biplanes could be a better proposition in many ways. I have already commented on the somewhat arbitrary ban imposed on monoplanes by the British War Office in 1912, ostensibly on the ground that such machines were unsafe. This eliminated the possibility of further official research or comparative trials, and in the long term probably handicapped Britain's planemakers in the early 1930s when the rest of the world had already switched to monoplanes. But back in 1913, when the Tabloid first flew, it is doubtful that any monoplane could have equalled the compactness, robust yet light structure and good all-round performance of this trim biplane. Any structural engineer will know how easy it is to create a rigid yet light biplane, and how much more difficult to do the same with a monoplane when the structural material used is wood. Monoplanes in 1913 had to carry large king-posts projecting above and below the fuselage to anchor the numerous wires that braced the wing. Sopwith's Tabloid seemed more attractive and sensible and confirmed the belief that the biplane idea was superior.

By the end of the first year of the First World War Sopwith had produced many hundreds of excellent biplanes of many types, the majority of them seaplanes assembled and launched at Hamble, near Southampton. By the end of 1915 the oddly-named Sopwith 1½-Strutter was in the air, and it has a major niche in history as possibly

Left: Probably the first production Camel (N6330). Compared with the prototype it has the revised gun fairing and large inspection cover on each side of the front fuselage.

Below: The original 1F.1 prototype, first of four built by Sopwith. It is not known if it had an RFC serial number. The cut-out in the upper centre-section was the first modification.

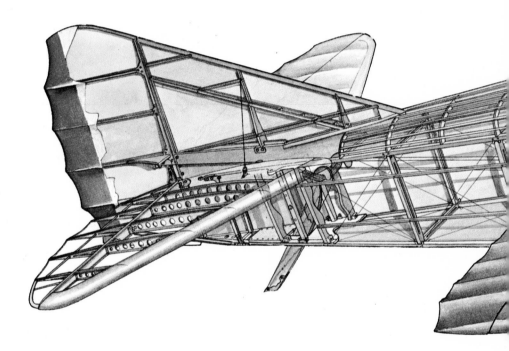

Top: *This reproduction Spad XIII has been finished in the insignia of America's greatest First World War ace, Capt 'Eddie' Rickenbacker, one of the giants of aviation and 35 years later chairman of Eastern Air Lines. Most of his 26 victories were gained with the Spad, in eight months flying with the 94th (Uncle Sam's hat in the ring) Aero Squadron which he soon commanded.*

One of John Batcherlor's most satisfying drawings is this beautiful Spad XIII, actually an aircraft of the US Army AEF (American Expeditionary Force) with which it was No 1 combat aircraft in 1918. Had the war continued it would probably have seen large-scale use in the RAF also. Fighter technology had come a long way since the Fokker monoplane.

SPECIFICATIONS

Types VII, 72 and 62
Engine: one 150 hp (later 189 and 200 hp) Hispano-Suiza 8Aa vee-8 water-cooled.
Dimensions: span 25 ft 7¾ in (7·81 m) (about 26 ft 4 in with 180 200 hp engines) ; length 20 ft 2½ (or 3½) in (6·18 m) ; height 6 ft 11½ in (2·13 m).
Weights: empty, 1 124 lb (510 kg) ; maximum loaded 1 632 lb (740 kg).
Performance: maximum speed 119 mph (192 km/h) ; initial climb 900 ft (275 m)/min ; service ceiling 17 500 ft (5 334 m) ; range, about 225 miles (360 km).

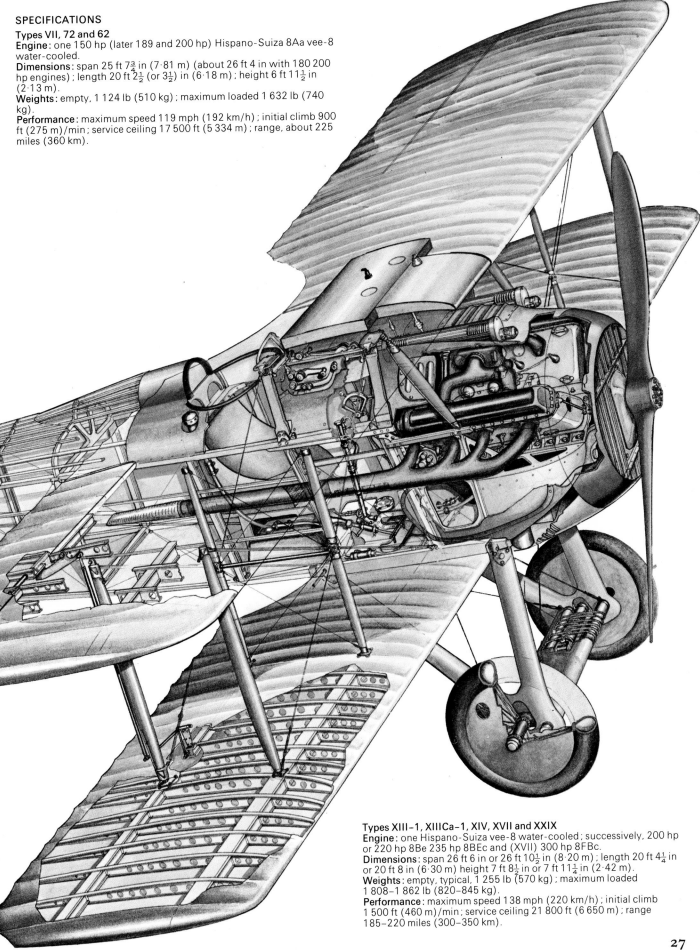

Types XIII-1, XIIICa-1, XIV, XVII and XXIX
Engine: one Hispano-Suiza vee-8 water-cooled ; successively, 200 hp or 220 hp 8Be 235 hp 8BEc and (XVII) 300 hp 8FBc.
Dimensions: span 26 ft 6 in or 26 ft 10½ in (8·20 m) ; length 20 ft 4¼ in or 20 ft 8 in (6·30 m) height 7 ft 8½ in or 7 ft 11¼ in (2·42 m).
Weights: empty, typical, 1 255 lb (570 kg) ; maximum loaded 1 808–1 862 lb (820–845 kg).
Performance: maximum speed 138 mph (220 km/h) ; initial climb 1 500 ft (460 m)/min ; service ceiling 21 800 ft (6 650 m) ; range 185–220 miles (300–350 km).

the first true combat aircraft. This is a matter for some argument, but certainly the 1½-Strutter had been designed from the start to carry a forward-firing Vickers gun, with an interrupter gear, an observer with a free Lewis gun on a specially designed mounting behind him, and bombs on underwing racks. The interrupter gear was usually the Vickers on RFC machines and the Scarff-Dibovski on those for the RNAS, and despite Fokker's claim, both mechanisms were flying in service on 1½-Strutters long before the first example of the Fokker gear fell into Allied hands on 8 April 1916.

On the other hand there is little doubt that the Fokker monoplanes did have a direct influence on the Pup, the delightful little Sopwith fighter that flew in February 1916. This was designed chiefly by Herbert Smith, and was so small and neat that it was beyond doubt the fastest armed combat aircraft ever powered by the 80 hp Gnome or Le Rhône rotary engines, exceeding 111 mph in full fighting trim. Altogether 1770 of these little fighters were built, for both the RNAS and RFC, and it is tragic that none survives today. No aircraft in history has ever been so universally liked, so sweet to fly, so tractable and docile or so perfect in every way. Its marvellous flying qualities more than made up for its low power and single gun until long after it might have been expected to become obsolete. In 8 Squadron RNAS, the famous 'Naval Eight', which saw some of the fiercest fighting at the time of the Somme offensive, one flight had Pups and another the Nieuport XI. Direct comparison soon led to the Pup becoming standard throughout the squadron.

Between this delightful little scout and the more famous Camel came a fighter built in only modest numbers yet which caused a greater stir in the ranks of the enemy than any other Allied warplane. By 1916, combat aircraft design had begun to settle down and follow fairly predictable lines of development. The Fokker monoplane had been accepted as a deadly little freak, and apart from a handful of manufacturers led by Morane-Saulnier, all production was concentrated on biplanes. Imagine the shock then, in early April 1917, when in the bitter fighting at Arras, No 1 Squadron RNAS roared into battle with the Sopwith Triplane! Herbert Smith gave the Triplane three almost-equal-size wings in an attempt to combine the utmost manoeuvrability with good pilot view, and the result was certainly effective. Powered by the 110 hp Clerget engine and carrying a single gun, the Triplane had the same 26½-ft span as the Pup, but the aggregate area of its three narrow wings was less than that of the two wings of the Pup. As the more powerful

Batchelor has drawn various Camel cutaways; this one shows a regular 1F.1 with two Vickers.

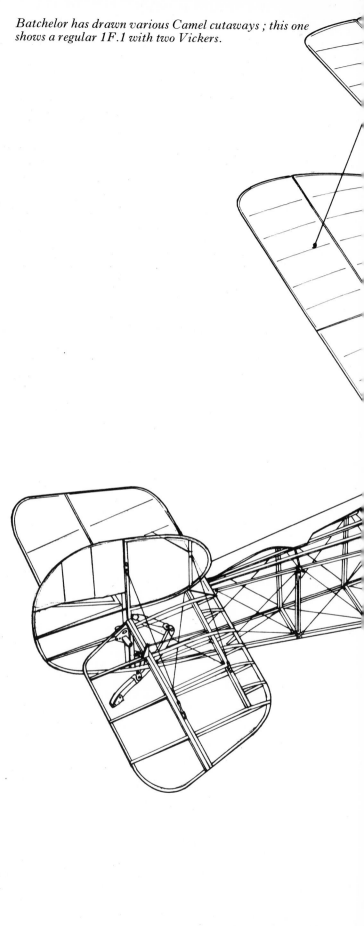

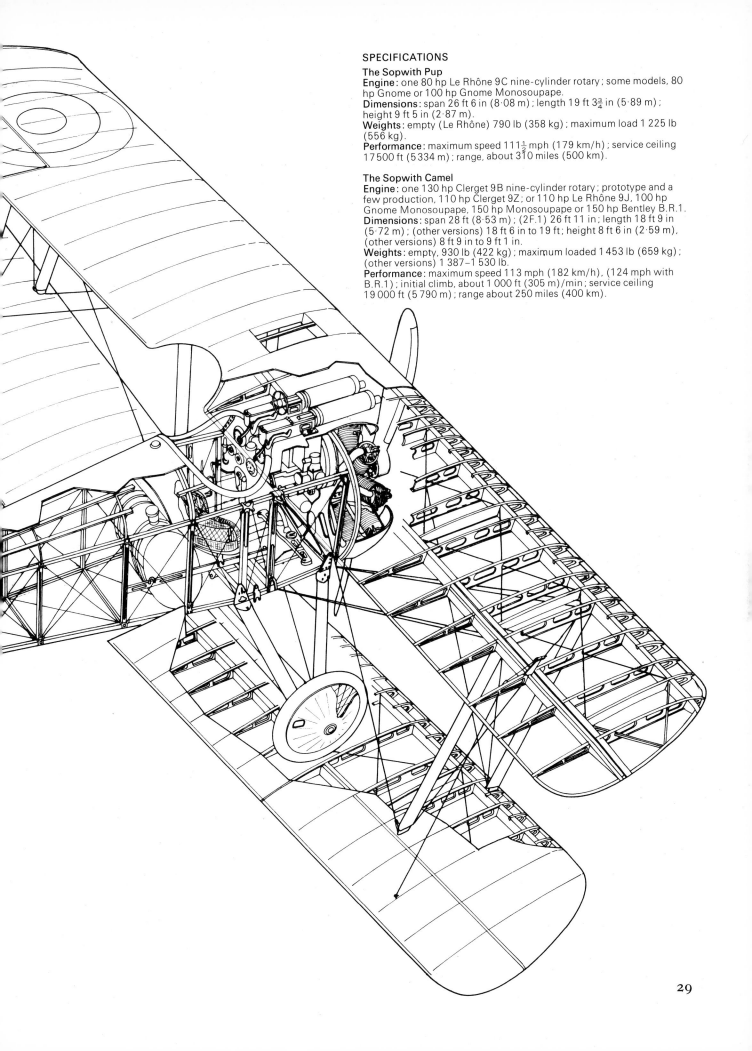

SPECIFICATIONS

The Sopwith Pup
Engine: one 80 hp Le Rhône 9C nine-cylinder rotary; some models, 80 hp Gnome or 100 hp Gnome Monosoupape.
Dimensions: span 26 ft 6 in (8·08 m); length 19 ft 3¾ in (5·89 m); height 9 ft 5 in (2·87 m).
Weights: empty (Le Rhône) 790 lb (358 kg); maximum load 1 225 lb (556 kg).
Performance: maximum speed 111½ mph (179 km/h); service ceiling 17 500 ft (5 334 m); range, about 310 miles (500 km).

The Sopwith Camel
Engine: one 130 hp Clerget 9B nine-cylinder rotary; prototype and a few production, 110 hp Clerget 9Z; or 110 hp Le Rhône 9J, 100 hp Gnome Monosoupape, 150 hp Monosoupape or 150 hp Bentley B.R.1.
Dimensions: span 28 ft (8·53 m); (2F.1) 26 ft 11 in; length 18 ft 9 in (5·72 m); (other versions) 18 ft 6 in to 19 ft; height 8 ft 6 in (2·59 m), (other versions) 8 ft 9 in to 9 ft 1 in.
Weights: empty, 930 lb (422 kg); maximum loaded 1 453 lb (659 kg); (other versions) 1 387–1 530 lb.
Performance: maximum speed 113 mph (182 km/h), (124 mph with B.R.1); initial climb, about 1 000 ft (305 m)/min; service ceiling 19 000 ft (5 790 m); range about 250 miles (400 km).

Above: *Dick Day's reproduction Sopwith Camel shares Old Rhinebeck aerodrome with Cole Palen's marvellous array of First World War scouts and several other reproductions including Dick King's Pup. The original aircraft, crashed by the hundred, never had such care lavished on them.*

Left: *A painting by Kenneth McDonough showing Spad XIIIs of SPA.3 Les Cicognes about to tangle with Fokker 'Tripehounds'. In the foreground, Le Vieux Charles of Guynemer.*

Below: *A beautifully restored and flyable P–26A, in the markings of the 34th Attack squadron. Aircraft 33–123 is at Planes of Fame in California; 33–135 is at the National Air and Space Museum in Washington.*

A Camel used as a fighter-pilot trainer. The characteristic humped appearance has been altered by removal of the twin Vickers and installation of a Hythe camera-gun on the centreline.

triplane was heavier the result might have been poor, but in fact there was little to choose between the two. Today we can probably form a balanced judgement, and this must be, I think, that triplane fighters, like the sesquiplane Nieuports, were interesting experiments only. At the same time, the fighting record of the Sopwith Triplane remains unsurpassed, mainly because it was used by some of the very finest units of the RNAS. I cannot resist naming 'Black Flight' of No 10 Squadron, commanded by Raymond Collishaw (No 3 British, or rather Canadian, ace with 60 confirmed victories), which between May and July 1917 destroyed 87 enemy aircraft. Collishaw himself shot down 16, 14 of them single-seater fighters, in 27 days.

That remarkable unit would probably have done as well with Pups, Spads or any other of the better fighters, but the Triplane did strike a note of fear into the German pilots that was, in retrospect, based more on the Triplane's exponents than on any magical properties of the three-wing layout. General von Hoeppner, commander of the entire Idflieg, personally praised the new machine and within days the

entire aircraft industry of the Central Powers was put to producing triplane fighters. However, before 1916 was out, back at Canbury Park Road, Herbert Smith had produced a new fighter that soon earned its place among the half-dozen most famous fighters of all time. Significantly it was not a triplane but a biplane. By using a more powerful rotary engine, it was able to carry two Vickers guns as standard armament, and its hump-backed appearance led to its nickname of 'Camel', which was used so universally that it became official. By this time Sopwith had worked out a designation system for its products, and the company knew the new fighter as the F.1 (Fighter, Type 1). A special RNAS version, often called Ships' Camel, was designated 2F.1, and had smaller wings and a detachable rear fuselage. It was intended to operate from ships, using short foredeck platforms, and even from lighters towed at high speed by destroyers.

Camels were powered by almost all the rotary engines then in production of over 110 horsepower, but the usual types were either the 130 hp Clerget or the 150 hp Bentley B.R.1. Possibly Sopwith should, by December 1916, have recognised that he was building in obsolescence by selecting a rotary for the Camel, though there was precious little else to be had. The engine-supply situation for the Farnborough (Folland) designed S.E.5a, with its intrinsically far superior Hispano or Wolseley V-8, was so desperate that aircraft were delivered with engines known to be faulty, this being judged better than no engine at all. However, the record of the Camel speaks for itself, and on this score Sopwith's engine choice must be considered right for the time, even though its big fast-spinning rotary, exerting an immense gyroscopic effect on the nose of such a small and stumpy fighter, was to give the Camel flight characteristics that made it the terror of pupil pilots. Hundreds died in its trim cockpit before they encountered the enemy. Some could never master just when or by how much to lean-off the rich mixture after takeoff, which was the kind of thing it should have been possible to teach without having a dual-control aircraft, but for some reason it caused endless fatal engine-cuts. Many trainee pilots died because they simply could not manage such a highly strung, lopsided racehorse, which became doubly dangerous because its reputation put fear into the raw pupil and prevented cool judgement.

Just why the Camel was so tricky is something I have never understood, and I am confirmed in my puzzlement by the inability of articulate men who flew the Camel to explain it either. Somewhere I read that the Camel took the same time to turn 270° to the right as to turn 90° to the left, so Camel pilots tended never to turn left. I do not believe this, and it certainly cannot be explained by any logical theory. But obviously a right-hand turn, with an engine running clockwise as seen from the cockpit, would pull the nose down, while a left-hand turn would pull the nose up,

and all pilots are agreed that heavy use of the rudder, often the opposite to what one might expect, was needed to make a co-ordinated turn. So all in all it took a little longer to learn how to master the Camel and execute tight manoeuvres without ending up in a spin, which was often lethal. Learning how to dogfight and aim the guns accurately took longer still. But it was worth it, and the view ahead over the two Vickers guns is often held to have been the most exciting in aerial warfare. The 2F.1 usually had only one Vickers, plus a Lewis on a Foster mount.

Despite the handicap of its rotary engine, the Camel had an excellent performance with two guns, and could also carry four 25 lb Harris bombs. Even a 112 lb bomb could be carried, which was a remarkable feat. Many Camels were used for close-support over the battlefield, suffering such heavy casualties from ground fire that Sopwith developed the armoured T.F.1 (Trench Fighter Type 1) followed by the purpose-designed T.F.2 Salamander. Other Camels were boldly flown at night and, from the summer of 1917, were among the most successful aircraft used against the Gotha and Zeppelin-Staaken heavy bombers over England. The blinding flash of the twin Vickers at night soon led to their replacement by two Lewis guns on the upper wing, with the pilot's cockpit moved further aft. But most of the Camel's 1294 confirmed victories, more than those gained by any other fighter of the First World War, were achieved by day over the Western Front. Some 5490 Camels were built, plus 340 2F.1 Ships' Camels. The latter had a very busy war, destroying two of the latest and biggest Zeppelins in a bombing raid (from the carrier *Furious*) on their base at Tondern and also being launched from a sling under HM Airship R.23.

Camels of No 8 (N) Sqn at Mont St Eloi, in the final months of the RFC in early 1918. Research by Chaz Bowyer has shown that the hoary old figure of '1,294 victories' is an under-estimate by getting on for 2,000; RFC/RNAS squadron victories alone add up to over 2,800, as explained in Bowyer's book Sopwith Camel – King of Combat.

Boeing P-26

Always known – in no sense derisively – as 'The Peashooter', the P–26 was built in small numbers and was much less important than many fighters of the inter-war period that are today almost forgotten. Examples of the latter are the British Gloster biplanes of the 1920s, the Bristol Bulldog and Hawker Fury, the French LGL family and Nieuport Delages, and many great fighters from Czechoslovakia, Poland, Italy and the Soviet Union. But the P–26 has unique charm, embodying in its snarling tubbiness many of the problems and the delights of fighter design.

Situated in Seattle, in the far American northwest, the Boeing Airplane Company established from the very start a reputation for technical innovation and bold management which in the inter-war years was to make it a towering giant in both military and civil aircraft production. Possibly its most significant single act was to take a close look at the 200 wartime-designed Thomas–Morse MB–3A fighters it was building for the US Army Air Service and decide, without being asked, that it could do better. The result was the company-funded Model 15, first flown on 2 June 1923. Apart from being aerodynami-

The Red Indian Thunderbird symbol adorned the 'Peashooters' of the Army Air Corps 34th Pursuit Sqn. The nimble Boeing's bases were literally fields. The P–26A needed runways.

cally superior to the MB–3A, it had a fuselage arc-welded from steel tubing, which was similar in weight and strength to other designs but much cheaper to make and – a vital point – always stayed the right shape without the need for re-rigging. As Boeing had hoped, the Army fell for the many improvements they had initiated, and eventually bought hundreds of fighters of progressively improved design, designated first PW–9 and then P–12. The Navy bought a parallel series called FB, F2B, F3B and F4B. They were among the best and most numerous biplane fighters ever built and the later P–12/F4B family are also blessed with a fanatical army of modern admirers. Frank Tallman's beautifully restored Boeing Model 100, in the colours of a Marine Corps F4B–1, is possibly the most prized vintage machine regularly flying.

On 29 September 1930 Boeing again pioneered the way by bringing out the Model 218, with a light-alloy monocoque fuselage. The steel tube structures, which were still thought rather new in the RAF, were judged by Boeing to be obsolete. The Army Air Corps (formed from the Air Service in 1926) tested the new fighter as the XP–925. It was then bought by China, suffering under aerial attack at the hands of the Japanese and eagerly trying to get military airpower from whatever source. An American mercenary, Robert Short, checked out in the new Boeing, and in 1932 single-handedly took on three Mitsubishi B1M3 carrier-based bombers escorted by three 2MT5 (Type 13–2) fighters. The lone Boeing shot down at least one, and probably two, of its enemies before being shot down itself. It was the first American-designed fighter ever to see combat.

By this time technology had advanced still further. The pioneers of stressed-skin construction had been the Germans, but Boeing were among the leaders in applying it to successful production aircraft. On 6 May 1930 Boeing had flown the first Monomail, a revolutionary new mailplane with a cantilever monoplane wing of advanced form and with stressed-skin construction throughout. It also had retractable landing gear and a ring cowl round the Hornet engine, and compared with the regular Model 40 biplane, carried twice as much about 30 per cent faster, using the same engine. Boeing could see that this was how future aircraft would be built. At the same time a British company, Armstrong Whitworth, was pressed to adopt stressed-skin construction but after long study it decided to stick to the old ways. The new ideas seemed complicated and heavy.

However, Boeing went ahead and the Model 247 soon appeared, the first of the modern breed of civil airliners, and some twin-engined bombers. What next? Why, a fighter, of course; but the trouble was money. The Army counted every nickel, and Clairmont L. Egtvedt, Boeing general manager, doubted if the company would get any support in the Depression for a new fighter.

In the event the Army did what it could. Boeing received Army technical collaboration from the start, a free Pratt & Whitney R-1340 Wasp engine, some instruments and equipment, and a small sum to pay for some static testing of the new fighter's stressed-skin wing. What the Army did not agree to was a retractable landing gear or a cantilever wing, so the resulting Model 248 was a curious blend of old and new. The new parts were obvious enough. By far the most important, from the viewpoint of fighter capability, was the monoplane wing. There had been parasol and low-winged monoplane fighters in the 1920s, but the little Boeing was clearly a more modern concept. The advantages were a higher speed, probably better climb, and certainly superior pilot view. The main drawback was a high takeoff and landing speed. In 1932 this was crucial. Though some US Army airfields were large and unobstructed, most were smaller grassy plots that imposed severe limitations on aircraft design. Not only was there not enough room, but the bumpy surfaces made life hard even for experienced pilots, and many aircraft overturned or broke landing gears. Aircraft such as the new Boeing fighter did much to bring in special paved runways.

Boeing flew the 248 on 20 March 1932. With a 522 hp SR-1340E engine driving a fixed-pitch Hamilton metal propeller the best level speed was 230 mph, some 40 mph faster than the best previous fighters with the same engine. Manoeuvrability was adequate, and not inferior to the biplanes. Pilots and generals liked the open cockpit, the fixed, spatted gear and the multiple bracing wires that tied it all together. Boeing might have preferred three different answers, but knew its conservative customer. In January 1933 the Army bought 111 of the new aircraft with the designation P–26A, and these were delivered in the first half of 1934.

The aircraft were different, and this invariably causes trouble. Pilots are quick to damn anything they do not know, especially when it turns out to be a handful to land at 73 mph on a field designed for the aircraft of the First World War. It says much for the Peashooter that it soon became not only respected but popular.

We must imagine ourselves posted to one of the new P–26A Pursuit Groups – the 1st, 16th, 17th, 18th, 20th, 32nd or 37th – to appreciate just how much the pilots and ground crews had to learn. The level of performance was up by about 25 per cent. The 500 hp R–1340–27 engine was familiar, but the installation contained new features. The cockpit was further forward than in

Boeing P–26 serial number 33–28, the first to come off the production line. Just visible behind the cockpit is the large arrowhead decal bearing the name WRIGHT. All Army Air Corps aircraft at this time had an arrowhead badge if assigned to a particular field for test purposes.

the biplanes, giving an excellent all-round view, but the instrument panel contained gyro instruments driven by suction from a venturi on the right-hand side, and this was still a fairly new idea. Flotation gear was standard, though the chances of a successful ditching were not very high. Above all, there was a complete two-way radio, with throat microphone and antenna mast just ahead of the windshield. The armament comprised two 0·30 in Brownings at first, but these were later changed for two of 0·5 in calibre, quite low on each side and with the barrels firing between engine cylinders inside the cowling.

Fatalities caused by nosing over on rough fields soon led to a strengthening and deepening of the headrest. By 1935 the Army's P–26As had been back to Boeing to be fitted with flaps. These were of the simple split type, worked by an engine-driven hydraulic pump or a handpump in emergencies, and they lowered the landing speed to about 65 mph. Boeing had experience of flaps already, and back in January 1934 had flown some on the Model 264, tested by the Army as the YP–29A, which was almost a P–26 with slimmer body, cantilever wing, retractable landing gear and a sliding cockpit canopy. The 264 was Boeing's idea of the next-generation fighter, and one is led to believe the Army liked it – except for all the improvements! Likewise the Navy tested the Model 273 as the XF7B–1, but again found this quite different and truly modern fighter not yet quite believable, and carried on buying fabric-covered biplanes.

Boeing did sell the Army 25 slightly later P–26B and P–26C fighters with direct-injection engines (600 hp SR–1340–33) and flaps, as well as a dozen Model 281 export versions, one of which went to Spain (to the regular air force before the start of the civil war) and 11 to China, where they no doubt saw much action.

From 1936 the waspish little Boeings gradually faded from the scene. Their replacements, of course, had cantilever wings, retractable landing gear and enclosed cockpits, all things Boeing could have given the P–26. But the customer was only just ready for these ideas when Seversky built the P–35 and Curtiss the P–36. As for the retired Peashooters, they soldiered on with the air forces of the Philippines and Guatemala, having been snapped up by those countries nearest to Clark Field and Albrook Field (Canal Zone) where the aircraft happened to be at the end of their original careers. Some of the Philippine aircraft went into action against the Japanese in December 1941, but it is doubtful if they lasted more than a few days against the new foe. In Guatemala a few were still flying in 1957, at Puerto Barrios and San José.

SPECIFICATIONS

Engine: 600 hp Pratt & Whitney SR-1340-33; Wasp direct-injection nine-cylinder radial.
Dimensions: span 27 ft 11½ in (8·82 m); length 23 ft 9 in (7·28 m); height 10 ft 0½ in (3·1 m).
Weights: empty about 2 200 lb (998 kg); loaded 3 075 lb (1 395 kg).
Performance: maximum speed 235 mph (378 km/h); cruising speed 200 mph (322 km/h); initial climb, 2 500 ft (762 m)/min; service ceiling, over 28 000 ft (8 530 m); range 635 miles (1 100 km).

Another picture of the first production P–26. It is almost certainly at Wright Field, close to Huffman Prairie where the Wrights carried out their development flying in 1904–5.

Above: *An historic photograph of the 'XP–936', later the XP–26, serial 32–412, taken on 17th March 1932, three days before the first flight. Today the hillside beyond the railroad is populated.*

Below: *One of the best surviving pictures of a Peashooter. The print still bears its original caption, crediting the Army Air Corps 23rd Photo Section, dated 2 May 1937 (when the P–26A was being replaced).*

Polikarpov I-16

When, in the late 1930s, details of this stumpy little fighter gradually seeped through to what we today call 'the West', it was hardly taken seriously. It did not look like a fighter, and most closely resembled the equally stumpy Gee Bee Super Sportster, built specially to take the world landplane speed record, which it did in 1932 at 294 mph. Racers are poles apart from fighters, which unlike the Gee Bee have to be manoeuvrable and tough. Moreover, the odd Russian machine had a crude homebuilt appearance, and this, combined with a basic belief that all Russian aircraft were inferior to or mere copies of Western designs, encouraged the conclusion that the I–16 hardly rated as a warplane at all.

Much the same kind of argument coloured Western thinking on Japanese aircraft. In both cases a poor opinion was based upon ignorance. Worse, it was ignorance compounded by deep-seated beliefs that made it hard to view Soviet aircraft objectively until the MiG–15 suddenly made Western observers wake up in 1951, as did the Japanese Zero a decade earlier. Today we can see that the I–16 was really a remarkable fighter, fully deserving its place in this book. With hindsight we appreciate what observers at the time forgot or did not know. Instead of comparing it with the Spitfire, which was entering service when news of the I–16 reached the West, it should have been measured alongside its true Western contemporaries which were fabric-covered biplanes with two Vickers guns.

Today we have learned a little more about the fabulous number of trial installations and special experimental fighters evaluated by the Soviet Union from 1927 onwards. Taking 1927–37 as the decade in which the I–16 was created, it is at once obvious that – like 1945–55 – this was a period of exceptional technical change. In the previous decade developments had been confined to weeding out the pushers and rotary engines, improving methods of construction by adopting amongst other things welded steel-tube structures that needed no maintenance, and fitting engines of increasing power. But by 1927 a designer could see several possibilities.

1. All-metal stressed-skin construction, of which experience had already been gained in Germany and the United States (and on an ignored 1920 prototype in Britain), promised to make aircraft stronger, smoother and faster without much change in weight, but at the cost of drastic changes in factory tooling and the skills of the labour force.

2. This method of construction opened the way to the cantilever monoplane, which appeared likely to be faster and more efficient than any biplane, where previous wire-braced and strutted monoplanes had been inferior.

This is probably an I–16 Type 18, operating over the Eastern Front in 1942. Curiously, neither the cockpit canopy nor the apparent 'bonedome' helmet are right for the period, though the Soviet caption describes it as 'a fighter in the Great Patriotic War'.

3. Retractable landing gear offered the prospect of a further reduction in drag, though early examples were often clumsy and heavy, and needed either laborious cranking or an on-board power system which had yet to be developed.

4. A variable-pitch propeller allowed the engine to run at maximum speed on take-off and then slow down to an economical cruising setting, when the aircraft was airborne. This, like most other possible changes, would be expensive initially.

5. With the prospect of increased speeds, the issue of the traditional open cockpit became questionable; it was no longer possible for pilots to wave to each other, or point to enemies – unless they kept their hands inside the cockpit. Nor

could they crane their heads outside to look for foes behind or below, so a transparent canopy was needed which not only improved comfort but considerably reduced drag.

6. New types of armament were emerging from various test programmes and vied for a place beside, or instead of, the rifle-calibre machine gun. America had a gun of 0·5 in (12·7 mm) calibre, and there were numerous cannon of 20, 23 or 37 mm calibre, together with various large-calibre recoilless guns and rocket launchers.

7. There was now the possibility of fitting slats or flaps to wings, to reduce the landing speeds of the new monoplanes and enable them to use the still rather primitive airfields. Wheel brakes allowed the use of a tailwheel instead of a skid, and other new things were radio, oxygen and pilot armour. Still in the laboratory were the self-sealing fuel tank and reflector sight.

In 1930 the French had written a specification for a new fighter which resulted in the Dewoitine D.500, first flown in June 1932. Though a contemporary of the Boeing P–26, the French fighter was far more advanced, having a light-alloy stressed-skin structure, wing machine guns, and a 20 mm cannon firing through the propeller hub. But the powerful geared engine needed a large propeller and, after studying stalky retracting landing gear to accommodate this, the French team chose a fixed gear with spats. In 1932 the Kremlin in its turn issued a requirement for a new fighter which stipulated a monoplane with retractable landing gear and enclosed cockpit.

For 1932 this was bold. One does not know how far these features were requested just to see if they worked or whether they were to be forced on the VVS (army aviation) regardless of how successful they were, but it was a forward-looking decision taken in advance of any other country.

Two prototypes emerged, one designed by Pavel Sukhoi at Tupolev's TsAGI and the other by Nikolai N. Polikarpov's team at the TsKB, by far the most important design teams in the Soviet Union at that time. Even today under the Soviet system, except when it would make poor economic sense, there are always two new prototypes in competition for each major requirement, and their evaluation is often prolonged. In the case of the 1932 fighter, it was to be 1936 before Sukhoi's ANT–31 (I–14) was finally dropped. Moreover, alongside both monoplanes was an outstanding Polikarpov biplane, the TsKB-3 (I–15) which had superb manoeuvrability and at some heights was faster than the monoplanes. It went into production and gave rise to the I–15bis and I–153, which from 1939 were often used as replacements in units previously equipped with the I–16 monoplane. This was partly because of fierce dogfighting over Mongolia and Manchuria, in which the Japanese Ki–27 and A5M, though inferior in other respects, had a definite edge in manoeuvrability over the I–16.

The TsKB–12 (I–16) first flew on the last day of 1933. It was a carefully considered compromise, poles apart from the biplane era yet still a long way from the later monoplanes of the Second World War. It did not use stressed-skin

This I–16 is probably a Type 24, but again there are features – such as the long channels behind the exhaust stubs – which do not tie in with the M–62 engine, and late type of windscreen.
This example was pictured on public display in the Soviet Union in the late 1960s.

construction, but had a wooden monocoque (single-shell, like a lobster claw) fuselage and a metal wing, with spars of Kolchug high-tensile chrome steel, and a skin of light alloy running back to the front spar, with fabric thereafter. Immense ailerons formed almost the entire trailing edge, but the inner sections were eventually developed to form split flaps to reduce the high landing speed. The robust wide-track landing gear retracted inwards, the generous soft-field tyres being accommodated in the fuselage and wing root and covered by doors hinged to the leg fairing. Retraction took 44 turns of a hand-crank, the final dozen or so of which were extremely hard work. Had the I–16 been a Western fighter, pilots would soon have escaped this labour by doing a half-roll before completing the cranking; Soviet pilots were not allowed such deviation from the rules.

But the main interest of the I–16 design centred on the fuselage. At the front was a 450 hp M–22 (Bristol Jupiter engine built under licence), which looked far too big for the amazingly small fuselage. Behind the engine was an aluminium fuel tank, and then came the cockpit, so far aft that the pilot could look diagonally ahead past the trailing edge. A one-piece metal-framed unit formed both the windscreen and canopy, opened by sliding it forwards along two tracks on the fuselage decking. Inside the wings, outboard of the propeller arc, were two of the brilliant new ShKAS 7·62 mm machine guns, firing 1800 shots/min each, fed by belts from magazines easily reloaded by an armourer by leaning over the trailing edge.

As it weighed under 3000 lb loaded the I–16 could hardly fail to have a good performance, and the first example reached 224 mph at sea level and showed good all-round manoeuvrability. By the late spring of 1934 Factory 1 in Moscow and Factory 21 at Gorki were preparing to build the I–16 Type 1, and deliveries began before the end of the year. Formations in VVS service flew over Red Square in the 1935 May Day parade, and at least 200 participated in the large-scale autumn manoeuvres in the Ukraine, yet for some reason the I–16 seemed not to have been noticed in the West until, two years later, it was in large-scale service with the Spanish Republicans, who called it the Mosca (Fly). For some equally obscure reason it was the derogatory name of Rata (rat), bestowed by its Nationalist opponents, that caught on in the West, where in 1938–41 it was imagined to be the last word in Soviet fighters! One must be careful not to over-rate the I–16. In comparison with other fighters in service in the mid-1930s it was comparable in manoeuvrability, better in all-round performance, superior

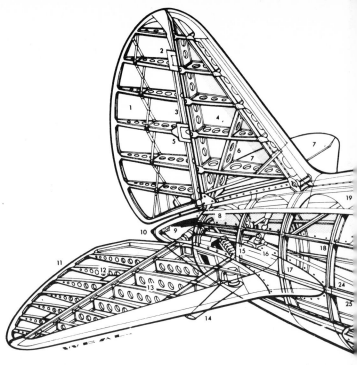

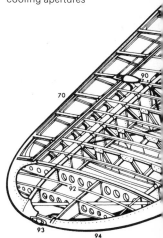

1 Rudder construction	44 Aileron hinge fairing
2 Rudder upper hinge	45 Fabric skinning
3 Rudder post	46 Port navigation light
4 Fin construction	47 Aluminium leading-edge skinning
5 Rudder lower hinge	
6 Fin auxiliary spar	48 AV–1 two-pitch metal propeller
7 Port tailplane	
8 Rudder actuating mechanism	49 Conical spinner
9 Tail cone	50 Hucks-type starter dog
10 Rear navigation light	51 Hinged mainwheel cover
11 Elevator construction	52 Port mainwheel (27·5-in/70-cm diam)
12 Elevator hinge	
13 Tailplane construction	53 Intake
14 Tailskid	54 Adjustable (shuttered) cooling apertures
15 Tailskid damper	
16 Control linkage (elevator and rudder)	
17 Tailplane fillet	
18 Fuselage half-frames	
19 Fin root fairing	
20 Dorsal decking	
21 Fuselage monocoque construction	
22 Main upper longeron	
23 Rudder control cable	
24 Elevator control rigid rod	
25 Main lower longeron	
26 Control linkage crank	
27 Seat support frame	
28 Vertically-adjustable seat	
29 Padded headrest on 8-mm armour plate	
30 Open cockpit	
31 Cockpit entry flap (port side only)	
32 Rearview mirror	
33 Curved one-piece windscreen	
34 Aldis sight (four-power magnification and incorporating crosshairs)	55 Propeller shaft support frame
	56 Machine gun muzzles
	57 Shvetsov M–25V nine-cylinder radial engine
35 Instrument panel	58 Oil tank
36 Mainwheel retraction handcrank	59 Starboard synchronised 7·62-mm Shpital'ny-Komaritsky (ShKAS) machine gun
37 Control column	
38 Rudder pedal	
39 Fuslage fuel tank of 56 Imp gal/254 litre) capacity	60 Exhaust exit ports
	61 Engine bearers
40 Fuel filler caps	62 Firewall/bulkhead
41 Ammunition magazines (650 rpg)	63 Centre-section trussed-type spar carry-through
	64 Wheel well
42 Fairing for port synchronised ShKAS gun	65 Fuselage/front spar attachment point
43 Dural-framed fabric-covered split-type ailerons	

One of Weal's truly valuable drawings is that of the I–16 Type 10. Not one vestige of this detail was known generally in the Second World War, when thousands of such aircraft existed and many had flown for years in Spain.

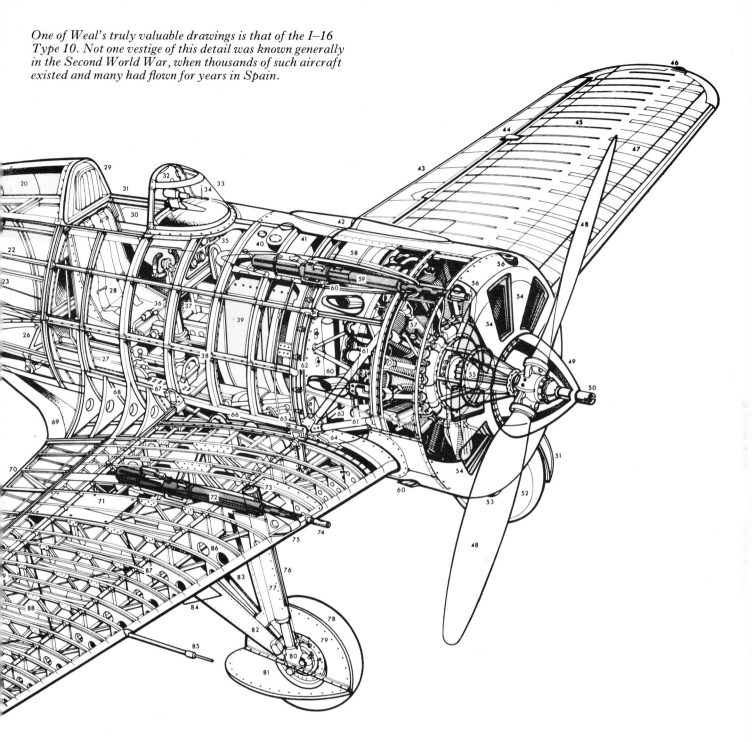

66 Retraction linkage
67 Fuselage/rear spar attachment point
68 Wing root frames
69 Wing root fillet
70 Aileron construction
71 Ammunition access panel
72 Starboard wing 7·62-mm Shpital'ny-Komaritsky (ShKAS) machine gun
73 Undercarriage pivot point
74 Machine gun muzzle
75 Centre/outer wing section break point
76 Mainwheel oleo leg
77 Leg cover plate
78 Starboard mainwheel

79 Mainwheel cover plate
80 Axle
81 Hinged wheel cover flap
82 Actuating rod cover
83 Retraction actuating rod
84 Cover flap
85 Pitot head
86 Leading edge construction
87 Chrome-molybdenum steel-alloy front spar
88 Alternate dural ribs
89 Rear spar
90 Aileron hinge fairing
91 Wire cross bracing
92 Wingtip construction
93 Starboard navigation light
94 Wingtip reinforcement strip

SPECIFICATIONS

I–16 Types 1, 4, 5, 10, 17, 18, 24, SPB and UTI

Engine: (Type 1) one 480 hp M–22 (modified Bristol Jupiter) nine-cylinder radial; (Type 4) 725 hp M–25A (modified Wright Cyclone); (Types 5, 10, 17) 775 hp M–25B; (Types 18 and 24) 1 000 hp Shvetsov M–62R (derived from M–25).

Dimensions: span 29 ft 6½ in (9·00 m); length (to Type 17) 19 ft 11 in (6·075 m); (18, 24 and UTI) 20 ft 1¼ in (6·125 m); height (to 17) 8 ft 1¼ in (2·45 m); (18, 24) 8 ft 5 in (2·56 m).

Weights: empty (1) 2 200 lb (998 kg); (4, 5, 10) 2 791 lb (1 266 kg); (18) 3 110 lb (1 410 kg); (24) 3 285 lb (1 490 kg); loaded (1) 2 965 lb (1 345 kg); (4) 3 135 lb (1 422 kg); (5) 3 660 lb (1 660 kg); (10) 3 782 lb (1 715 kg); (17) 3 990 lb (1 810 kg); (18) 4 034 lb (1 830 kg); (24) 4 215 lb (1 912 kg) (24 overload, 4 546 lb, 2 062 kg).

Performance: maximum speed (1) 224 mph (360 km/h); (4–18) 280–288 mph (450–465 km/h); (24) 326 mph (525 km/h); initial climb (4–24, typical) 2 790 ft (850 m)/min; service ceiling (typical) 29 500 ft (9 000 m); range (1–18) 500 miles (800 km); (24) 248 miles (400 km), (with two 22 gal drop tanks, 435 miles, 700 km).

Part of a large formation of I–16s photographed long before the Second World War as they flew over Red Square, Moscow, with large letters painted underneath to form a word (these three appear to read T-R-IV). Oddly, little was known of the I–16 until the Second World War, when it was called by the offensive nickname Rata bestowed in Spain.

in firepower and probably cheaper to build. But it was a tricky machine. It had most of the main masses very near the centre of gravity, and this made the aircraft only just stable longitudinally, like the Sopwith Camel. Indeed, though surviving reports are somewhat conflicting, it appears that in turns or a steep climb the I–16 was unstable, and if not flown with the utmost concentration could get out of control, not ideal when combined with laborious cranking of the landing gear on take-off. Should the aircraft get into a spin, recovery was made much more difficult by the ineffectiveness of the elevators in the disturbed airflow. Like several other great fighters, the I–16 was formidable in the hands of a master but dangerous to an inexperienced pilot. For this reason, from 1935 one aircraft in every four produced was a UTI–4 (I–16UTI) trainer version, carrying less fuel, and with a fixed landing gear and tandem seats. A few dual-control trainers were converted early-model fighters, retaining the retractable landing gear.

Back in February 1934 Valeri P. Chkalov, who did most of the test flying, began trials with a second prototype powered by a 700 hp M–25 (licence-built Wright Cyclone), with advanced installation ideas that later appeared on the I–153. The fixed-pitch metal propeller was carried on an extension shaft, terminating at the front in dogs to engage a Hucks starter, a ground vehicle used to start the engine. This needed a long conical support for the front bearing. The front of the cowl formed a rotary shutter: upstream of each of the nine cylinders was a variable aperture, closed or opened by the pilot using a handcrank. Nine separate exhaust stacks discharged around the rear of the cowl, which tapered to meet the slim fuselage. Speed jumped to 282 mph, but the first M–25 version, the Type 4, was a handful to fly and was a major factor in a 1936 plan to give military airfields runways.

In the Spanish civil war large numbers of similar Type 6 fighters gave good service, but the Russian adherence to unsuitable tactics negated the monoplane's advantages and made victory

hard over the agile Fiat C.R.32. In the Type 10, also widely used in Spain, two more ShKAS guns were added above the engine and the canopy was replaced by a large fixed screen and open cockpit. Pilots preferred the open view and had complained of the sliding canopy jamming after forced landings. There followed an immense profusion of I–16 variants and derivatives, including the Type 17 with 20 mm ShVAK wing cannon, the TsKB–18 ground-attack aircraft with six machine guns, bombs and extra armour, the TsKB–29 with pneumatically actuated flaps and landing gear, and the I–16SPB dive bomber which shortly after the German invasion of the Soviet Union in the summer of 1941 made an epic attack on a Danube bridge, pairs of aircraft being carried near to the target slung under the wings of TB–3 bombers.

While Moscas (Ratas) in Spain took on the Messerschmitt Bf 109B on roughly level terms, considerably greater numbers saw very extensive active service against the Japanese in China, Manchuria and Mongolia in 1937–41. But the sternest test for the I–16 came after 22 June 1941 when it bore the brunt of the first year's valiant defensive fighting against the Luftwaffe. The versions in front-line use in 1941 were the Type 18 with a developed M–25 called the Shvetsov M–62, rated at 1000 hp, and the similar Type 24 with wing cannon. The final versions were powered by the 1100 hp M–63 engine with VV–1 constant-speed propeller, and attained speeds in excess of 320 mph despite weighing over 50 per cent more than the prototype. Total production has been estimated at 7000, excluding spares, of which 4000 were used in the Second World War.

By 1941 the I–16 was long overdue for retirement, but it was used with sustained courage – and sometimes in unconventional and even deliberately suicidal ways – to give the Soviet Union a little more time to gather enough strength to halt the invader. That it was able to make any impression on the Luftwaffe is testimony enough, because the contemporaries of the first I–16s were the P–26, Bulldog and Gauntlet.

Messerschmitt Bf 109

Seldom can a fighter have had a more inauspicious beginning, and though it had abundant 'character', the 109 was hardly beautiful. Some of the later versions were thoroughly unpleasant to fly, and earlier sub-types suffered from various severe faults. Like many aircraft of Hitler's Luftwaffe, the 109 had to carry on longer than it should because there was nothing with which to replace it, other than the dramatic new jets. In 1944, despite the pulverization of German cities, output of the 109 reached an all-time high of 14212, and the total of some 33000 built exceeds that of all other fighters except the Soviet Yak family. I hesitate to call the 109 the greatest fighter of all, if only for the reason that almost every example built was in some major way deficient or over-demanding; but what fighter was greater? Which one saw more action, in more places, and shot down more enemies? Perhaps the courage and skill of its pilots, many of whom had no rest from operations for almost six years, transformed a fighter that the RAF would never have accepted at all into one of the classic aircraft of history.

The 109's inauspicious beginning stemmed from the violent antipathy between Willi Messerschmitt, its designer, and Hitler's Secretary of State for Air Erhard Milch, which was fanned until the planemaker was almost ostracized by the Reichsluftfahrt-ministerium (RLM). In mid-1933 Messerschmitt was officially rebuked because his Bayerische Flugzeugwerke had accepted a development contract from Romania. Messerschmitt produced his answer: sadly, he had been given no contracts by the RLM. So, in August 1934, he was instructed to build a new sporting machine for the 4th Challenge du Tourisme Internationale. Helped by Walter Rethel, who had been top engineer at Arado and was one of the most experienced stressed-skin designers, Messerschmitt created the Bf 108A for the Challenge. From this stemmed the Bf 108B Taifun, by far the best four-seat lightplane of the pre-war era and used in large numbers by the Luftwaffe and Luftdienst until 1945. The few still flying look modern today.

In January 1934 the RLM issued a specification for a new fighter. To prevent Messerschmitt from complaining that he was being ignored, he was sent a copy – whilst being openly told by the officials that he would never receive a production contract. At this time he was offered a professorship at Danzig, and the RLM strongly advised him to take it, as he was considered of no use to Germany. Milch allowed Messerschmitt to build a fighter prototype only because he was certain it would show up badly

It is difficult to identify this Bf 109 but it appears to be a late-model B–1. Features include cropped spinner
for a VDM constant-speed propeller, small oil cooler, early stub exhausts and no wing guns.
At first derided, the rakish fighter from Augsburg flew rings round its rivals.

alongside the rival Arado Ar 80, Heinkel He 112 and Focke-Wulf Fw 159. Messerschmitt had no experience of high-speed aircraft, and was completely discounted by almost the entire official establishment.

Those who were waiting to laugh at Messerschmitt's fighter should have studied the Bf 108 predecessor, which had the cleanest lines, neatest retracting landing gear and simplest all-metal stressed-skin structure anywhere in Europe if not in the world. And the fighter, the Bf 109, was conceived along exactly similar lines. It had a long and slender fuselage, splayed-out main landing gear far forward at the leading edge of the wing roots, retracting outwards to lie flat in the wings, and a rather shallow cockpit canopy, hinged along the right side. The wing was remarkably small. Though the 109 was going to be a weighty machine in the 1000 horsepower class, the wing had an area of only 174 square

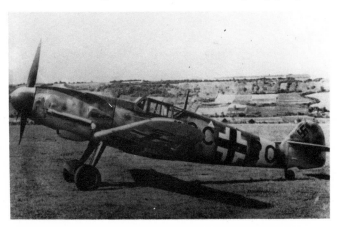

CC + PO was one of the first Gustavs (Bf 109G). It has been identified as a DB 603-engined G-0 development aircraft and also, and more probably, as a standard production G-2.

feet, compared with 293 sq ft for the He 51 bi-plane fighter then being built for the Luftwaffe and over 257 sq ft for the Hurricane, a monoplane destined to be one of the 109's chief rivals. The first service version of the 109 had a wing loading in excess of 27 lb/sq ft, which worried RLM officials who did not allow for the powerful, high-lift system of full-span leading-edge slats and a fully hinged trailing edge, the inboard sections of which were slotted flaps and the outer sections slotted ailerons.

No suitable German engine being available, the first prototype, with civil registration D-IABI, flew at Augsburg-Haunstetten in early September 1935 with a British Rolls-Royce Kestrel. To the mixed amazement, chagrin and embarrassment of Milch and the officials, the severe and rakish Messerschmitt out-performed and out-flew all the opposition. Later prototypes

Clark drew the Bf 109F in June–July 1941, entirely from inspection of one shot-down specimen. He called it the 'Me 109F series I'; until late in the war true designations were usually unknown, and one had such incredible things as 'He 111K Mk VA'. Clark knew perfectly well that Luftwaffe machine guns were of 7·92 mm calibre.

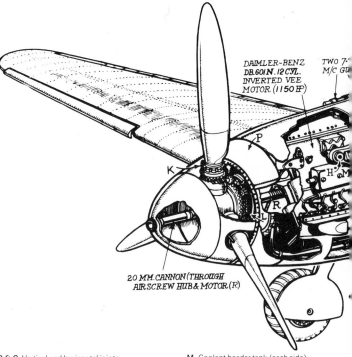

B & C Vertical and horizontal joints for spar
D Horizontal pin for front fix of wing
E Undercarriage electric interlock
F Supercharge air inlet
G Ejector exhausts
H Rubber anti-vibration motor mount pads
K De-icing spray pipe
L VDM electrically-operated controllable-pitch and constant speed airscrew
M Coolant header tank (each side)
N Undercarriage hand (emergency) retracting gear
P Oil tank
Q 'L' shaped fuel tank (Rubber bag in plywood casing)
R Cannon between cylinder banks
S Master compass (Repeats on dashboard)
T 10 mm armour behind pilot's seat

SPECIFICATIONS

Types Bf 109B, C, D, E, F, G, H and K series, S–99 and 199, Ha–1109–1112
Engine: (B, C) one 635 hp Junkers Jumo 210D inverted-vee-12 liquid-cooled; (D) 1 000 hp Daimler-Benz DB 600Aa, same layout; (E) 1 100 hp DB 601A, 1 200 hp DB 601N or 1 300 hp DB 601E; (F) DB 601E; (G) 1 475 hp DB 605A–1, or other sub-type up to DB 605D rated 1 800 hp with MW50 boost; (H–1) DB 601E; (K) usually 1 550 hp DB 605ASCM/DCM rated 2 000 hp with MW50 boost; (S–199) 1 350 hp Jumo 211F; (HA–1109) 1 300 hp Hispano-Suiza 12Z–89 upright vee-12 or (M1L) 1 400 hp R-R Merlin 500–45.
Dimensions: span (A to E) 32 ft 4½ in (9·87 m); (others) 32 ft 6½ in (9·92 m); length (B, C) 27 ft 11 in; (D, E, typical) 28 ft 4 in (8·64 m); (F) 29 ft 0½ in; (G) 29 ft 8 in (9·04 m); (K) 29 ft 4 in; (HA–1109–M1L) 29 ft 11 in; height (E) 7 ft 5½ in (2·28 m); (others) 8 ft 6 in (2·59 m)
Weights: empty (B–1) 3 483 lb; (E) 4 189 lb (1 900 kg) to 4 421 lb; (F) around 4 330 lb; (G) 5 880 lb (2 667 kg) to 6 180 lb (2 800 kg); (K, typical) 6 000 lb; maximum loaded (B–1) 4 850 lb; (E) 5 523 lb (2 505 kg) to 5 875 lb (2 665 kg); (F–3) 6 054 lb; (G) usually 7 496 lb (3 400 kg); (K) usually 7 439 lb (3 375 kg).
Performance: maximum speed (B–1) 292 mph; (D) 323 mph; (E) 348–354 mph (560–570 km/h); (F–3) 390 mph; (G) 353 to 428 mph (569–690 km/h); (K–4) 452 mph (729 km/h); initial climb (B–1) 2 200 ft/min; (E) 3 100 to 3 280 ft (1 000 m)/min; (G) 2 700 to 4 000 ft/min; (K–4) 4 823 ft (1 470 m)/min; service ceiling (B–1) 26 575 ft; (E) 34 450 ft (10 500 m) to 36 090 ft (11 000 m); (F, G) around 38 000 ft (11 600 m); (K–4) 41 000 ft (12 500 m); range on internal fuel (365–460 miles (700 km).

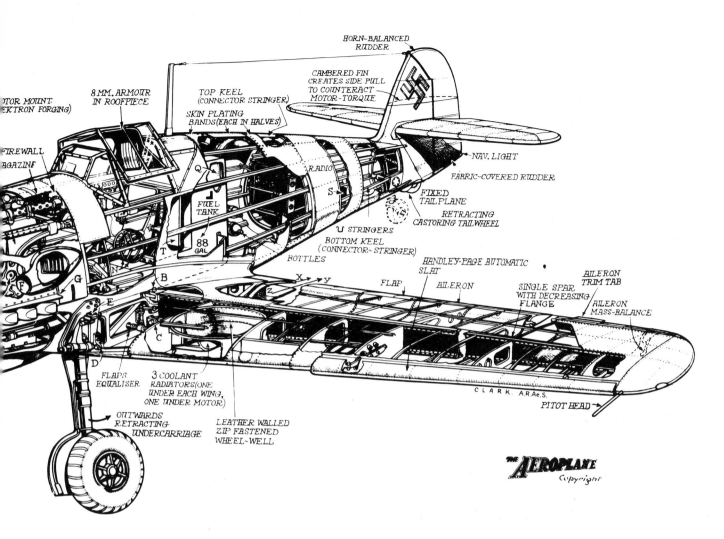

HORN-BALANCED
RUDDER

CAMBERED FIN
CREATES SIDE PULL
TO COUNTERACT
MOTOR-TORQUE

8 MM. ARMOUR
IN ROOFPIECE

TOP KEEL
(CONNECTOR STRINGER)

SKIN PLATING
BANDS (EACH IN HALVES)

OTOR MOUNT
EKTRON FORGING)

RADIO

NAV. LIGHT

FIREWALL
AGAZINE

FABRIC-COVERED RUDDER

FIXED
TAIL PLANE

FUEL
TANK

RETRACTING
CASTORING TAILWHEEL

88
GAL.

U STRINGERS

BOTTOM KEEL
(CONNECTOR-STRINGER)

BOTTLES

HANDLEY-PAGE AUTOMATIC
SLAT

AILERON
TRIM TAB

FLAP

AILERON

SINGLE SPAR
WITH DECREASING
FLANGE

AILERON
MASS-BALANCE

FLAPS
EQUALISER

3 COOLANT
RADIATORS (ONE
UNDER EACH WING,
ONE UNDER MOTOR)

CLARK. A.R.Ae.S.

PITOT HEAD

OUTWARDS
RETRACTING
UNDERCARRIAGE

LEATHER WALLED
ZIP FASTENED
WHEEL-WELL

THE AEROPLANE
Copyright

Whereas the first 109 to fall into Allied hands had been an E–3, given RAF serial AE479, this aircraft (DG200) was assembled from parts of at least five E-models. It is seen flying with the canopy removed and with the spinner of an E–4.

The Daimler-Benz engine and wing guns identify this aircraft as an E, and the matt-finished propeller blades probably rule out an E–0 development prototype. It is probably an early E–1, such as served with JG 20 and JG 51, the Legion Kondor and Swiss Fliegertruppe.

were powered by the 640–680 hp Jumo 210, giving much better nose lines with the Schwartz fixed-pitch propeller. It had two 7·92 mm MG 17 machine guns mounted in the top of the forward fuselage and in most respects was markedly superior to the He 112, its only serious rival. Its only significant deficiencies appeared to be a narrow and cramped cockpit, a hood that could not be opened to improve view, and an obstructed view when taxiing because of the steep ground angle. But the clear superiority of the first Messerschmitt fighter in prolonged trials at Rechlin was reinforced in January 1937 by the outstanding performance of prototypes 4, 5 and 6 in the Spanish war, even before they had completed their development programme at Augsburg. A month later the first production Bf 109B for the Luftwaffe left the assembly line, some of the B-series having a third MG 17 firing through the hub of the variable-pitch VDM-Hamilton propeller used in later models. Most of the Bf 109C series had four guns, two in the top of the fuselage and two in the wings, while the 109D (Dora) of 1938 introduced the 1000 hp Daimler-Benz DB 600Aa engine and three-bladed VDM propeller. It had a much better nose with a shallow oil cooler under the engine, the coolant radiators being moved to the underside of the wing roots immediately ahead of the

flaps. A 20 mm MG FF cannon fired through the propeller hub, backing up the two fuselage-mounted MG 17s, and speed leaped from 295 to 357 mph.

In early 1939 delivery began of the supposed definitive 109, the E (Emil). Though almost identical otherwise to Dora, this had the 1175 hp DB 601A engine with direct fuel injection, giving engine performance unaffected by negative g and thus allowing the Emil to push over into a dive and escape from an opponent whose engine had a carburettor. New plants were built at Augsburg, Regensburg and Wiener Neustadt, with further production by Erla at Leipzig and Fieseler at Kassel, so that between 1 January and 31 August 1939 (when the Luftwaffe went into action against Poland) no fewer than 1091 Emils were delivered. This was real strength, and from that time onwards the Bf 109 played the central role in making the Luftwaffe, not just more powerful in its enemy's minds – which thought had been instilled from 1935 onwards by the Nazi propaganda machine – but more powerful in fact. After twenty-seven days all resistance in Poland was crushed, and the Luftwaffe began transferring units to the West where, as Hitler had predicted, the powerful French and British combined forces had missed their chance and done nothing. Messerschmitt's enormous pro-

A puzzling picture of an aircraft identified as a G–6 but obviously altered by some post-war 'restorer' and apparently combining German balkenkreuz fuselage markings with under-wing crosses faintly resembling a style used by Bulgaria and Hungary. There is no evidence of provision for Rüstsatz wing racks, suggesting post-war modification.

ductive capacity continued to tick over on single-shift working, and it was even possible to export 109s to Switzerland, a country which chose the 109B, C and E as standard fighters and made the Emil under licence. Spain did likewise, and went into production itself with later versions.

Basically the 109E was smaller and lighter than a Spitfire, and rather more powerful with 1175 or 1200 hp against the 1030 hp of the early Merlins, yet the level speed of the 109E was actually inferior at around 354 mph, and it would be unwise to ascribe this solely to the strut-braced tailplane. Take-off and climb of the 109 were better than any contemporary fighter, handling at low speeds was excellent, and all-round manoeuvrability in the air was good. But one has memories of severe deficiencies. It was essential to keep sustained pressure on the left rudder pedal in order to fly straight at high speeds because there was no rudder trimmer, though this could easily have been added and did appear later. Worse, the flight controls tightened up drastically as speed increased beyond 300 mph, which was particularly severe in a roll because the pilot had to hold his arms straight out in front and could not get a good leverage on the stick except for fore and aft movement. In tight manoeuvres, which quickly became tiring, the slats snatched open and shut, causing sudden yaw (weathercocking)

which made accurate aiming of the guns impossible. There were many other tricky features, yet the JG (Jagdgeschwader, fighter wing) pilots considered it the best fighter in the world, and perhaps they had a case. It could climb and dive better than anything else, stand off and destroy enemies with up to three cannon (some had an MG FF firing through the propeller hub) and was extremely formidable in the hands of a pilot with experience, which was the reason why so many of these strangely deficient machines scored so many victories. With growing skill a pilot could master the 109, instinctively coping with all its bad features, and making full use of the good ones, but I do not understand why so much effort should have been expended in developing later versions without ever rectifying the obvious shortcomings. Not until the final months of the war, when virtually all the old *Experte* pilots had been killed, did geared trim tabs begin to appear on the control surfaces, which had been needed from the beginning.

Instead the proven superiority over such opposition as the PZL P.11c, Morane-Saulnier 406 and I–16 led to a concentration on development rather than improvement. There was one notable exception, and this was the first major new model introduced during the war, the 109F. With this the Messerschmitt team greatly im-

47

proved the 109 flying qualities as a result of a complete redesign, which could be seen most obviously in the rounded wingtips, but in fact left few parts unchanged. Usually powered by a 1 300 hp DB 601 E engine, the F was judged the best of all 109s to fly but usually had only one cannon (MG FF or the new 15 or 20 mm MG 151) and two machine guns. Like most of the later Emils there were bomber and reconnaissance versions, and among a growing list of optional additions were underwing cannon gondolas, a 66-gallon drop tank and a large sand filter ahead of the engine air inlet on the left side. With the inherently superior Fw 190, the F gave the RAF Spitfire V a hard time in 1941–42.

What should Messerschmitt do next? By this time the despised outcast had become Germany's favourite industrial leader, and his empire was swelling daily with new plants and thousands of willing or unwilling workers from all over Europe. One might have thought that the best answer was to build on success. Joe Smith did this to the full with the Spitfire, and to some degree so did Tank with the Fw 190, but Messerschmitt never found the ultimate fighter for the Luftwaffe, unless it was the 262. The Me 209 was a complete failure, a design that grew out of a little racer of 1938–39 which, for propaganda purposes, was publicised as a version of the 109. The Me 309 of 1942 was a new fighter making the fullest use of 109 experience and fitted with a tricycle landing gear, but it was eventually abandoned. In 1942–43 there emerged a far better fighter, designated Me 209–II. This had a

Another puzzle : this photograph – almost certainly showing a G–6/R2 Trop with WGr 21 rocket tubes and dust filter – is said to show service on the Russian Front, yet the width and shade of the theatre band suggest the Mediterranean. At least the 3-gruppe symbol is unequivocal.

A Bf 109F, with unbraced tailplane, MG 17 fuselage guns and quarter-light windows below the side windscreens. Unit codes or badges, or even a theatre band, are absent.

1750 hp DB 603 engine with an annular nose radiator, very wide-track landing gear, additional wing-span and many other good features, and was far better than any Bf 109. It was eventually dropped for the inadequate reason that it would disrupt production and that it was not much better than the Dora 9 (Fw 190D–9) then about to enter service.

This would not have been serious had subsequent 109 versions been superior, but in my view they were in most respects anything but this. During 1942, production switched to the 109G (Gustav), which was essentially an F with a 1475 hp DB 605A engine. Other basic changes common to most G sub-types included a pressurized cockpit and a change from the rifle-calibre MG 17 fuselage guns to the 13 mm MG 131, with ammunition feeds being accommodated in large flattish external bulges. Most were fitted with GM-1 nitrous-oxide injection to boost the power of the engine in emergencies, and later sub-types had a much better tail made of wood and a clear-view 'Galland' type cockpit hood. But not only did all the old deficiencies remain; most were accentuated. The G became heavier and heavier as more armament, armour

and special equipment was added, but the wing did not get any bigger and the heavy and badly arranged flight controls became, if anything, worse. The basic tendency of the narrow landing gear to induce a swing on take-off or landing appeared to be accentuated with the heavier, higher-torque Gustav, despite the report that in 1939–42 about 1500 Emils and 109Fs had been badly damaged or written off as a result of such swings. So the most important fighter of the Luftwaffe continued to be a thoroughly unsatisfactory machine, which in inexperienced hands was dangerous, and which became formidable only in the hands of a skilled pilot who knew how to cloak its inadequacies.

It was the most important fighter nevertheless. Production, which had been running at around 100 per month in the first two years of war, soared to 6418 in the calendar year of 1943 and, despite round-the-clock bombing of factories making it, to a remarkable 14,212 in 1944. It should be said, however, that there is some doubt about this figure, because production czar Albert Speer later said that it included hundreds of major airframe portions bombed before completion, subsequently salvaged, and then built into later

One of Michael Turner's fabulous action paintings, showing a scene that was all too common in May 1940. The Bf 109E–3 is clearly that of the Gruppenkommandeur of III/JG 53, the famed Werner Mölders, who began the Second World War with a

head start having gained 14 victories with the Legion Kondor in Spain. He went on to down 16 French aircraft – one of them this luckless Hawk 75C–1 of GC.II/5 – and was killed on 22 November 1941 with his score (including Spain) at 115.

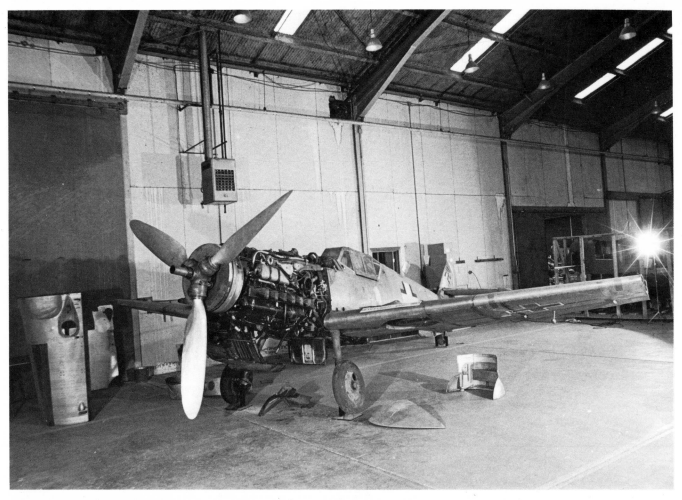

'Restoring' a 109 in the United States. Obviously the same aircraft as that shown on page 47, this view reveals that the Swastika has been painted on the wrong way round (the print has not been reversed).

aircraft which were counted afresh. These far outnumbered all previous versions, and were used by all the Axis air forces including the ARSI (fascist Italy after the September 1943 armistice), Slovakia, Croatia, Finland, Hungary, Bulgaria and Romania. Czechoslovakia, Hungary and Romania built the Gustav under licence, and Spain procured a licence but did not get into production until 1947.

There was no standard 109G armament, but it usually included two fuselage-mounted MG 131s and various arrangements of 20 mm MG 151 and 30 mm MK 103 or 108 cannon, often supplemented by 21 cm rocket launchers, various bombs up to 1102 lb, and a great diversity of special weapons. Many Gustavs were captured and evaluated against Allied fighters, and on the whole showed up badly. Despite the use of GM–1, the only aspect of performance in which it was competitive was rate of climb and dive, and increasingly the 109G pilots found themselves not only outnumbered but outclassed. Even the final model, the 109K, merely touched the edges of the problems and incorporated only various

detail changes. The 109H was a long-span high-altitude model which was abandoned along with the grossly developed Me 155, which was later passed to Blohm und Voss as the BV 155. The Bf 109T was planned as a family of carrier-based versions for the *Graf Zeppelin*, and another stillborn type was the 109Z (Zwilling) twin-fuselage Zerstörer (destroyer or heavy fighter).

After the Second World War, Czechoslovakia assembled a version called the S99, ran out of engines, and eventually fitted the Jumo 211F (intended for He 111 bombers) to produce the S199, which had flying characteristics markedly worse even than the Bf 109G. A substantial number served with the post-war Czech Air Force, where they were appropriately called Mezek (Mule); others were bought by Israel. A much better post-war family was built in Spain by Hispano Aviación, the HA–1109 series having Hispano-Suiza 12Z engines and the HA–1112 Buchón (Pigeon) having the British Merlin. On an autumn day in 1958 the last Buchón came off the assembly line at Seville. It was 23 years and 33 000 aircraft later than the first 109.

Hawker Hurricane

This great aircraft, upon which fell the brunt of the air fighting of the RAF in the first two years of the Second World War, was deliberately conceived as a blend of new and old. Stemming from a line of fighter biplanes, it was designed by Sydney Camm to be the best fighter that Hawker Aircraft could develop within a reasonable time and put into mass production with their existing resources. Camm could have held out for stressed-skin construction, and such refinements as a constant-speed propeller and cannon armament. Though it would have been possible to produce a hand-built prototype of such a fighter, more impressive than the Hurricane, the Battle of Britain would have found few in service and the rate of production low. The error might have been fatal to Britain.

Camm began to scheme a monoplane fighter in 1933. Twenty years earlier the British military

of biplane obsolescent within a few years. Unfortunately Hawker Aircraft had no facilities for making stressed-skin aircraft, and the way ahead beyond the Fury biplane was uncertain.

As a start Camm planned a monoplane version of the Fury, for which he chose the Goshawk engine. There was a sliding cockpit canopy and four Vickers guns were mounted, two in the sides of the forward fuselage and two in the wing roots. This was the armament specified in the latest RAF fighter specification (F.7/30), for which Camm had created the P.V.3 biplane, and it marked the first timid move away from the entrenched belief that a fighter pilot had to be able to reach his guns and clear stoppages by hand with a mallet. Camm considered the Fury Monoplane a practical 270 mph fighter which should be welcomed by the RAF, but his proposal met with only polite enthusiasm.

The Hawker High-Speed Monoplane, built to specification F.36/34, pictured at Brooklands in September 1935. One of the first changes was to add extra frames to the sliding canopy ; many more modifications led to the Hurricane I.

establishment had prohibited the monoplane. By 1933, though the service was becoming more open-minded, there remained doubts that monoplanes could offer any advantage. There had been attempts to effect direct comparisons, with inconclusive results, but by 1933 the growing trend towards stressed-skin monocoque construction, allowing a monoplane to have a thin wing section yet still be a pure unbraced cantilever, appeared likely to render most classes

Britain was hardly out of the industrial depression, the official policy was International Disarmament, and Hitler was someone not to be offended. As for RAF production orders, two years were still to elapse before the RAF would decide to place a contract for the biplane Gladiator! As it turned out, lack of action by the RAF was a blessing in disguise. If it had been ordered, the Fury Monoplane would have been a major type

Above: *Erla-built Bf 109E–3 beautifully restored at RAF St Athan. It was shot down on 27 November 1940 while flying with 2/JG 51 at Wissant, and the fuselage formed the basis for RAF DG200, flown hard until 1943. Today it has 1/JG 51 badges, but is much more authentic than most would-be 109s.*

Below: *Undoubtedly the best – almost the only – Bf 110 in existence, this G–4d/R3 was captured at Knokke, Belgium, apparently coded D5 + RL and on the strength of a gruppe in NJG 3. This was the final night-fighter sub-type, with improved low-drag SN–2 (FuG 220b) Lichtenstein radar. After sporadic flying with the RAF, Werke-Nr 730301 was crated, then restored as shown, and is now re-restored almost back to its original NJG 3 state.*

Above: *Merlin-engined Hispano HA–1112s neither look nor sound like a Bf 109, and this one combines British camouflage with incorrect gruppenkommandeur markings.*
Below: *A loose gaggle of Bf 110 Zerstörers over the Eastern Front in 1941 or 1942. So few ZG units were involved at this stage that further identification should be easy, but the Luftwaffe colour film has lost much of its definition. The sub-type is probably C–4/B and a hint of a Wespe (wasp) on a more distant machine suggests II/SKG 210.*

John Weal is a fine, clean draughtsman. He has filled in many of the gaps in the cutaway scene, and also produced better drawings of some famous aircraft, such as the Hurricane IIC, which, of course, had the stressed-skin wing. Most previous Hurricane cutaways were not so finely detailed. Wartime artists had no mechanical tint to pick out engines, cannon and tankage.

1 Starboard navigation light
2 Starboard wingtip
3 Aluminium alloy aileron
4 Self-aligning ball-bearing aileron hinge
5 Aft wing spar
6 Aluminium alloy wing skinning
7 Forward wing spar
8 Starboard landing light
9 Rotol three-blade constant-speed propeller
10 Spinner
11 Propeller hub
12 Pitch-control mechanism
13 Spinner back plate
14 Cowling fairings
15 Coolant pipes
16 Rolls-Royce Merlin XX engine
17 Cowling panel fasteners
18 'Fishtail' exhaust pipes
19 Electric generator
20 Engine forward mounting feet
21 Engine upper bearer tube
22 Engine forward mount
23 Engine lower bearer tubes
24 Starboard mainwheel fairing
25 Starboard mainwheel
26 Low pressure tyre
27 Brake drum (pneumatic brakes)
28 Manual-type inertia starter
29 Hydraulic system
30 Bearer joint
31 Auxiliary intake
32 Carburettor air intake
33 Wing root fillet
34 Engine oil drain collector/breather
35 Fuel pump drain
36 Engine aft bearers

37 Magneto
38 Two-stage supercharger
39 Cowling panel attachments
40 Engine RPM indicator drive
41 External bead sight
42 Removable aluminium alloy cowling panels
43 Engine coolant header tank
44 Engine firewall (armour-plated backing)
45 Fuselage (reserve) fuel tank (28 Imp gal/127 litre)
46 Exhaust glare shield
47 Control column
48 Engine bearer attachment
49 Rudder pedals
50 Control linkage
51 Centre-section fuel tank
52 Oil system piping
53 Pneumatic system air cylinder
54 Wing centre-section/front spar girder construction
55 Engine bearer support strut
56 Oil tank (port wing root leading-edge)
57 Dowty undercarriage ram
58 Port undercarriage well
59 Wing centre-section girder frame
60 Pilot's oxygen cylinder
61 Elevator trim tab control wheel
62 Radiator flap control lever
63 Entry footstep
64 Fuselage tubular framework
65 Landing lamp control lever
66 Oxygen supply cock
67 Throttle lever
68 Safety harness
69 Pilot's seat
70 Pilot's break-out exit panel
71 Map case

72 Instrument panel
73 Cockpit ventilation inlet
74 Reflector gunsight
75 Bullet-proof windscreen
76 Rear-view mirror
77 Rearward-sliding canopy
78 Canopy frames
79 Canopy handgrip
80 Plexiglas canopy panels
81 Head/back armour plate
82 Harness attachment
83 Aluminium alloy decking
84 Turnover reinforcement
85 Canopy track
86 Fuselage framework cross-bracing
87 Radio equipment (TR9D/TR133)

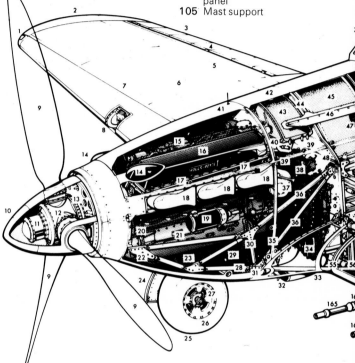

88 Support tray
89 Removable access panel
90 Aileron cable drum

91 Elevator control lever
92 Cable adjusters
93 Aluminium alloy wing/fuselage fillet
94 Ventral identification and formation-keeping lights
95 Footstep retraction guide and support rail
96 Radio equipment (R3002)
97 Upward-firing recognition apparatus
98 Handhold
99 Diagonal support
100 Fuselage fairing
101 Dorsal identification light
102 Aerial mast
103 Aerial lead-in
104 Recognition apparatus cover panel
105 Mast support

106 Wire-braced upper truss
107 Wooden fuselage fairing formers

Z3778, painted in abnormally small characters, identifies this Mk IIC from a batch of 1,000 built by Hawker Aircraft in 1941–2. It is serving with No 1 Sqn, RAF.

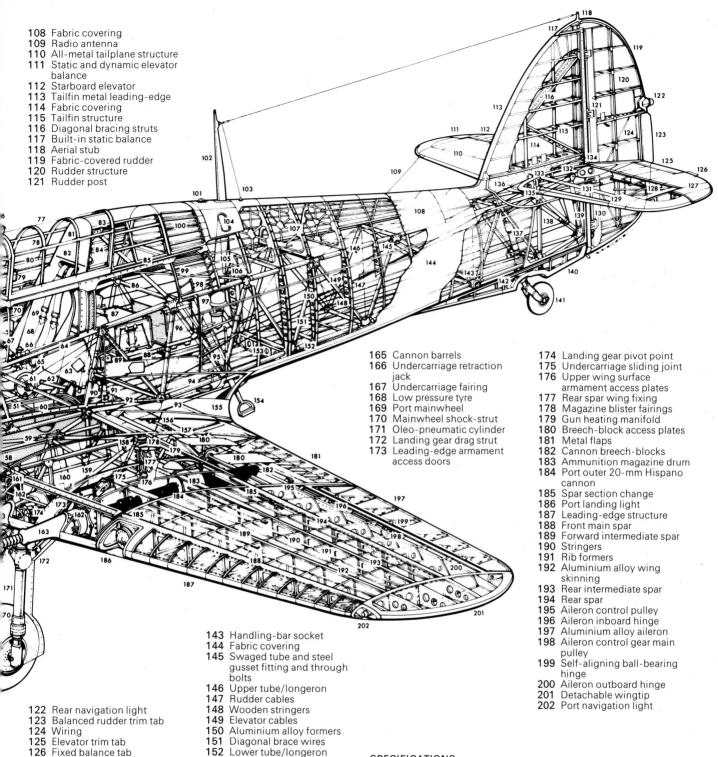

108 Fabric covering
109 Radio antenna
110 All-metal tailplane structure
111 Static and dynamic elevator balance
112 Starboard elevator
113 Tailfin metal leading-edge
114 Fabric covering
115 Tailfin structure
116 Diagonal bracing struts
117 Built-in static balance
118 Aerial stub
119 Fabric-covered rudder
120 Rudder structure
121 Rudder post

122 Rear navigation light
123 Balanced rudder trim tab
124 Wiring
125 Elevator trim tab
126 Fixed balance tab
127 Fabric-covered elevator
128 Tailplane rear spar
129 Tailplane front spar
130 Rudder lower hinge
131 Rudder operating lever
132 Connecting rod
133 Control pulleys
134 Elevator operating lever
135 Tailplane spar attachments
136 Aluminium alloy tailplane/fuselage fairing
137 Tailwheel shock-strut
138 Angled frame rear structure
139 Sternpost
140 Ventral fin
141 Dowty oleo-pneumatic fixed self-centering tailwheel
142 Fin framework

143 Handling-bar socket
144 Fabric covering
145 Swaged tube and steel gusset fitting and through bolts
146 Upper tube/longeron
147 Rudder cables
148 Wooden stringers
149 Elevator cables
150 Aluminium alloy formers
151 Diagonal brace wires
152 Lower tube/longeron
153 Aluminium alloy former bottom section
154 Retractable entry footstep
155 Wingroot fillet
156 Flap rod universal joint
157 Aileron cables
158 Fuselage/wing rear spar girder attachment
159 Main wing fuel tank (port and starboard: 33 Imp gal/150-litre each)
160 Ventral Glycol radiator and oil cooler
161 Front spar wing fixings
162 Cannon forward mounting bracket
163 Cannon fairing
164 Recoil spring

165 Cannon barrels
166 Undercarriage retraction jack
167 Undercarriage fairing
168 Low pressure tyre
169 Port mainwheel
170 Mainwheel shock-strut
171 Oleo-pneumatic cylinder
172 Landing gear drag strut
173 Leading-edge armament access doors

174 Landing gear pivot point
175 Undercarriage sliding joint
176 Upper wing surface armament access plates
177 Rear spar wing fixing
178 Magazine blister fairings
179 Gun heating manifold
180 Breech-block access plates
181 Metal flaps
182 Cannon breech-blocks
183 Ammunition magazine drum
184 Port outer 20-mm Hispano cannon
185 Spar section change
186 Port landing light
187 Leading-edge structure
188 Front main spar
189 Forward intermediate spar
190 Stringers
191 Rib formers
192 Aluminium alloy wing skinning
193 Rear intermediate spar
194 Rear spar
195 Aileron control pulley
196 Aileron inboard hinge
197 Aluminium alloy aileron
198 Aileron control gear main pulley
199 Self-aligning ball-bearing hinge
200 Aileron outboard hinge
201 Detachable wingtip
202 Port navigation light

SPECIFICATIONS

Type I to XII

Engine: one Rolls-Royce Merlin vee-12 liquid-cooled.
Dimensions: span 40 ft (12·19 m); length 32 ft (9.75 m); (Mk I) 31 ft 5 in; (Sea Hurricanes) 32 ft 3 in; height 13 ft 1 in (4 m).
Weights: empty (I) 4 670 lb (2 118 kg); (IIA) 5 150 lb (2 335 kg); (IIC) 5 640 lb (2 558 kg); (IID) 5 800 lb (2 631 kg); (IV) 5 550 lb (2 515 kg); (Sea H.IIC) 5 788 lb (2 625 kg); loaded (I) 6 600 lb (2 994 kg); (IIA) 8 050 lb (3 650 kg); (IIC) 8 250 lb (3 742 kg); (IID) 8 200 lb (3 719 kg); (IV) 8 450 lb (3 832 kg); (Sea H. IIC) 8 100 lb (3 674 kg).
Performance: maximum speed (I) 318 mph (511 km/h); (IIA, B, C) 345–335 mph (560–540 km/h); (IID) 286 mph (460 km/h); (IV) 330 mph (531 km/h); (Sea H. IIC) 342 mph (550 km/h); initial climb (I) 2 520 ft (770 m)/min; (IIA) 3 150 ft (960 m)/min; (rest, typical) 2 700 ft (825 m)/min; service ceiling (I) 36 000 ft (10 973 m); (IIA) 41 000 ft (12 500 m); (rest, typical) 34 000 ft (10 365 m); range (all, typical) 460 miles (740 km), or with two 44 Imp gal drop tanks 950 miles (1 530 km).

Another splendid Michael Turner painting, showing the Spitfire IX of J. E. 'Johnny' Johnson, from Melton Mowbray, leading his tough Canadian wing in a Rhubarb attack before D-day. On such a sortie a Mk IX usually started with bombs or rockets as well as loaded guns. From 1941 it was common practice for wing leaders to use their personal initials instead of

squadron codes. One can forgive The Aeroplane Spotter *for captioning a 1943 picture 'A mixed formation of Spitfires from two squadrons, IR and UF . . .' IR–G was the aircraft of wing leader Ian R. Gleed.*

59

in Fighter Command at the time of the Battle of Britain, and it would have been outclassed.

There had for many years been keen competition between the air-cooled radial and the water-cooled 'V' types of engine. Roy Fedden, at Bristol, maintained that the former represented a simpler, cheaper, lighter and more compact form of propulsion, which could offer flight performance comparable to a water-cooled unit, and gave an aircraft using it superior manoeuvrability because it was shorter. In addition it was likely to be less vulnerable in battle, because it needed no radiator and 'plumbing', and it offered immediate starting and good performance in all climates. Its coolant – the slipstream – could not freeze; and as the air acted directly on the hot cylinders without the intermediary of relatively cool water there was always a large difference in temperature which made for extra efficiency, even in very hot climates. All this was true enough, but the Air Ministry insisted that for the highest possible speed to be reached there was no alternative to the water-cooled 'V'. Its argument rested largely on the superlative performance of Rolls-Royce water-cooled engines in the succession of Schneider Trophy races, which tended to create a situation expressed by the tag 'I've made up my mind; don't bother me with the facts.'

Back in those crucial years of 1933–34 the Rolls-Royce V-12 engines were the only ones seriously being considered. The engine preferred for the F.7/30 trialists was the Goshawk. This was a development of the Kestrel (used in most of Camm's biplanes), in which the cooling-water was allowed to evaporate to steam in the cylinder blocks, subsequently being re-cycled through condensers built into the airframe. The system worked, and as the condensers could be shaped to the leading edge of a wing or any other suitable part, their drag was less than that of a conventional water/air radiator. But the installation proved heavy, cumbersome and vulnerable, and the Goshawk suffered from problems. Rolls-Royce was confident that it could develop the Kestrel to give more than the 700-odd horsepower of the Gosawk, but towards the end of 1933 a new engine began to come into the picture. This was the Rolls-Royce PV.12, a conventional V-12 and slightly larger than the Kestrel. It was first run on 15 October 1933, and at 3000 rpm the prototype gave about 900 horsepower. Though it suffered more than the expected number of mechanical problems, Rolls-Royce told Camm that, for design purposes, he could count on a further ten per cent power being available – in other words around 1000 hp. This was sufficient to call for major changes in Camm's monoplane

fighter and he decided to attempt adding a retractable landing gear.

New armament, the second major reason for change, stemmed from research at the Aeroplane and Armament Experimental Establishment, Martlesham Heath. Assuming that only rifle-calibre guns would be available, studies had indicated that 250 hits would be needed to 'assure destruction' of an enemy bomber. Calculations suggested that in future combat, between high-speed monoplanes, a fighter could not count on having a target in its sights for longer than two seconds. This led to an apparent need for fighter armament capable of delivering not fewer than 250 bullets in two seconds, or about 8000 in a minute. At the then current nominal firing rate of 1000 rounds/min this meant using eight guns, or more if any were synchronized. Squadron Leader (later Air Marshal Sir Ralph) Sorley was instrumental in promoting this thinking and making it official policy within the Operational Requirements branch at Air Ministry. This led to a new specification, F.5/34, calling for a fighter with eight unsynchronized guns. After extensive work on a four-gun installation, Camm succeeded by January 1935 in fitting eight guns and approximately 2400 rounds of ammunition (about 20 seconds' firing, the same as for a four-gun installation) into a new design of wing. In July 1935 BSA was authorized to begin tooling to manufacture the Browning gun, converted to 0·303 in rimmed ammunition, under licence from the Colt Automatic Weapon Corporation, of Hartford, Connecticut. Soon afterwards Camm considered he could drop the eight Vickers gun scheme he had planned as an alternative.

Hawker Aircraft had received a contract for 'one High Speed Monoplane', K5083, on 21 February 1935. The contract mentioned the original four-gun specification, F.36/34, but throughout Camm had designed K5083 as a private venture. The PV.12 engine and eight guns were his own choices, and it was also his choice in the summer of 1935 to begin the design of an entirely new wing of stressed-skin construction. This was a long-term project, and the company did not have the funds to tool up for this type of manufacture.

Though the new wing went ahead, K5083 was thus wholly fabric-covered. The fuselage was based on a primary structure of light-alloy tubes, joined by riveted plates and braced by steel wires. On this was fastened a secondary structure of formers and stringers of wood, and the fabric was stitched to the stringers. The wings had two widely separated spars, linked by diagonal Warren-truss bracing, with sheet webs and Hawker-patented polyhedral 'bulb flanges'

RAF No 85 Sqn, which had seen action in these parts 22 years earlier with S.E.5a scouts, scrambles from its base on the Franco-Belgian border during the Phoney War of 1939–40. At least No 85 had variable-pitch propellers.

where a modern spar would have booms. To form the aerofoil profile, light channels ran chordwise at frequent intervals above and below, and had Simmonds nuts into which were screwed channels securing the fabric, the groove being faired with strips of doped fabric. Ahead of the front spar were D-nose ribs covered by sections of flush-riveted metal skin. Fabric covering was used elsewhere except for the metal cowling panels, which were held in place by Dzus quick fasteners, and the rearward-sliding canopy.

P. W. S. 'George' Bulman flew K5083 at Brooklands on 6 November 1935. Ballast took the place of the unavailable guns, but the aircraft was easy to fly. The only visible modifications needed were to remove the hinged wheel doors from the bottoms of the leg fairings, remove the tailplane bracing struts, stiffen the canopy, enlarge the radiator, alter the fin and rudder, add a rear underfin after the start of production and make the tailwheel a fixed one. More complicated changes were needed later to accommodate the first production PV.12 engine, the Merlin II.

Early in 1936 the Hawker board took a chance and ordered material and jigs and tools for the manufacture of 1000 of the new monoplane fighters. Thus, when the first official order for 600 was received in June 1936, production was already in hand and the only delay was caused by the engine. By this time the aircraft was named Hurricane. The first production machine flew on 12 October 1937. By the end of the year nearly 40 had been built and No 111 squadron was converting to them at Northolt. By 3 September 1939 no fewer than 497 had been delivered, and rate of production trebled by bringing in factories at Langley and at Gloster Aircraft, with much greater speed of production yet to come, augmented in 1940 by aircraft built in Canada. The first metal-skinned wing was tried out in the air in April 1939, a modern structure with two main spars, two intermediate spars and sheet ribs aligned fore-and-aft. In August 1938 the vital need for a better propeller than the old wooden

Watts was partially met by the first Hurricane flight with a DH (Hamilton licence) two-position bracket-type, which had three light-alloy blades. Later the Rotol constant-speed RX.5/2 with densified-wood blades became the preferred propeller on British-built Hurricanes, though DH (Hamilton) constant-speed propellers with slimmer, metal blades were common. In 1939 all Hurricanes received an armour bulkhead ahead of the cockpit and a bullet-proof windscreen; rear armour arrived in 1940.

In France with 1 and 73 Squadrons the fabric-wing Hurricane with fixed-pitch propeller demonstrated its suitability for front-line use; sporadic encounters with the BF 109E confirmed the German fighter's much higher speed, but the Hurricane could turn in a tighter radius. It was appreciably larger than the Spitfire or 109. The gross weight, estimated in the initial design at 4600 lb, had climbed to 6600 lb and was soon to exceed 8000 lb. With an engine rated at 1030 hp this was really too much. The large size of the aircraft made it difficult for the pilot to climb in: he put his right boot in an extended spade-grip under the left wing root, reached for a push-in hand-hold, with his left foot off the ground, and then swung his left foot round to a kick-in step on the left-hand side of the cockpit. He then disengaged his right foot and brought this up and into the cockpit followed by the left foot, taking care not to stand on the seat parachute pack which was usually left in the aircraft. A member of the ground crew would then follow and, with feet in the two steps, help strap the pilot in and check his parachute harness, R/T and oxygen connections. There was no authorised walkway and the fuselage, and in some versions the wing, had fabric covering.

Invariably the pilot would leave the canopy open even in flight, for comfort and possible emergency escape. The 'Hurry' rode the grass rather heavily, the forward view was better than a Spitfire, and for really good sight-line in a difficult situation it was possible to release the

Above: *Genuine colour photographs of British Second World War aircraft are rare. Vidicolor Ltd transformed a faded purple 35 mm transparency into this fine picture of refuelling in 1940. The number '313' confirms this Mk I Hurricane as Canadian-built, with original Watts propeller.*

Below: *Two of the best-known of all British fighters are Hurricane IIC LF363 and Spitfire VB AB910, photographed with the Battle of Britain Flight at Coltishall. Apart from missing cannon, completely phoney six-stub exhausts and horribly wide code-letters they look almost genuine – which, of course, they are under all that new-specification paint.*

When this photograph was taken this represented almost the sum total of airworthy Second World War fighter-PR aircraft in RAF hands, all of them with Battle of Britain Flight. They comprised (from the front): two Spit VBs, two Hurry IICs and two Spit PR.XIXs.

Above: *Hurricane IIAs of No 151 Wing – formed from two hastily-created squadrons, Nos 81 and 134 – serving in the defence of Murmansk in the Soviet Union in September 1941. The wing lost one Hurricane in combat and scored 16 destroyed, four probables and seven damaged before handing over its aircraft to the Russians in mid-October. According to the CO of 134 'The Russians would turn up and demand training in the most appalling weather'. Later the Russians were sent 2,952 Hurricanes.*

Below: *Possibly slower even than the aircraft in Malta (right), this Canadian-built machine had a British Merlin and tropical filter. Later Canadian Hurricanes had Packard engines and Hydromatic propellers.*

Above: *Among the slowest Hurricanes ever invented, this tropicalized Mk I bomber is seen on naval charge in the defence of Malta in early 1942. They harried Kesselring's lines of communication to Libya.*

Sutton harness and almost stand up in order to see the ground about twenty feet in front of the nose. The only snag was that the aircraft seemed tail-light and nose-heavy, and sharp braking could bring disaster if you were in such a position. However, taking off was no problem, the only essentials being to reach 140 mph before climbing, and the need to fly the aircraft properly whilst working the undercarriage lever, which required sustained force and could appear to jam, for there was a lock that could spring back just at the wrong moment.

The Hurricane's climb was not spectacular, and it was a struggle to get much higher than 30000 ft. At full throttle a Mk I could reach a maximum speed of about 320 mph though less with a fixed-pitch propeller. Above or below the best altitude this maximum fell away to about 285 mph at 10 000 ft and barely 250 mph at sea level. Speed in a dive was poor compared with a 109 or even a Ju 88, but on the credit side the Hurricane had a comfortable cockpit, pleasant controls, a reasonable rate of roll in either direction, a good radius of turn at all heights, adequate armour protection, and the ability to fire its eight Brownings without deviating noticeably from the target. In addition, despite the Merlin's vulnerable glycol cooling system, the Hurricane could absorb severe battle damage. The airframe was extremely robust and easier to repair than stressed-skin structures, which called for dismantling the aircraft and return of the damaged part to the factory or to a civilian repair unit.

Owing to its less than excellent performance the Hurricane was used as far as possible against bombers, and in general below 20000 ft. Under these conditions, when flown by an experienced pilot, the Hurricane could give a good account of itself. Pilots of Hurricanes often killed the pilot of an enemy bomber with the first burst and, seeing no immediate effect, they would continue firing. Up to 2660 rounds could be exhausted within 20 seconds, and these long and unnecessary bursts would exhaust the ammunition. Conversely some pilots became so excited on getting into a firing position that they forgot to turn the brass ring which surrounded the firing button on the control column from SAFE to FIRE.

The Hurricane was as easy to land 'dead-stick' as any fighter in history; conversely, if one had to put on power to avoid an undershoot the nose came up strongly, so that little back-pressure on the control column was needed to do a three-point landing. Small windows in the cockpit floor gave a direct view of the position of the wheels, though (the book said) the only proof that the wheels were locked down was the indicator with its green lights. Most Hurricanes also had a horn which blared if the throttle was closed without both legs being down and locked. If a wheels-up landing was inevitable the Hurricane design was ideal, for the radiator took the main impact. Later the more hazardous technique of open-sea ditching became routine when working with the catapult-armed merchant (CAM) ships, whose Hurricanes often had no other way of coming

From the largest single batch of British combat aircraft ever ordered (1,500 Hurricanes in the serial range KW969 to LA144), this Mk IV is equipped with the two Vickers S 40 mm tank-busting guns originally fitted to the IID. The Hurricane IV had a low-blown Merlin with four-blade propeller and could be equipped for almost any tactical duty.

down. On landing, a tired or injured pilot would throttle back, approach at 90–95 mph with the undercarriage down, and just let the aircraft hit the airfield, thereafter landing off the first bounce. There were not many other fighters which could be taxied back in after such a landing, where the pilot was not in proper control, and Hurricane pilots remember this great warplane as rock-solid, reliable and effective. If you got behind a target you could hit it. If something got behind you, you could go into fine pitch with full power and slam the control column into one corner of the cockpit. One squadron sent a formal deputation to protest to their CO on hearing a rumour that they would be re-equipping with Spitfires.

By 1941, production had switched to the Hurricane II with the 1 280 hp Merlin 20 engine giving speeds up to 340 mph. It had modified outer wings accommodating an armament of four 20 mm Hispano cannon or twelve 0·303 in Brownings, and had racks for two 250 lb (later

500 lb) bombs or drop tanks, which could also take any of a range of other stores including SBCs (small bomb containers), smoke generators or, in the Mk IID, 40 mm Rolls-Royce or Vickers cannon for anti-tank missions. In 1943 the Mk IV brought together all the improvements and had wings able to carry all the above stores or gun armament as well as eight 60 lb rocket projectiles. By this time the gross weight had climbed to 8 500 lb, but performance was maintained by the use of the 1 620 hp Merlin 24, 27 or the (Packard-built) 28. In the final three years of the war the Hurricane served valiantly by day and night in North Africa, Sicily, Italy, the Balkans, Burma, the Soviet Union and from catapult ships and carriers in the Atlantic. Almost 3000 Mk II and IV Hurricanes served with the Soviet air forces, and others with the Fleet Air Arm, in Egypt, in India, Portugal, Finland, Belgium, Eire and other countries. Total production was about 14231, of which 1451 were built by Canadian Car & Foundry at Fort William.

Supermarine Spitfire

Reginald Mitchell, chief designer of Supermarine (part of the Vickers group of companies), had rarely been a rival of Sydney Camm of Hawker. He concentrated on flying boats, and the Schneider Trophy seaplanes which had little in common with RAF warplanes. But when the challenging F.7/30 specification was issued in December 1930 both Vickers and Supermarine submitted designs, and contrary to the official preference, both were monoplanes. Mitchell's Supermarine 224 was a pedestrian machine of mixed construction, with a faired landing gear on a cranked wing of almost 46 feet span, the leading edges of which accommodated the flush radiators for the 660 horsepower steam-cooled Goshawk engine. In accordance with the specification there were four Vickers guns, two low in the sides of the fuselage, accessible to the pilot, and the others on the inner sides of the undercarriage fairings. Like Camm's Fury Monoplane, if it had gone into production, it would have been quite outclassed in 1940, and Mitchell soon moved on to a smaller machine which had an uncranked wing and retractable landing gear, split flaps and an enclosed cockpit. He followed with a further refinement which had all four guns set in a broader wing, a deeper rear fuselage faired into the cockpit canopy, and an undercarriage on two single legs retracting outward.

These new machines were much better than the 224 but the Air Ministry had at last begun to get to grips with the problems of a future instead of a past war, and prodded by Squadron Leader Ralph Sorley, had issued Specification F.36/34 as mentioned in the preceding chapter. Mitchell, like Camm, decided the new PV.12 (Merlin) was the right choice of engine, but despite the demand for eight guns stuck to the small size of his second revised design. He decided that all the guns should be in the wings, and in 1935 plans crystallized for manufacture under licence in Britain of the American Browning of 0·303in calibre. To hold them Mitchell finally designed an elegant stressed-skin wing with a single spar assembled from channel sections, which changed to angle sections outboard. The graceful, elliptical shape looked right and gave a good chord measurement outboard to house the outermost guns, but otherwise there was little advantage and it made the aircraft more difficult to build. The wing had split flaps immediately behind a radiator on the right and an oil cooler on the left, immediately ahead of which were the bays for the outward-retracting landing wheels. The fuselage was the smallest that could fit behind the big P.V.12 engine, which had a traditional wooden propeller, and other features included a capacious cockpit with sliding hood, tailskid, flush exhaust stubs, and fabric-covered control surfaces.

In March 1936 Captain 'Mutt' Summers, chief test pilot of the Vickers group, flew the Supermarine 300 prototype at Eastleigh, now Southampton Airport. Air Ministry specification F.37/34 had been written around it, though the actual design, like Camm's Hurricane, had been a private venture. The prototype, K5054, appeared at various times unpainted (for the first

A pleasing formation above ragged stratus in the middle war years. EN821 and its companions with BL serials were all Mk V B Spitfires built at Castle Bromwich, serving with 152 Sqn.

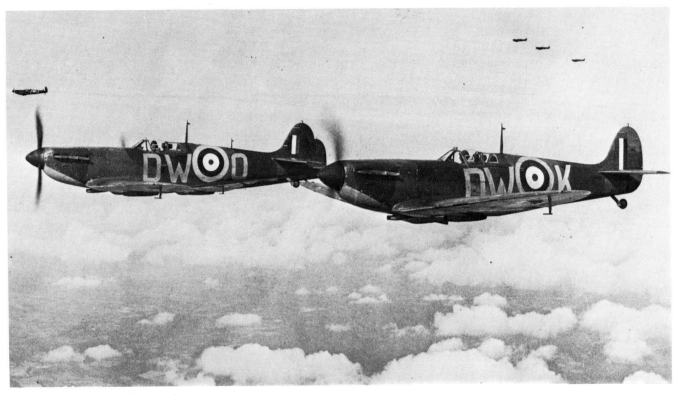

Above: *Battle of Britain photograph, showing a combat patrol by aircraft of 610 (County of Chester) Sqn, AAF, then based at Biggin Hill. The nearest aircraft (N3029, 'K') was one of the second production batch of 200 Mk I ordered from Supermarine in 1937. In 1943 it was lost while being shipped overseas – after surviving four years of air combat.*

Below: *An original photograph of 'the latest Spitfires with four-blade propellers'. The Aeroplane Spotter used to refer to this as the 'Mk ??' hinting that its Roman numeral had two characters. It was, of course, the hastily contrived Mk IX, a Mk V airframe with the two-stage engine, seen here with No 611 (West Lancashire) Sqn, AAF.*

flight), in cream seaplane enamel, glossy grey and PRU turquoise blue. Powered by a 1045 hp P.V.12, later changed for a Merlin C, the new fighter not only reached 346 mph but was found to be a sheer delight to handle both on the ground and in the air. There was probably a measure of luck in this, for Mitchell had no experience of fighters and precious little of stressed-skin construction other than in flying-boat hulls. Yet the Type 300 provided a basis from which emerged one of the best fighters in the world. Sadly, Mitchell did not live to see the full outcome because for many years he had suffered from tuberculosis and he died at the age of 42 on 11 June 1937.

By this time the Type 300 had been named Spitfire, the name previously given (unofficially) to the Type 224. A year earlier 310 Mk I Spitfires had been ordered to a revised specification, F.16/36, and the Vickers group had a tremendous job setting up adequate capacity for building them until, with Air Ministry funding, the Nuffield organisation built a large factory at Castle Bromwich, east of Birmingham, specifi-cally to build the Spitfire. In 1938 Vickers reorganised to become Vickers-Armstrongs, and Mitchell's place as chief designer was taken by Joe Smith, who headed the team right to the end of the Scimitar programme in the 1960s. However, in 1938 the desperate need was to get production going; nobody knew then the engineering development that would go into the Spitfire in the course of time, and it must match that of any other aircraft in history.

Slowly – much more slowly than the Hurricane, which was started first, was more traditional and came from a larger factory complex – production of the Spitfire got under way. Deliveries began to 19 Squadron (previously equipped with Gloster Gauntlets) in July 1938, and so slow was the transformation of the RAF into a force that could stand up to the Luftwaffe that, by the time of the Munich crisis in October 1938, the entire strength of Fighter Command still consisted of fabric-covered bi-planes, except for five squadrons of Hurricanes and five Spitfires (five machines, not five squadrons). The Mk I Spitfire had the 1030 hp Merlin

Early Seafire IBs converted from Spitfire VBs by Air Service Training in 1942. The aircraft nearest the camera had originally been Spitfire AD354, built at Castle Bromwich. The tips of the A-frame arrester hooks are just visible.

Totally different in almost every way from earlier Spitfires, the great Griffon-engined versions – especially those, like this one, with two-stage Griffons – were impressive performers. TP265 was an FR.XVIII, with rear-fuselage cameras in a bay which in the F.XVIII was occupied by extra fuel.

II engine, an Airscrew Company wooden, fixed-pitch propeller, Browning guns (only four at first, because of short supply), ejector exhaust stacks, tailwheel, and radio. Experience with those machines not damaged or written off by pilots unfamiliar with modern aircraft led to further changes, including a bulged cockpit hood, a thick, bullet-proof windscreen, armour behind the engine, and an engine-driven hydraulic pump for the flaps and landing gear, which were previously pumped up and down by hand. Nuffield developed an improved radiator; a new radio aerial mast and primitive IFF (identification friend or foe) was fitted, and, after 77 aircraft had been delivered, the outmoded wooden propeller was replaced by a DH-Hamilton or (later) Rotol metal three-bladed two-pitch type. In June 1940 de Havilland sent teams to Spitfire stations to fit constant-speed propellers.

Back in 1938 a 'B' wing had been designed mounting a 20 mm Hispano cannon and two Brownings, and 30 Mk IB aircraft were delivered in the first half of 1940. However, the drum feeds tended to jam and these potentially more formidable aircraft were withdrawn, even though a belt feed for the Hispano had been developed by Bristol. Total Mk I production was 1516 by Vickers-Armstrongs (Supermarine) plus 50 by Westland at Yeovil. A further 920, designated Mk II, were built at Castle Bromwich, with Merlin XII engines and fitted with armour from the start. A few Mk II aircraft had a non-

jettisonable, 40-gal fuel pod on the left wing, but later the standard long-range fitting was a 30, 45 or 90-gal slipper tank under the fuselage.

Though there were such oddities as the Speed Spitfire racer, a 'plastic' Spitfire to conserve aluminium, a Mk III, two Mk IVs, the IIC for air/sea rescue, and two types of float seaplane, the next mainstream model was the V, built in greater numbers (6479) than any other. The main advance in this was the strengthening of the fuselage longerons to take the 1470 hp of a Merlin 45-series, often with the use of a better propeller. The VA had eight machine guns, the VB two 20 mm cannon and four machine guns, and the VC four 20 mm cannon. In 1941, one aircraft had two 20 mm cannon and four 0·5 in Brownings, which led to a third standard wing, the 'E', with two cannon and two (not four) 0·5 in guns. The V had 125, 152 or 193 lb armour, and carried a 115 or 175 gal slipper tank or a 500 lb bomb, or two of 250 lb under the wings. Many had the wing-tips removed to become LF.V ground-attack aircraft (span 32 ft 7 in instead of 36 ft 10 in), while machines for the tropics had a Vokes filter in a large fairing under the nose. Though in some respects outclassed by the Bf 109F and, especially, the Fw 190A, the Spitfire V was the best Allied fighter available in 1941–42 and served on every front in defensive and offensive roles. Large numbers were supplied to the USAAF and Soviet Union, and other users included Turkey, Portugal and Egypt.

Since before the war Rolls-Royce had been

LA541 was the penultimate member of the family, a Seafire 46. The first production Mk 46, it had non-folding wings and was a navalized Spitfire 22. The final model, the 47, was built in several sub-types, all with folding wings, the final type having the carb-air intake immediately below the spinner.

working on a Merlin with a two-stage super-charger, both impellers being geared from the engine and with an intercooler between them. An experimental Merlin 60 was fitted to the only Spitfire III, but the Mks VII and VIII were designed as the definitive aircraft with the production Merlin 61 engine, rated at 1565 hp and holding power to high altitudes, giving, in fact, twice the power of early Merlins at 30000 feet. This lifted the 'Spit' to a level of performance at least as good as its enemies, but the need for these aircraft was so pressing by late 1941 that a hasty modification was put into production as the Mk IX. This was a slightly reinforced Mk V airframe with a Merlin 61 engine, which necessitated a longer nose of better shape, multi-stack exhausts, a four-blade Rotol propeller and symmetric glycol, oil and intercooler radiators under the wings. Deliveries began in July 1942, and this hastily conceived stop-gap continued to pour out of the factories almost to the end of the war, 5665 being built. There were LF (32 ft 7 in), F (36 ft 10 in) and HF (40 ft 2 in) wings, with the usual armament schemes, and bomb load rising to 1000 lb. Other features included metal-skinned ailerons and a broader rudder. Slipper and pod drop tanks were provided, but the Spitfire's very small internal fuel capacity prevented it from flying long escort missions of the kind done as routine by the US 8th Fighter Command. Again, large numbers of the IX served with all Allied air forces.

In 1941 a special extreme-altitude Spitfire was

rushed through to combat the Ju 86P. This, the Mk VI, had a high-blown (single-stage) Merlin 47, a primitive pressure cabin, HF wings, a four-blade Rotol propeller and (usually) B-type armament; 100 were built. In 1942 this type was succeeded by the HF.VII with a Merlin 61 engine, C-type wing with shorter ailerons, retractable tailwheel and double-glazed hood, late examples of the 140 which were built having a broad, pointed rudder. In my view the nicest of all Spitfires, the Mk VIII, was intended as the standard but it was continually delayed and displaced by repeated orders for the stop-gap IX. Usually powered by a 1720 hp Merlin 66, the VIII had most features of the VII except the pressure cabin. It came in LF, F and HF forms, and virtually all of them were built from 1943 onwards for use in Italy and Burma.

The last Merlin fighter variant was the XVI, virtually a stop-gap IX with a Packard Merlin 266 engine. Most had the LF wing and broad pointed rudder, and later examples of the run of 1054 had a cut-down rear fuselage and bubble canopy, as flown on the prototype VIII. The usual armament was E-type (two 20 mm cannon and two 0·5 in guns) and the XVI served widely with 2nd Tactical Air Force from Normandy to VE-day. By far the most important of the wartime PR (photo-reconnaissance) versions was the XI, basically a pressurized IX without armament and with the whole leading edge forming fuel tanks; with the addition of a deep slipper tank the range was well over 2000 miles, the enlarged oil tank resulting in a deeper nose. Various camera installations were fitted, and nearly all the aircraft had the broad pointed rudder and retractable tailwheel.

In 1942 a batch of 100 Spitfires was modified to use the 1735 hp Griffon II or IV, a larger engine than the Merlin, which increased speed at low level for catching 'hit and run' Fw 190s. Half were based on the VC and half on the VIII, the main difference being the bigger bulged nose and the fact that on take-off the aircraft swung to the right and not the left. In 1943 a far better, but still interim, Griffon Spitfire emerged as the Mk XIV, with the 2050 hp two-stage Griffon 65, deep symmetrical radiators, a five-blade Rotol propeller, and a new fin and rudder of greatly increased chord. The latter was needed to counter the longer nose, and when later F and FR (fighter recce.) versions appeared with a cut-down rear fuselage and teardrop hood the directional stability became marginal. These were tremendous machines, quite unlike earlier Spitfires. They were fast enough to chase and catch flying bombs and shoot down the Me 262, and the 957 delivered were the final Spitfires in action in the Second World War. Later came the XVIII, the XIX photo-reconnaissance, and the redesigned 21 to 24 which served post-war.

Going back, from early 1941 about 100 Mk V aircraft were transferred to the Fleet Air Arm, and many were fitted with arrester hooks. From these, Air Service Training derived a purpose-built Seafire IB, which equipped 807 Squadron in June 1942. This was followed by the IIC, which was basically a Spitfire VC with universal wing, hook and catapult spools, which was followed by the main wartime Seafire, the III. This usually had a Merlin 32 or 55 driving a four-blade Rotol propeller, and manually folding wings; Westland made 870 and Cunliffe-Owen 350. The last wartime Seafire was the XV, rather like the Griffon-engined Spitfire XII, but post-war Seafires were redesigned two-stage-Griffon engined machines, representing the pinnacle of Spitfire development.

When Joe Smith took over the Spitfire in 1938 it had 1030 horsepower, weighed 5800 lb and was likened to a ballerina. The Seafire 47, the final aircraft that developed from the Spitfire, had up to 2375 horsepower, weighed up to 12750 lb, and yet could outperform the early Spitfires by the wide margin of about 100 mph on the level. It was this amazing process of development that kept the Spitfire/Seafire in the forefront of the air battle, and extended production to 22890. So when people argue about whether or not the Spit was the greatest fighter, they should say which mark they mean.

1. Aerial stub attachment
2. Rudder upper hinge
3. Fabric-covered rudder
4. Rudder tab
5. Sternpost
6. Rudder tab hinge
7. Rear navigation light
8. Starboard elevator tab
9. Starboard elevator structure
10. Elevator balance
11. Tailplane front spar
12. IFF aerial
13. Castoring non-retractable tailwheel
14. Tailwheel strut
15. Fuselage double frame
16. Elevator control lever
17. Tailplane spar/fuselage attachment
18. Fin rear (fuselage frame extension)
19. Fin front spar (fuselage frame extension)
20. Port elevator tab hinge
21. Port elevator
22. IFF aerial
23. Port tailplane
24. Rudder control lever
25. Cross shaft
26. Tailwheel oleo access plate
27. Tailwheel oleo shock-absorber
28. Fuselage angled frame
29. Battery compartment
30. Lower longeron
31. Elevator control cables
32. Fuselage construction
33. Rudder control cables
34. Radio compartment
35. Radio support tray
36. Flare chute
37. Oxygen bottle
38. Auxiliary long-range fuel tank (29 gal/132 litre)
39. Dorsal formation light
40. Aerial lead-in
41. HF aerial
42. Aerial mast
43. Cockpit aft glazing
44. Voltage regulator
45. Canopy track
46. Structural bulkhead
47. Headrest
48. Plexiglas canopy
49. Rear-view mirror
50. Entry flap (port)
51. Air bottles (alternative rear fuselage stowage)
52. Sutton harness
53. Pilot's seat (moulded Bakelite)
54. Datum longeron
55. Seat support frame
56. Wingroot fillet
57. Seat adjustment lever
58. Rudder pedal frame
59. Elevator control connecting tube
60. Control column spade grip
61. Trim wheel
62. Reflector gunsight
63. External windscreen armour
64. Instrument panel
65. Main fuselage fuel tank (48 gal/218 litre)
66. Fuel tank/longeron attachment fittings
67. Rudder pedals
68. Rudder bar
69. King post
70. Fuselage lower fuel tank (37 gal/168 litre)
71. Firewall/bulkhead
72. Engine bearer attachment
73. Steel tube bearers
74. Magneto
75. 'Fishtail' exhaust manifold
76. Gun heating 'intensifier'
77. Hydraulic tank
78. Fuel filler cap
79. Air compressor intake

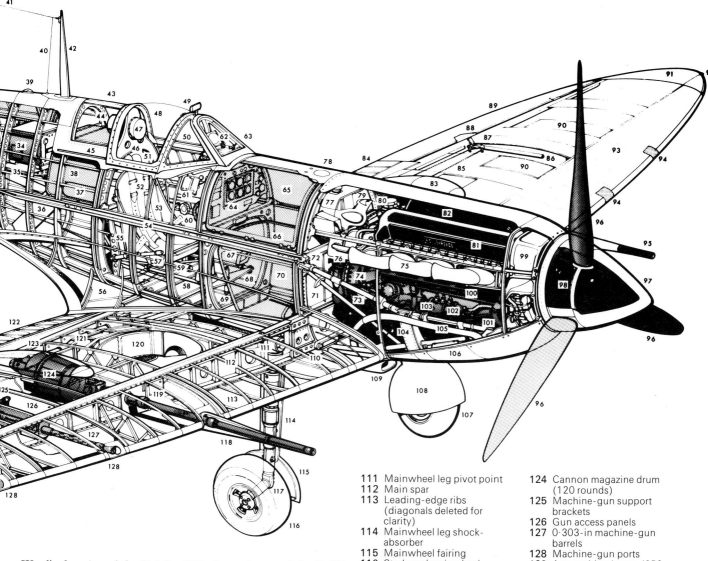

Weal's drawing of the Spitfire VB, the mainstay of the RAF during the tough middle war years. The Spit is a difficult aircraft to draw convincingly and this is a first-class drawing in all respects.

111 Mainwheel leg pivot point
112 Main spar
113 Leading-edge ribs
    (diagonals deleted for
    clarity)
114 Mainwheel leg shock-
    absorber
115 Mainwheel fairing
116 Starboard mainwheel
117 Angled axle
118 Cannon barrel support
    fairing
119 Spar cut-out
120 Mainwheel well
121 Gun heating pipe
122 Flap structure
123 Cannon wing fairing

124 Cannon magazine drum
    (120 rounds)
125 Machine-gun support
    brackets
126 Gun access panels
127 0·303-in machine-gun
    barrels
128 Machine-gun ports
129 Ammunition boxes (350
    rpg)
130 Starboard aileron
    construction
131 Wing ribs
132 Single-tube outer spar
    section
133 Wingtip structure
134 Starboard navigation light

80 Air compressor
81 Rolls-Royce Merlin 45
   engine
82 Coolant piping
83 Port cannon wing fairing
84 Flaps
85 Aileron control cables
86 Aileron push tube
87 Bellcrank
88 Aileron hinge
89 Port aileron
90 Machine-gun access panels
91 Port wingtip
92 Port navigation light
93 Leading-edge skinning
94 Machine-gun ports
   (protected)
95 20-mm cannon muzzle

96 Three-blade constant-speed
   propeller
97 Spinner
98 Propeller hub
99 Coolant tank
100 Cowling fastening
101 Engine anti-vibration
    mounting pad
102 Engine accessories
103 Engine bearers
104 Main engine support
    member
105 Coolant pipe
106 Exposed oil tank
107 Port mainwheel
108 Mainwheel fairing
109 Carburettor air intake
110 Stub/spar attachment

SPECIFICATIONS

Mks I to 24

Engine: one Rolls-Royce Merlin or Griffon vee-12 liquid-cooled.
Dimensions: span 36 ft 10 in (11·23 m), clipped, 32 ft 2 in, or, more often, 32 ft 7 in (9·93 m), extended, 40 ft 2 in (12·24 m) ; length 29 ft 11 in (9·12 m), later, with two-stage engine, typically 31 ft 3½ in (9.54 m), Griffon engine, typically 32 ft 8 in (9.96 m) ; height 11 ft 5 in (3·48 m), with Griffon, typically 12 ft 9 in (3·89 m).
Weights: empty (Mk I) 4 810 lb (2 182 kg) ; (IX) 5 610 lb (2 545 kg) ; (XIV) 6 700 lb (3 040 kg) ; (Sea 47) 7 625 lb (3 458 kg) ; maximum loaded (I) 5 784 lb (2 624 kg) ; (IX) 9 500 lb (4 310 kg) ; (XIV) 10 280 lb (4 663 kg).
Performance: maximum speed (I) 355–362 mph (580 km/h) ; (IX) 408 mph (657 km/h) ; (XIV) 448 mph (721 km/h) ; (Sea 47) 451 mph (724 km/h) ; initial climb (I) 2 530 ft (770 m)/min ; (IX) 4 100 ft (1 250 m)/min ; (XIV) 4 580 ft (1 396 m)/min ; range on internal fuel (I) 395 miles (637 km) ; (IX) 434 miles (700 km) ; (XIV) 460 miles (740 km).

Messerschmitt Bf 110

In 1934 several air forces began independently to study a new type of fighter with two engines. There were several reasons for having two engines, among them being higher speed, more armament could be carried, and there was greater ability to survive engine failure or combat damage. But the most important reason was that such aircraft could carry more than twice as much fuel as single-engined fighters, and thus have greater range. The results which emerged from this thinking were diverse. The US Army Air Corps tested the Bell XFM–1 Airacuda, an extraordinary machine which, among other things, had a gunner in the front of each pusher nacelle, aiming a 37 mm cannon, a scheme previously tried out in 1916. France built so many twin-engined fighter prototypes, related *Multiplace de Combat* and fighter/reconnaissance or attack machines, that they were submerged beneath a welter of possible options – though a few types did get into production, notably the Potez 63 family and Breguet 693–695. In Britain the long-range twin appeared to be overlooked. The F.37/35 specification resulted in the unsuccessful

Whirlwind which happened to have two engines, but this was not a long-range aircraft and could just as well have been single-engined. With war seemingly imminent the absence of a long-range British fighter was noticed and an urgent programme was put in hand to convert Blenheim bombers to fighters, a compromise that could not survive except by night.

As might be expected, the German RLM left little overlooked in the mid-1930s, and studied the Zerstörer and Kampfflugzeug (literally, destroyer and battle aircraft) classes of aircraft carefully. The former was a heavy fighter, while the latter was a fast fighter-bomber. There was something that appealed to the German mentality in these concepts, which involved penetrating deep into other people's airspace, probably escorting bombers, and demolishing any aerial opposition. In contrast Britain's fighters, right up to the supersonic Lightning, were tailored to a narrow defensive concept that called for barely enough fuel to cross county boundaries, let alone cross the Channel! But one seldom gets something for nothing, and the German Zerstörer

A frame from a German film of mid-1941 showing early Bf 110C models (lacking the extended rear fuselage for a dinghy) of ZG26, the first Zerstörergeschwader to fight through Greece to North Africa. Though painted regulation Sand Yellow, the far aircraft still has its four-letter factory code.

Though unable to survive over southern England, the Bf 110C was still an extremely valuable long-range aircraft that subsequently gave important service in the Soviet Union (as seen here, in the summer of 1941) and Mediterranean theatre.

inevitably had to be substantially bigger than other fighters. This might not harm performance but made it virtually impossible to achieve the manoeuvrability needed to win a dogfight. To a first approximation, the rate of roll is a function of span, and the figures just did not allow a span remotely similar to the ten metres of a Bf 109. So, rather haphazardly, the Zerstörer took shape as something rather lumbering which would make up for this deficiency (if it could) with increased firepower.

Though there were other German Zerstörer and Kampfflugzeug contenders, the most important by far was the Bf 110 from BFW (later Messerschmitt AG) of Augsburg. This needed two of the new Daimler-Benz DB 600 engines, each of 1000 hp, and two of these powered the prototype when it flew on 12 May 1936. But the undeveloped engine gave prolonged trouble, and the Bf 110A–0 development batch had to have Jumo 210 engines of 680 hp, with which the maximum speed was only 268 mph. By 1938 production was proceeding on the B4 110B series, still with the Jumo 210, but with a better-shaped nose with two 20 mm MG FF cannon supplementing the original forward-firing armament of four MG 17 machine guns. The radio-operator/gunner in the rather remote rear seat had a manually aimed MG 15. Manoeuvrability was judged adequate, and with more power the performance was acceptable, though pilots found the tendency to swing on take-off or landing too

pronounced for comfort. Technically the 110 was thoroughly modern, and like the 109 had a smooth stressed skin, radiators under the wing (except in the interim Jumo versions) and single-leg landing gears. But it was not until the end of 1938 that Daimler-Benz finally cleared the DB 601A, the definitive development with fuel injection that replaced the DB 600, so that production could begin in January 1939 of the Bf 110C.

By this time the ZG (Zerstörergruppen) had emerged as the élite of the élite; Goering's Luftwaffe was itself the favourite of the Nazi propaganda machine, and Goering's own paternal love centred on the new Bf 110 units, which, he said 'will be like Hannibal's cavalry protecting the elephants; the bombers are my elephants'. Focke-Wulf, Gotha and MIAG helped to swell the rate of production, and the propaganda machine told the world the ZG were invincible. What is more, Goering and the Bf 110 crews believed it. Nothing could stand up to the Zerstörers, winging their way far into the enemy airspace and blasting everything sent against them with cannon and machine guns. The final six months of peace were hectic as the new ZG were formed and, in partnership with special 'instructional units', worked out how the formidable Bf 110 should be used.

In the Polish campaign few fighters managed to get airborne from the blasted Polish fields, and though once or twice the Bf 110 seemed to come

75

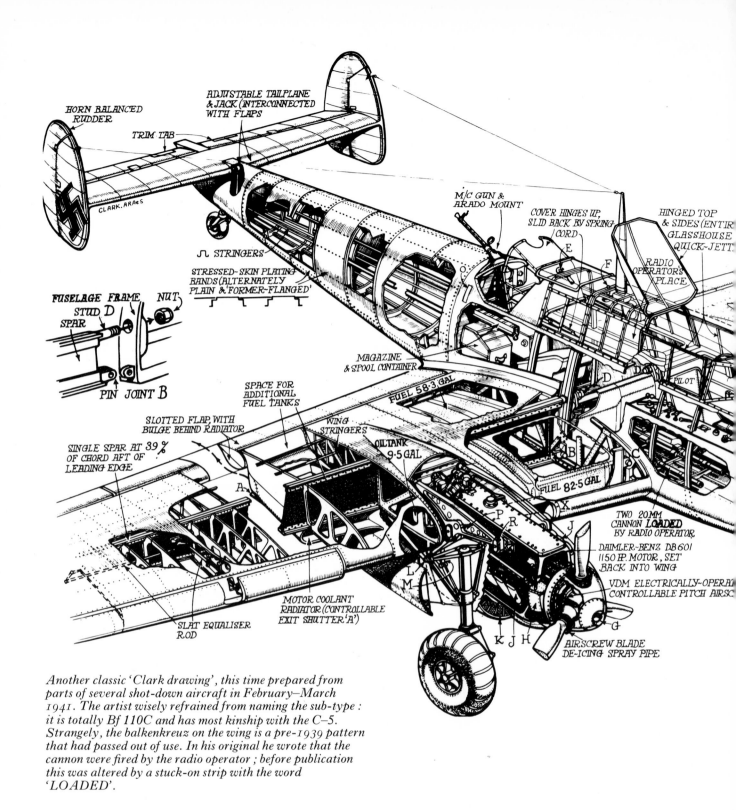

HORN BALANCED RUDDER

TRIM TAB

ADJUSTABLE TAILPLANE & JACK (INTERCONNECTED WITH FLAPS)

CLARK.ARAeS

∏ STRINGERS

STRESSED-SKIN PLATING BANDS (ALTERNATELY PLAIN & 'FORMER-FLANGED')

FUSELAGE FRAME

STUD D

SPAR

NUT

PIN JOINT B

SLOTTED FLAP, WITH BULGE BEHIND RADIATOR

SINGLE SPAR AT 39% OF CHORD AFT OF LEADING EDGE

SPACE FOR ADDITIONAL FUEL TANKS

WING STRINGERS

OIL TANK 9·5 GAL

SLAT EQUALISER ROD

MOTOR COOLANT RADIATOR (CONTROLLABLE EXIT SHUTTER 'A')

M/C GUN & ARADO MOUNT

COVER HINGES UP, SLID BACK BY SPRING CORD

HINGED TOP & SIDES (ENTIR GLASSHOUSE QUICK-JETT.

RADIO OPERATOR'S PLACE

MAGAZINE & SPOOL CONTAINER

FUEL 58·3 GAL

FUEL 82·5 GAL

PILOT

TWO 20MM CANNON **LOADED** BY RADIO OPERATOR

DAIMLER-BENZ DB 601 1150 H.P. MOTOR, SET BACK INTO WING

VDM ELECTRICALLY-OPERA CONTROLLABLE PITCH AIRSC

AIRSCREW BLADE DE-ICING SPRAY PIPE

Another classic 'Clark drawing', this time prepared from parts of several shot-down aircraft in February–March 1941. The artist wisely refrained from naming the sub-type : it is totally Bf 110C and has most kinship with the C–5. Strangely, the balkenkreuz on the wing is a pre-1939 pattern that had passed out of use. In his original he wrote that the cannon were fired by the radio operator ; before publication this was altered by a stuck-on strip with the word 'LOADED'.

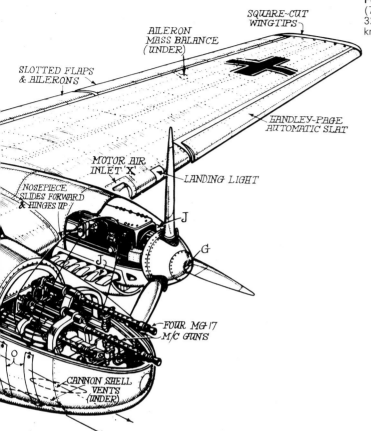

SQUARE-CUT WINGTIPS

AILERON MASS BALANCE (UNDER)

SLOTTED FLAPS & AILERONS

HANDLEY-PAGE AUTOMATIC SLAT

MOTOR AIR INLET 'X'

LANDING LIGHT

NOSEPIECE SLIDES FORWARD & HINGES UP

J

G

FOUR MG·17 M/C GUNS

CANNON SHELL VENTS (UNDER)

SPECIFICATIONS

Types Bf 110C-4/B
Engines: two 1 100 hp Daimler-Benz DB 601A; (later C-4s) 1 200 hp DB 601N 12-cylinder inverted-vee liquid-cooled; (G, H) two 1 475 hp DB 605B, same layout.
Dimensions: span 53 ft 4¾ in (16·25 m); length 39 ft 8½ in (12·1 m); height 11 ft 6 in (3·5 m).
Weights: empty 9 920 lb (4 500 kg); loaded 15 430 lb (7 000 kg).
Performance: maximum speed 349 mph (562 km/h) at 22 966 ft (7 000 m); climb to 18 045 ft (5 500 m), 8 minutes; service ceiling 32 800 ft (10 000 m); range 528 miles (850 km) at 304 mph (490 km/h) at 16 400 ft (5 000 m).

off second-best against the obsolete but nimble P.11c, only 12 were lost in the entire campaign. Conversely they destroyed numerous Polish aircraft both in the air and on the ground, and lack of manoeuvrability against an obsolete fabric monoplane designed in 1930–32 was not considered important. Further proof of the Bf 110's effectiveness came on 18 December 1939, when the RAF sent a formation of Wellingtons to look for the German fleet, and Bf 110C–1s of ZG 76 (the Haifisch wing with a fierce shark-mouth painted on its aircraft) shot down nine out of twenty-four, to which Bf 109s added another three. For the Norwegian campaign in April 1940 the 110 was just what was needed, quickly overcoming almost all aerial opposition, despite the long flying distances involved. One ZG 76 unit under Lt Hansen eliminated opposition over Oslo Fornebu airport, but the Ju 52 troop

carriers which should have arrived then were delayed by bad weather. Hansen waited, and when the Bf 110 tanks were almost dry, he audaciously led his fighters down to capture the airport, successfully holding the field until the Ju 52s appeared. This action fitted in perfectly with the impressive image created around the Zerstörers.

But in the month of May came a douche of cold water: the ZG wings lost 82 aircraft, nearly all in combat after the invasion in the west on 10 May. Against a motley and disorganised rabble of opponents, the big fighter did not have it all its own way. As a destroyer of bombers and other unwieldy aircraft it was unrivalled, but other fighters gave it very real problems. It could not bring its heavy armament to bear, except by 'jumping' its enemy unawares; and it was hard pressed to evade an enemy's subsequent attack.

Before the collapse of France the Luftwaffe had agreed that the 110 was not a dogfighter, and that new tactics had to be worked out, so that more than once the proud Zerstörers had to get into a defensive circle, like the helpless bombers of the First World War!

What did the Zerstörergruppen think as they got ready for Adlertag, the opening of the assault on Britain? They knew this would be their sternest test yet, but never doubted their ability to win. It was vital that they should. Even in the

pecially designed to show them in their worst light, because when opposed by stoutly-flown single-seaters they had little chance. Many ZG were disbanded, while the few that continued to fly over England found themselves, the supposed escorts, having to be escorted by the hard-pressed short-range Bf 109s!

This disaster was not the end of the Bf 110, but merely the end of its misguided beginning. It retired to lick its wounds to find itself on the threshold of a whole succession of new careers, all

Though bearing their badge of Britain in a gunsight, these Bf 110D escorts are pictured on the Eastern Front at least two years after the Battle of Britain. S9 was the code of EGr.210, which was decimated over England. Subsequently it became SKG 210, and was the only complete Bf 110 unit, other than one gruppe of ZG 26, to take part in Barbarossa, the invasion of the Soviet Union in June 1941.

situation (wholly unforeseen by the British) where Luftwaffe fighters could operate from bases along the whole length of the Channel coast, the Bf 109 could penetrate only a little way into England, and could not safely escort bombers as far as London. Escort was therefore mainly up to the Bf 110, which, as the C–4 and C–5, was now a mature and well-liked machine, with a speed of up to 350 mph. However, despite this, the Battle of Britain that followed proved far worse than even the most pessimistic ZG crew had feared. The 110 started out with the psychological advantage of formidable power, which had penetrated the Fighter Command squadrons in France. Yet, within the first week, the big twin-engined fighter had ceased to be a bogey-man and instead was regarded as easy meat. The ZG attrition was crippling. Before the end of August 1940 another 120 had been lost, nearly all in combat in the twenty days from Adlertag on 10 August. This crucial test of the much-vaunted Zerstörers might have been es-

of which brought forth new versions from the prolific Messerschmitt organization. In the summer of 1940 a need for greater range, to protect Norwegian sea convoys, produced the grotesque Dackelbauch (dachshund belly) tank, which was troublesome and soon replaced by two 66 or 198-gal tanks slung under the outer wings. Most of the D-series could carry two tanks and two 1102 lb bombs, while many E-models could carry a 2645 lb bomb load. This made the aircraft slow and sluggish, and failure of one engine made things dangerous. Probably even more dangerous and one of the 'hairiest' regular tasks in the history of flying, was the Troika-schlepp, a vic (vee formation) of three 110s linked by separate cables to a Messerschmitt Me 321 Gigant glider. Numerous 110 tow-planes came to grief carrying out this programme, which was ended by the development of the five-engine He 111Z and by turning the 321 into the powered 323.

Although accepted as no longer a fighter for

close combat, the willing 110 took on ever-greater burdens, and needed more power. The F-series had the 1350 hp DB 601 F engine, and with earlier models appeared with a great diversity of special armaments and equipment. In 1943–44 most versions then in service were in the forefront of day defence against the US 8th Air Force and other Allied bomber assaults, carrying cannon, rockets, recoil-less guns and even air-to-air bombs. But by far the most important family were the G-series night fighters. The Bf 110 was the first aircraft chosen as a Luftwaffe night fighter, Oberst Kammhuber using the 110C to form I/NJG 1 on 20 July 1940. From this small beginning grew the biggest and most efficient arm of the Luftwaffe, which after a slow start received priority in equipment. Production of the 110, due to phase out in 1941–42 in favour of the Me 210, rose by 300 per cent to 1580 in 1943, a further 1525 being delivered in 1944. Virtually all were of the Bf 110G family with 1475 hp DB 605B engines. Failure of the Me 210 put a heavy responsibility on the 110, which responded nobly. Gradually the NJG wings received more

effective aircraft with FuG 202 radar, and then SN–2 (FuG 220) radar, Flensberg (for homing on the tail-warning radars added to British bombers to protect them), a third crew-member to work the extra equipment, large flame-damped exhausts, and powerful new armament. Some sub-types had as many as eight cannon, two of them being mounted diagonally in the rearmost cockpit in the deadly Schräge Musik (Jazz) installation. With this the pilot, if he was an *experte*, could slide in under the defenceless belly of a bomber and, using a special roof sight, aim exactly at the wing spars between the engines. Schnauffer, the greatest *experte* with 121 kills, once shot down a Lancaster that was violently corkscrewing in the approved way to prevent a night fighter from formating with it.

A few Bf 110H-series were built in 1944–45, very like the G, bringing output to about 6050. Though of little use in its original design role, the 110 proved to be a docile and most valuable workhorse that – partly because of the failure of its successors – soldiered on to the end of the war in Europe.

One of the most important of all Bf 110s, the DB 605-powered G–4/R3 night fighter. Despite flame-damped exhausts, and the weight and drag of both BC and SN–2 types of Lichtenstein radar, drop tanks, a crew of three and heavy cannon armament, this docile aircraft retained ample performance margin over the ill-planned RAF heavy bombers, which bristled with defences except where it mattered.

Lockheed
P-38 Lightning

After so much about the war in Europe, it is pleasant to turn to the blue skies of sunny California and to what, in 1937, was one of the many friendly and talented planemakers striving to climb out of the depression. Lockheed Aircraft had a lot going for it. At the helm was Robert S. Gross, who had already shown he had the stuff successful businessmen are made of. In a nearby office was Hall L. Hibberd, chief engineer since 1932, whose aerodynamically clean creations – the round-the-world Vega, the speedy Orion airliner and the twin-engined Electra 10, 12 and 14 caused such a sensation the Nazis had asked him to Berlin to give them a lecture in 1935. In a smaller office was young C. L. 'Kelly' Johnson, soon to be appointed chief research engineer and later to be one of the most famous names in fighter design. It was a good enough team to take a chance and try to meet a specification that some other companies said was too ambitious, which had just been received from the Air Corps. Calling for a new interceptor, it specified a top speed of 290 mph at sea level and at least 360 mph at 20000 feet, an endurance of one hour at full throttle at that height, and the ability to take off and land over a 50 foot barrier within a distance of 2200 feet.

At this time the Air Corps still had squadrons of the P–26 with 550 hp engines and two guns. Hibberd could find no way to meet the required performance with one engine, even with the much more powerful ones about to become available, and eventually decided to use two of the new Allison (General Motors) liquid-cooled V–1710 vee-12s, which had just completed their first type-test at 1000 hp. It took a little longer to finalise on the twin-boom layout, in which, on each side, the engine, turbocharger, radiator and vertical tail all fell neatly behind each other in a straight line, while the pilot and guns fitted into a very small central nacelle. Tunnel tests showed that the arrangement had low drag, thus confirm-

ing the advantages of a configuration which at the time was most unusual and which, six years later, was to lead to Luftwaffe pilots calling the P–38 'Gabelschwanz Teufel' (fork-tailed devil). In fact the P–38 was not the world's greatest fighter; but it was so nice to fly, so capable and generally useful in all theatres in the Second World War that it richly deserves its place in this review.

The prototype XP–38 had a short but eventful life. Taken by night under police guard to March Field, it suffered brake failure on taxi runs and ran into a ditch. On its first flight, on 27 January 1939, it experienced flutter of the advanced Fowler flaps, which had been fitted to counter the very high wing loading. On 11 February with the same pilot, Lt Kelsey of the Air Corps, the precious machine flew on an extraordinary two-stop flight to Mitchell Field, New York. On arrival he undershot badly, and the XP–38 was destroyed. But it had completed the flight in a time, then hardly credible, of 7 hr 2 min. Two months later a service-test batch of 13 YP–38s was ordered, followed in August by 66 production machines designated the P–38 Lightning. The following year, before any of them had flown, the British Air Commission ordered 667; the Air Corps ordered a further 607, and Lockheed's main problem was one of productive capacity.

Armament of the service-test machines comprised guns of three calibres, all grouped in the nose: one 37 mm, two 0·5 in and two 0·30 in.

To get aboard, the pilot of a Lightning pulled a latch at the rear of the nacelle, immediately under the trailing edge and on the centreline of the wing, extracted a pivoted ladder, climbed up this and across the wing to settle into an extremely comfortable cockpit. American cockpits tended to look haphazard to British eyes used to the standard blind-flying panel, but they were lavishly equipped and the only odd thing about the P–38 was that, instead of a conventional

One of the best-ever air-to-air peel-off shots was taken over California in early 1942. The aircraft are P–38F Lightnings, working up as a squadron prior to overseas deployment. Even at that early time the P–38 was in action in the Pacific, Aleutians, Iceland and (within weeks) England.

central column, it had an aileron control wheel on a massive, angled column down the right side of the cockpit. Two starter buttons got the twin Allison engines turning. They rotated in opposite directions, most production machines having Curtiss Electric propellers, revolving anticlockwise on the left and clockwise on the right.

Taxiing was simple with the well-sprung tricycle landing gear, steering with toe-operated brakes. On take-off you opened up to, say, 44 in manifold pressure, at which time the engines had a powerful though muted note because the exhaust, instead of crackling out of stubs, was ducted to turbos far behind on top of the booms, and flowed from here in a gentle stream. When a P–38 flew past one never ceased to be amazed at the quiet sighing sound, even less obtrusive than that of a sleeve-valve Beaufighter. For takeoff the handed propellers made the aircraft sheer joy, provided one had space ahead to hold the aircraft down after lift-off until the speed was over 130 mph – if possible well over. In the air the Lightning was sedate, stable, forgiving and extremely pleasant – but no dogfighter. With a 52-foot wing span, the roll was majestic rather than fast, and the poor leverage the pilot could exert on the control yoke did not help. However, in the longitudinal plane things were better, and with the Fowler flaps half-out and acting as manoeuvre flaps, it was possible to pull tight turns and stay with the opposition. Even at extreme

limits, when the wing began to stall, it did so from the root outwards, leaving the ailerons fully effective. In its own sedate way the P–38 could do almost anything.

One group of early models were really quite terrible. The first British batch had ordinary propellers both turning the same way, and because export clearance had not been granted there were no turbos. They were gutted of most equipment so, being light, they scrambled well enough, but as they climbed they got increasingly sluggish until, above 10 000 feet, they were useless. As they were not even nice to fly Boscombe rejected AE978 and its camouflaged successors, which eventually wound up as RP–322 trainers at Williams Field in Arizona. If pilots survived these, they were allowed real P–38s, truly a Cadillac among warplanes.

After a fair amount of bother, Lockheed cleared the P–38D, the first combat-worthy model, in August 1941. It had armour, self-sealing tanks and all other essentials, and within an hour of America's entry into the war on the morning of Pearl Harbor, one based in Iceland shot an Fw 200C into the Atlantic. By this time the production version was the P–38E in which the 37 mm cannon was swapped for a 20 mm with six times the number of rounds. Previously the 0·3-in guns had been replaced by 0·5-in, giving quite a fair punch. But most pilots were not crack shots, and the fact that all five guns were in a tight

A striking P–51D Mustang, US civil register NL5747, on a welcome visit to England. Like several other Mustangs, including N2251D of the Confederate Air Force, it bears the nose marking of the 8th AAF 353rd Fighter Group ; but the black/yellow 'invasion stripes' are poetic licence.

Above: *One of the first of the J-model Lightnings to reach combat status in England was* Betty A III, *in olive-drab finish. It flew with the 383rd Fighter Squadron of the 364th FG, based at Honington, Suffolk. The 364th claimed 256½ enemy aircraft in the air plus 193 in ground straffing.*

Below: *The most numerous Lightning was the P–38L, which was by far the most important in the final year of war. Lockheed built 3,810, and Vultee another 113. The turbos and coolant radiators can be seen clearly, the chin inlets serving the oil radiators and intercoolers.*

This P–38L has the final rocket installation, with five-a-side hung on single wing hardpoints. Previously seven were hung in a row along the underside of each wing.

group, aligned parallel, made it harder to score hits than in most fighters. Just the same, if that narrow hail of lead happened to hit an enemy it did him no good at all.

With the P–38G, the engines were up-rated to 1325 hp, and a little way into this run of 1082 aircraft the B–13 turbo was introduced, giving even better altitude performance. Along with numerous unarmed F–4 and F–5 photographic versions, many of which were conversions from other types, the G saw much action from the autumn (fall) of 1942. With two 300 US gal drop tanks on pylons under the inner wings it was the first American fighter to fly non-stop to Britain, usually in large groups escorted by a B–17 or B–24 with two navigators. The first major P–38 theatre of action was Tunisia, and though it could not tangle easily with a 109F or Fw 190 it struck fear into the Axis pilots, reaching out as far as 250 miles out over the Mediterranean. Other F and G models used their long range in the Pacific, where on 18 April 1943 the 339th Fighter Squadron made one of the most brilliant interception missions in history. By picking up a Japanese message and breaking the code it was learned that Admiral Yamamoto, the great Pacific Commander-in-Chief, was flying on that day at a certain time from Rabaul to Buin. A consignment of drop tanks was delivered to the 339th's base at Guadalcanal and 16 aircraft flew the 550 miles to the planned interception. They arrived dead on schedule, and despite facing an escort of A6M Zeros shot Yamamoto's Ki–21 into the sea. The man who led the Americans, Lt Tom Lanphier, later became a noted Lockheed test pilot.

In May 1943 the H entered service with 1425 hp engines, improved cannon, 1600 lb bomb pylons and automatic engine cooling. Three months later came the J, the first of the new breed with deep, chin air inlets and with the leading-edge intercoolers relocated between the oil coolers under the engines. This enabled the full high-altitude potential of 1425 hp at 26500 feet to be realised, making the J the fastest of all Lightnings at around 420 mph at that height. Three of the 13 P–38J groups were in the Pacific, where the P–38 destroyed more Japanese aircraft than any other USAAF type. The top-scorer, Richard Bong gained all his 40 kills on a P–38 in the Pacific.

The final major wartime model of the Lightning was the L, with V–1710–89/91 engines with war emergency power of 1600 hp at 26500 feet. The L appeared in 1944 with a row of seven rockets under each wing, later changed to a 'tree' of five on each side. Others carried two 2000 lb bombs, released by P–38s in formation on the command of a bombardier in a two-seat 'droop-snoot' lead-aircraft fitted with a Norden sight in a transparent nose. Sometimes it had a 'Micky' BTO, for bombing through overcast, a kind of radar used when the target was under cloud cover.

Total Lightning production was 9942, completed in September 1945. The final wartime model was the two-seat black-painted P–38M night fighter, with ASH radar in a pod under the nose. The XP–49 had Continental XI–1430 engines, a pressure cabin and heavier armament, while the monster XP–58 was a bomber destroyer with two 3000 hp double Allison V–3420 engines and devastating armament. Lightnings towed gliders, carried pairs of stretcher casualties, operated on skis and flew many target-marking and ECM missions. It was a most forgiving aircraft, and the late J and L models had hydraulically boosted ailerons and so could even win victories in a tight scrap with single-engined fighters. Unfortunately they did not arrive until most aircraft of the Luftwaffe and Rising Sun had already been beaten.

Another fine Confederate Air Force Mustang, P–51D N10601, previously USAAF 44–73843, built at Inglewood and obtained from Guatemala in 1972 before restoration in Texas. It can be seen parked behind the CAF 'Bf 109' on page 55.

Based on Malta, the Beaufighter was used for anti-shipping strikes. Photograph June 1943.

For this Lightning cutaway John Batchelor chose the little-known P–38M. One can have fun tracing the oil, supercharger air, exhaust and coolant piping. Two exhaust valves per cylinder means 12 stubs from each bank.

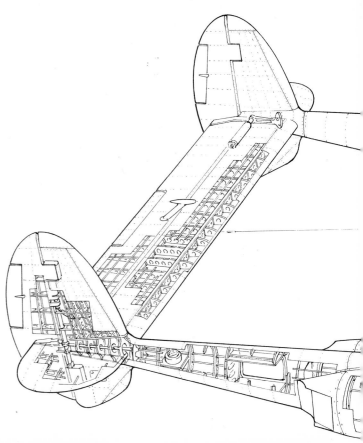

Often thought of as a mere prototype programme, in fact the two-seat P–38M was a night fighter which saw service in the Pacific, at least 75 being built as field conversions. The radar operator worked an APS–6 with 3-cm dish in a nose pod and receiver aerials under the wings.

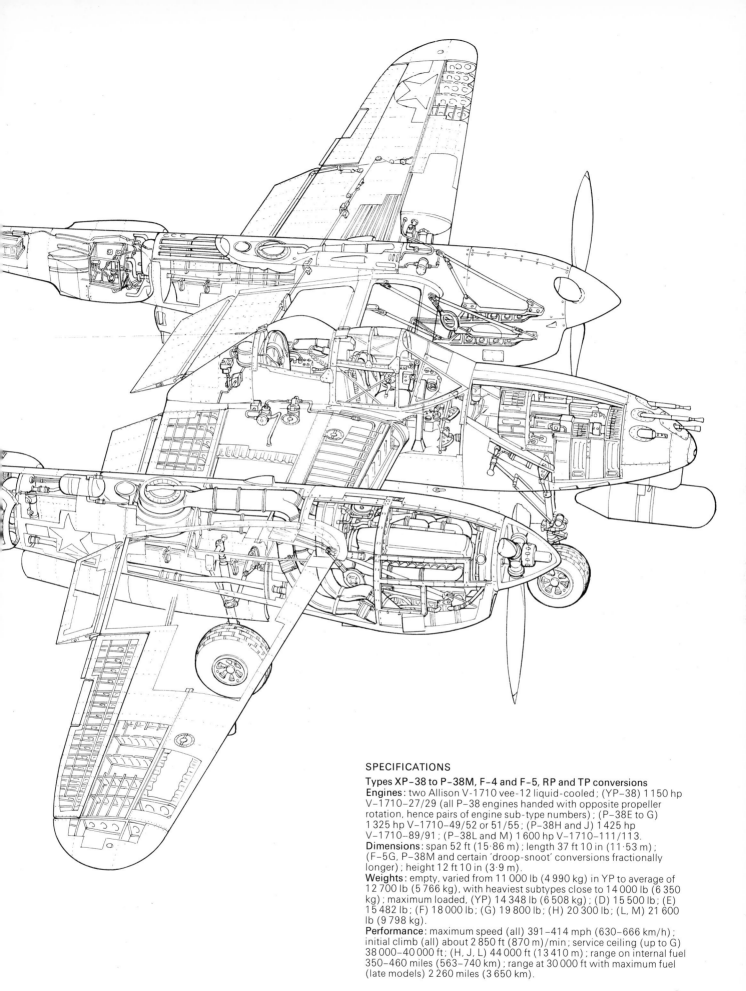

SPECIFICATIONS

Types XP-38 to P-38M, F-4 and F-5, RP and TP conversions

Engines: two Allison V-1710 vee-12 liquid-cooled; (YP-38) 1150 hp V-1710-27/29 (all P-38 engines handed with opposite propeller rotation, hence pairs of engine sub-type numbers); (P-38E to G) 1 325 hp V-1710-49/52 or 51/55; (P-38H and J) 1 425 hp V-1710-89/91; (P-38L and M) 1 600 hp V-1710-111/113.

Dimensions: span 52 ft (15·86 m); length 37 ft 10 in (11·53 m); (F-5G, P-38M and certain 'droop-snoot' conversions fractionally longer); height 12 ft 10 in (3·9 m).

Weights: empty, varied from 11 000 lb (4 990 kg) in YP to average of 12 700 lb (5 766 kg), with heaviest subtypes close to 14 000 lb (6 350 kg); maximum loaded, (YP) 14 348 lb (6 508 kg); (D) 15 500 lb; (E) 15 482 lb; (F) 18 000 lb; (G) 19 800 lb; (H) 20 300 lb; (L, M) 21 600 lb (9 798 kg).

Performance: maximum speed (all) 391–414 mph (630–666 km/h); initial climb (all) about 2 850 ft (870 m)/min; service ceiling (up to G) 38 000–40 000 ft; (H, J, L) 44 000 ft (13 410 m); range on internal fuel 350–460 miles (563–740 km); range at 30 000 ft with maximum fuel (late models) 2 260 miles (3 650 km).

N47DA is one of a whole squadron of Thunderbolts, most of them restored to flying condition, of the Confederate Air Force at Harlingen (pronounced Harlinjen), Texas. Originally AAF No 44–90471 was acquired from Peru in 1969 with five others.

The D/F loop 'acorn' betokens serious long-distance flying to air shows such as this (Transpo '72) ; note the STOL Caribou landing.

Yakovlev series 1-9

Most of us in the West interested in aviation must long for the day when the Soviet Union tells the world about the problems and achievements of its aircraft industry since the 1917 revolution. It is of intense technical interest, but very hard to research. One begins to fear that priceless records will be lost or, even worse, that true records may eventually be changed for political reasons and emerge in a twisted and misleading way. One of the few original sources available to us is the autobiography of Alexander S. Yakovlev. Though brief, disjointed and sadly vague – and probably so edited as to bear little resemblance to the original draft – it was at least based on what the great designer actually wrote in the 1950s. We are grateful to him, because his little book adds a few vestiges of human colour to the scarce facts concerning Soviet fighters built in greater numbers than any others have ever been, or ever will be. The total was about 37000.

Yakovlev was born in 1906. After creating successful gliders in 1924–26, he built a 60 horsepower tandem-seat biplane at the Air Force Academy, which flew on 12 May 1927 and was much like the original D.H. Moth. In 1932 Yakovlev first hit the headlines with a tandem-seat cabin monoplane which achieved 330 km/h (205 mph) on a 480 hp licence-built Jupiter. Two years later came a classic type of which nearly 7500 were destined to be produced. This was the AIR–9 (later Ya–9) and led to the Ya–10 which, in V–VS service, was called the UT–2. A low-wing monoplane trainer, it equipped virtually all Soviet pilot schools and clubs until superseded from 1948 by Yakovlev's own Yak–18. Subsequently his bureau, now grown large, produced a remarkable diversity of jet fighters, lightplanes, large and small jetliners, piston and jet trainers, aerobatic machines and helicopters.

Back in the mid-1930s his bureau was small, but he had ambition. He wrote: 'Every time during the fly-pasts over the Red Square, or at the Tushino airfield when the red fighters designed by Polikarpov streaked across the sky, to the general admiration of the spectators, my heart skipped a bit [beat?]. I was possessed by the idea of building a high-speed combat machine. In 1938 the Government suggested to several designers, myself included, that they should compete in creating a new fighter. I got down to work with great enthusiasm.'

Reading between the lines this suggests that Yakovlev was in no position to make any move himself, or even make suggestions, and one feels the sense of inexpressible joy that the benevolent Soviet leaders had at last allowed the pent-up energies of his design bureau to be translated into action. As the I–16 then in service had been designed fully six years earlier the competition for a new fighter came none too soon.

Forty years ago real achievement in Soviet aircraft design was widely discounted in the West. Soon after the Nazi invasion of the Soviet Union on 22 June 1941 that much-loved newspaper *The Aeroplane Spotter* published a page of Russian aircraft. One, the R–5 biplane, had 'designer unknown' beside it, despite the fact that 6000 had been built since 1928. The others, with one exception, were either said to be derived from Western types or were actually Western types said (erroneously) to be built under licence. The exception, the TB–6 heavy bomber, was described, in a rather sarcastic way, as being 'most original'. The idea that Soviet designers might be talented engineers like those in other countries was clearly difficult to swallow, but in fact they had to create aircraft that were not only highly competitive but were exactly tailored to the Soviet environment and manpower potential. There was plenty of land and plenty of human muscle, but woefully little of either technically skilled labour, light alloy, or paved runways. Until after 1945 the general situation did not change, and in the circumstances the aircraft with which the Soviets fought the Luftwaffe were remarkably good – and they were not copied from anyone else.

The three main new fighters that competed for production orders in 1939 were by Mikoyan and Gurevich (I–61, later MiG–1); Lavochkin, Gorbunov and Gudkov (I–22, later LaGG–1); and Yakovlev's I–26. Yakovlev's old friend

Yulian Piontkovsky flew the I–26 for the first time in March 1939. How well it performed is shown by the award of the Order of Lenin, a ZIS car and 100000 roubles to the designer during the following month.

There were good reasons, like the alloy shortages already listed, for not making the new fighter out of light-alloy stressed skin. So the wing was a wooden structure with two spars, ply skin and split flaps. The fuselage was of gas-welded steel tube, with metal panels over the front and ply/fabric aft. Movable surfaces were metal-framed with fabric covering, and the flaps, wide-track undercarriage and tailwheel were all retracted hydraulically. The engine was the 1100 hp M–105PA.

In engines the Soviets did at that time copy the West, and the M–105 was a development of the French Hispano-Suiza V–12. In the Second World War it was redesignated the VK–105 in honour of Vladimir Klimov, whose bureau produced it. The P in the designation signified provision for a *pushka* (cannon), firing through the constant-speed propeller hub. In the matter of aircraft guns the Soviets excelled, and the 20 mm ShVAK was lighter and smaller than the Hispano and fired 800 rounds/min as opposed to 550. Above the engine were two 7·62 mm ShKAS machine guns, of the kind mentioned in the I–16 story.

This may seem modest armament, but it was probably the best choice. Soviet designers had a hard struggle to achieve superior fighters in pre-jet days, because the steel and wood construction added significantly to the weight. The aircraft had to be as small as possible, for good performance and manoeuvrability, and with a heavy engine there was little weight available for guns and ammunition. Only with painful slowness could the designers increase the proportion of light-alloy stressed-skin structure and one of the important sources of light alloy was actually shot-down Axis aircraft!

In the early days there were plenty of small and large 'bugs' to be eliminated from the I–26, some in the prototype during development flying from the Moscow (Khimki) factory field. There were many more in 1940 when the usual service-test unit, with in this case a sensible quota of 36 aircraft, operated from a simulated advanced base with neither hangars nor runways. The V–VS designation was Yak–1.

Not one fighter had reached a combat unit when the Germans invaded, though small numbers were trickling through the pipeline and about 100 were with various test units. Just as production was beginning to roll, the Panzers were reaching out for Moscow and, in the biggest industrial move in history, completely new factories were speedily built far to the east, mostly in the Ural mountains and in Siberia. On 16 October 1941 Yakovlev himself drove out of Moscow on the first stage of the long journey to the new Yak plant at Kamensk-Uralsk, and according to legend, complete Yak–1 fighters were coming off the assembly line three weeks after the arrival of the first tooling from Moscow. Within three months output had passed the rate achieved before the move. The new plant, of course, was bigger.

Early Yak–1s were simple and austere, though they had armour, oxygen, a crude reflector sight and single-channel radio. The oil cooler was further forward than in the first development machines, the engine air inlets were moved to the wing roots, and the tailwheel fixed down. Later the radiator was moved forward and racks added for two 220 lb bombs or six of the exciting RS–82 rockets, the two ShKAS being replaced by a 12·7 mm Beresin BS, and the 1210 hp VK–105PF engine raised speed slightly to 372 mph. But the main line of development soon switched to a parallel type which had first flown in 1940 as the UTI–26, a dual trainer made highly desirable by the yawning gap between the UT–2 and Yak–1. From the start the new Urals factory produced the trainer alongside the fighter as the Yak–7V, with tandem sliding canopies. From this, around

One of the photographs taken at the old Yakovlev plant at Khimki, just north of Moscow, showing early batches of Yak–1 fighters. They had virtually all-wood structures.

A small-wing Yak–3. One of its distinguishing features, also shared by the post-war versions of Yak–9, was the absence of an oil cooler under the nose.

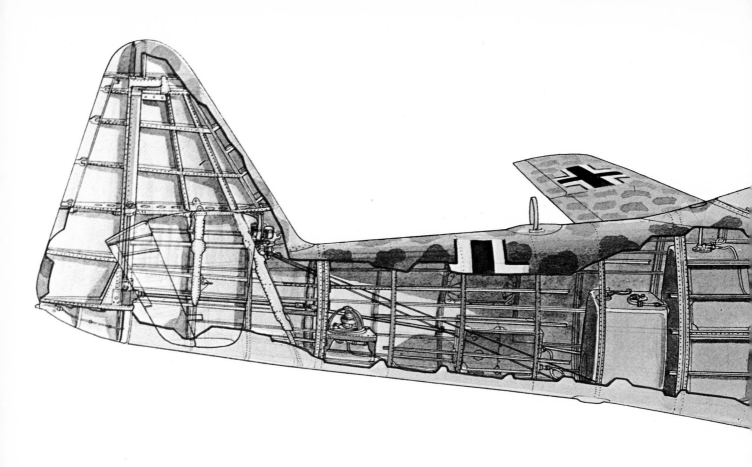

A John Batchelor drawing of the Me 262A–1a Schwalbe. Still looking superficially modern today, this remarkable fighter was planned in 1938–39 and in detail engineering design in 1940. The aerodynamics, structure and armament were more advanced than those of any contemporary Allied aircraft.

One of the relatively genuine Me 262s, this A–1a resides in the fine Swiss Transport Museum in Lucerne. Beyond (far right) is a Fliegertruppe Bf 109E–3, and at left is the tail of a Fokker D. VII.

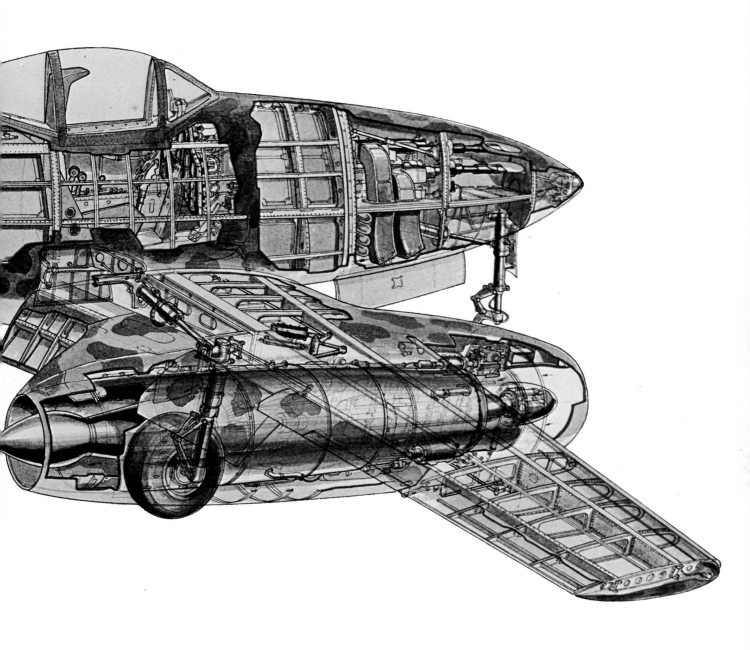

SPECIFICATIONS

Types Me 262A–1a Schwalbe, Me 262A–2 Sturmvogel, Me 262B–1a
Engines: two 1 980 lb (900 kg) thrust Junkers Jumo 004B single-shaft axial turbojets.
Dimensions: span 40 ft 11½ in (12·5 m); length 34 ft 9½ in (10·6 m), (262B–1a, excluding radar aerials) 38 ft 9 in (11·8 m); height 12 ft 7 in (3·8 m).
Weights: empty (A–1a, A–2a) 8 820 lb (4 000 kg); (B–1a) 9 700 lb (4 400 kg); loaded (A–1a, A–2a) 15 500 lb (7 045 kg); (B–1a) 14 110 lb (6 400 kg).
Performance: maximum speed (A–1a) 540 mph (870 km/h); (A–2a, laden) 470 mph (755 km/h); (B–1a) 497 mph (800 km/h); initial climb (all) about 3 940 ft (1 200 m)/min; service ceiling 37 565 ft (11 500 m); range on internal fuel, at altitude, about 650 miles (1 050 km).

Weal's Yak–9 is most satisfying, because such fighters had enough 'meat' to be interesting yet not too much to show clearly. An inset shows the internal bomb bay of the Yak–9B. But propellers are often hard to draw, and the reader may be puzzled to deduce the direction of rotation.

1 Muzzle of 20-mm Shpital'ny-Vladimirov cannon
2 Propeller spinner
3 VISh–61 P constant-speed metal propeller
4 Coolant header tank
5 Auxiliary intake
6 Oil cooler intake
7 Starboard mainwheel door fairing
8 Starboard mainwheel
9 Oil cooler installation
10 Oil cooler outlet shutter
11 Engine support frame
12 Engine main bearer
13 Klimov M–105PF–1 12-cylinder liquid-cooled engine
14 Exhaust stubs
15 Blast tube
16 Coolant piping
17 Gun trough
18 Filler cap
19 H-section steel wing spar
20 Starboard outboard fuel tank
21 Aileron control push-rod
22 Fuel filler cap access
23 Wing skinning (plywood)
24 Starboard navigation light
25 Starboard aileron
26 Yak–9B bomb installation (four 220-lb/100-kg bombs in individual forward-inclined tubes)
27 Starboard flap
28 Ammunition feed
29 Gun cocking mechanism fairing
30 Berezin UB 12,7-mm machine gun (portside only)
31 Gun support bracket
32 Cannon breech
33 Oil tank
34 Engine bearer support
35 Outlet
36 Wing root air intake duct
37 Supercharger intake
38 Port mainwheel well door inboard fairing plate
39 Port mainwheel well
40 Ventral radiator intake
41 Wing root/fuselage fairing
42 Rudder pedal bar
43 Control column
44 Bulkhead
45 Instrument panel
46 Trim tab control handwheel
47 Reflector gunsight
48 Armourglass windscreen
49 Aft-sliding cockpit canopy
50 Armourglass rear screen
51 Electrical switch panel
52 Pilot's seat
53 Engine control console
54 Oxygen cylinder
55 Seat support frame
56 Control linkage
57 Wing root frame fairing
58 Hydraulic reservoir
59 Radio equipment bay
60 Access hatch
61 Stringers
62 Steel-tube fuselage frame
63 Utility compartment (for emergency ferrying of equipment, baggage, mechanic, etc)
64 Aerial mast
65 Aerials
66 Fuselage decking
67 Dorsal formers
68 Diagonal bracing
69 Elevator control cables
70 Tail fin attachment points
71 Starboard tailplane
72 Starboard elevator
73 Elevator trim tab
74 Tail fin structure
75 Aerial attachment
76 Rudder post
77 Rudder structure
78 Rudder trim tab
79 Rear navigation light
80 Elevator trim tab
81 Elevator frame
82 Tailplane structure
83 Rudder lower hinge external fairing
84 Elevator control horns
85 Tailwheel doors
86 Retractable tailwheel
87 Tailwheel oleo leg
88 Access/inspection panel
89 Tailwheel retraction jack
90 Lifting tube
91 Ventral skinning
92 Wing root fillet
93 Inset flap structure
94 Aileron trim tab
95 Aileron frame
96 Port wingtip/aileron profile
97 Port navigation light
98 Front spar
99 Rear spar
100 Pitot tube
101 Rib structure

SPECIFICATIONS

The Yakolev Yak–1,
Types Ya–26, I–26, Yak–1, Yak–7
Engine: initially, one 1 100 hp VK–105PA (M–105PA) vee-12 liquid-cooled, derived from Hispano-Suiza 12Y; later, 1 260 hp VK–105PF.
Dimensions: span 32 ft 9¾ in (10 m); length 27 ft 9¾ in (8·48 m); height 8 ft 8 in (2·64 m).
Weights: empty (early I–26) 5 137 lb (2 375 kg); maximum loaded 6 217 lb (2 890 kg)
Performance: maximum speed 373 mph (600 km/h), 310 mph (500 km/h) at sea level; initial climb 3 940 ft (1 200 m)/min; service ceiling 32 800 ft (10 000 m); range, 528 miles (850 km).

The Yakolev Yak–9
Types Yak–9, –9D, –9T, –9U and –9P
Engine: (–9, D and T) one 1 260 hp Klimov VK–105PF vee-12 liquid-cooled; (U, P) one 1 650 hp VK–107A.
Dimensions: span 32 ft 9¾ in (10 m); length (–9, D, T) 28 ft 0½ in (8·54 m); (U, P) 28 ft 6½ in (8·70 m); height 8 ft (2·44 m).
Weights: empty (T) 6 063 lb (2 750 kg); (U) 5 100 lb (2 313 kg); maximum loaded (T) 7 055 lb (3 200 kg); (U) 6 988 lb (3 170 kg).
Performance: maximum speed (9) 373 mph (600 km/h); (D) 359 mph (573 km/h); (T) 367 mph (590 km/h); (U) 435 mph (700 km/h); (P) 416 mph (670 km/h); initial climb (typical 9, D, T) 3 795 ft (1 150 m)/min; (U, P) 4 920 ft (1 500 m)/min; service ceiling (all) about 34 500 ft (10 500 m); range (most) 520–550 miles (840–890 km); (D) 840 miles (1 350 km); (DD) 1 367 miles (2 200 km).

The longest-ranged of all the single-engined Yak fighters was the –9DD (ultra-long-range). These used every ounce of extra space in the metal wing to pack in 187 gal (225 US gal) of fuel.

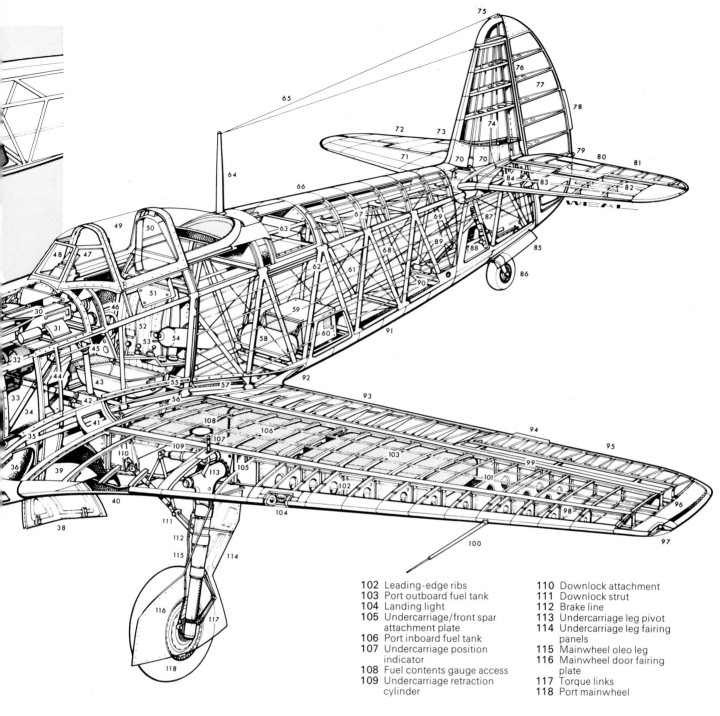

102	Leading-edge ribs
103	Port outboard fuel tank
104	Landing light
105	Undercarriage/front spar attachment plate
106	Port inboard fuel tank
107	Undercarriage position indicator
108	Fuel contents gauge access
109	Undercarriage retraction cylinder
110	Downlock attachment
111	Downlock strut
112	Brake line
113	Undercarriage leg pivot
114	Undercarriage leg fairing panels
115	Mainwheel oleo leg
116	Mainwheel door fairing plate
117	Torque links
118	Port mainwheel

One of a series of air-to-air photographs of a formation of Yak–9D long-range fighters over the Eastern Front in 1944. The unit was probably a crack Guards fighter regiment, despite the stuck tailwheel door.

January 1942, emerged the Yak–7A fighter, while the 7V was given a cut-down rear fuselage and modified canopy. The radiator was improved and moved back to its original position, and in early 1942 the Yak–7B became the main production fighter. It had a raised canopy and the cut-down rear fuselage (then ahead of its time) that was standard thereafter. Speed was 381 mph.

As the best Soviet fighters in the first two years of war, production of the Yak–1 and –7 was accelerated by every means possible. It is fair to claim that in most respects they were close enough in capability to a Bf 109F or Fw 190A for a battle between them to depend on pilot skill – and what a Soviet pilot might lack he made up for in courage and determination. In 1941–43 there was need of these qualities in the Soviet Union, but gradually the Yaks gained better radio, more armour, gyro instruments and even a gyro gunsight. Meanwhile supplies of strategic alloys improved, and around August 1942 Yakovlev tested a Yak–7B with light-alloy wing spars, retaining wooden ribs and skin. The wing was lighter, and as it gave room for more fuel, the resulting machine was called the Yak–7DI (DI standing for *Dalny Istrebitel*, long-range fighter). Quickly the improved machine replaced the –7B,

but its designation was changed to Yak–9 and ultimately 16769 were built, more than any other single Soviet type except the Il–2. It is true that there were about 26000 Lavochkin wartime radial-engined fighters, roughly evenly divided between the La–5 and –7, but they cannot be considered as one type.

When the Yak–9 appeared over the Stalingrad front in October 1942 it was found to have the edge over the 109G, except above 15000 feet. In 1943, Yakovlev's enlarged bureau produced a succession of new models. The Yak–9T had the cockpit moved back to make room for a 37 mm 11–P–37 cannon, one hit from which was usually lethal to an aircraft and often to armoured vehicles and ships. The –9M had a second BS gun, while the –9B had an internal bomb bay for an 880 lb load. The –9D had 143 gallons of fuel in the wings and the –9DD no less than 187 gallons, which allowed a large formation to make a non-stop 1120-mile flight early in 1944 to Bari in southern Italy in support of the Jugoslav partisans. Other D and DD models escorted American heavy bombers to and from Soviet bases.

The final wartime –9 was the –9U, in which the VK–107A engine of 1620 hp was combined with a mainly light-alloy structure and resulted in a dramatically superior fighter which was able to reach 434 mph and outfly the Luftwaffe.

Two years earlier, work had begun on a lightened fighter able to achieve the highest possible performance on the original engine. The result was the nimble Yak–3, with the 1222 hp VK–105PF–2 engine, which differed from a –9 chiefly in having a smaller wing. Manoeuvrability did not suffer and on many occasions the 403 mph Yak–3 so routed the enemy that Luftwaffe pilots were specifically instructed to

'Avoid combat below 5000 metres with Yakovlev fighters lacking an oil-cooler intake beneath the nose' (the –3 moved the oil cooler to the left wing root). The French Normandie-Niemen Group, with experience of the Spitfire, Airacobra, Mustang and all Soviet fighters, chose the Yak–3 when it re-equipped in October 1944 and scored most of its 273 victories on these capable aircraft. In circumstances of almost unrelenting adversity, Yakovlev's bureau created a dynamic series of fighters that gradually achieved ascendency even over the Luftwaffe.

Far left: *A most intriguing picture of part of the Normandie-Niemen (Yak–3) regiment watching an aerobatic display by one of their number. What makes it intriguing is that in the background are a Spitfire IX and a French Martin 167 (Maryland) in immaculate finish. Location is probably the French occupied zone in late 1945.*
Above left: *Described as a MiG–3 on the original photograph, this is, in fact, an unusual second-generation Yak–9, with oil cooler moved from the nose to the wing roots*

and with a centreline gun larger than the normal ShVAK. There were plenty of big-gun Yak–9T models, but these had the original oil cooler.
Above right: *A standard Yak–3 of the Normandie-Niemen fighter regiment. One of this famous group's Yaks is in the Paris Musée de l'Air.*
Below: *Testing a Yak–3, possibly one of the first development aircraft, near the vast factory at Kamensk-Uralsk in Siberia. The pilot is probably Mikhail Ivanov.*

Mitsubishi A6M

In all important respects the design of this carrier-based fighter of the Imperial Japanese Navy was ordinary to the point of being old-fashioned. It was, for example, almost identical in size, shape, weight, engineering detail design and performance to the British Gloster F.5/34 flown in December 1937, almost 18 months before the Japanese fighter. When the A6M went into action at Pearl Harbor it ought to have been familiar to the Allies, because it had already been in action in China for 18 months; and it should have posed few problems to Allied pilots. Instead, because Allied intelligence, psychology and equipment could hardly have been worse, the 'Zero' was allowed to sweep all before it. Swiftly it became the centre of a legend of invincibility that bordered on supernatural power. Just as the British public learned the name of the Spitfire's designer, Reginald Mitchell, so did the Japanese learn the name of their own miracle-worker Jiro Horikoshi, Mitsubishi Jukogyo's chief engineer. In an incredible succession of victories the Zero eliminated Allied air power from a greater area of the globe than had ever previously been conquered by one nation; roughly 12 million square miles in six months. Then, for the simple reason that nothing arrived to replace it except improved models of the same aircraft, this famous fighter's star waned. But it left a legend of grinning yellow faces and spitting cannon that was not entirely fiction and has become part of history.

In the 1920s the growing aerial strength of the Japanese nation was accompanied by the need to learn things already familiar to the Occidentals. Careful study by both the Army and Navy air forces led to the emergence of manoeuvrability as the paramount quality of fighter aircraft. Though there was no fixation on the biplane, as in Britain, or reactionary dislike of change, as in Italy, the new Japanese monoplane fighters of the mid-1930s – the Army Ki–27 and Navy A5M – had extremely low wing-loadings and manoeuvrability that can fairly be described as fantastic. This was gained at the expense of leaving out most equipment apart from two 7·7 mm Vickers guns, and of course the pilot and a little fuel. But the 12-Shi (1937) specification for a replacement for the much-liked A5M made life difficult for the Japanese designers. It called for, in addition to machine guns, two 20 mm cannon and a speed of 270 knots (the nautical mile was the Navy unit in Japan) together with a cruising endurance of six to eight hours. Full radio, and the ability to carry two 132 lb bombs, with manoeuvrability 'at least equal to that of the A5M' was also called for. Nakajima gave up, but Mitsubishi doggedly pressed on and eventually the A6M1, with a 780 hp Zuisei 13 engine, flew at Kagamigahara on 1 April 1939.

Officially its name was the Reisen and from the start it was obviously an outstanding fighter, but the maximum speed of 304 mph fell slightly short of the requirement. On 28 December 1939 the third prototype flew with a 925 hp Nakajima NK1C Sakae engine, and this not only exceeded 330 mph but also met or did better than every other requirement. Development for service use was rapid, and by July 1940 a trials batch of 15 A6M2 were on their way to China. Later production A6M2s joined them, destroying 99 Chinese aircraft in a year for the loss of two Zeros to ground fire.

From the 65th aircraft the outermost 20 inches of each wing were hinged to fold up manually to improve clearance on a carrier lift (deck elevator), and in June 1941 the A6M3 had these tips removed entirely, and also had substituted the 1130 hp Sakae 21 engine with two-speed supercharger, giving a better speed and rate of roll but a slightly poorer climb and turn radius. In November 1941 Nakajima's Koizumi plant added its output to that from Mitsubishi's Nagoya factory, and by the start of the Pacific war on 7 December more than 400 had been delivered, of which 328 were aboard carriers in the Pacific. Over Pearl Harbor the A6M arrived as a terrible shock, and nobody has ever explained what became of General Chennault's reports to Washington from Chungking about the deadly potential of the aircraft over the preceding 18 months.

To overcome the difficulty of discovering or remembering Japanese designations the Allied (i.e. American) commands adopted a code, using boys' names for fighters. Suddenly the A6M2, whose real designation was thought by the Allies to be S–00, became Ben, and then Ray and finally Zeke, while the A6M3 became Hap. Ray and Ben were soon dropped, while Hap was thought to sound too much like Jap – and might offend 'Hap' Arnold, USAAF Chief of Staff. It was changed first to Hamp and finally, when the clipped-winger had been identified as merely a version of Zeke, as Zeke 32. Today there is no reason for not using the Japanese designation, but at the time this very ordinary aircraft was so totally unknown it was considered a great achievement even to capture a small fragment. All attempts to piece a whole 'Zeke' together proved quite impossible. Hundreds – though because of their fantastic range which allowed them to show up at places thousands of miles apart on successive days, they seemed like thousands – swept away second-rate Allied fighters over countries as far apart as Ceylon, the Aleutians and the Coral Sea.

On 3 June 1942, Petty Officer Koga took off from *Ryujo* in a brand-new A6M2 to attack Dutch Harbour, in the Aleutians. Two bullets severed the fuel lines and he came down on the emergency landing ground on the island of Akutan, overturned on marshy ground and died of a broken neck. Five weeks later the most valuable prize of the Pacific war was discovered by the Americans, shipped to NAS North Island, San Diego, and test flown. Suddenly the Zero fighter was found not to be invincible at all, and in fact to possess numerous shortcomings.

It so happened that another aircraft took off on its first flight in June 1942, the XF6F, the Grumman Hellcat. For the remainder of the war this totally different style of fighter, partnered by the older but at least equally formidable F4U Corsair, was to blast the Zero or Reisen out of the sky wherever it was met. The American fighters were also carrier-based single-seaters, with aircooled radial engines, but these were Pratt & Whitney R–2800 Double Wasps of more than twice the power of the Sakae, which enabled them to outfly the A6M whilst carrying much heavier firepower, armour and additional equipment. Early A6Ms weighed around 5500 lb fully loaded, and late models about 6000 lb, whereas the US Navy fighters turned the scales at over 9000 lb empty and from 12000 to 15000 lb fully laden. The contrast is astonishing, and is elaborated upon in the introduction to this book. Horikoshi himself urged repeatedly that his next fighter should have a 2200 hp engine, and when it came it turned the scales at about 10500 lb, but it never even saw action.

While mainstream development led to the A6M3 Model 22, with folding rounded wing-tips restored, and then the mass-produced A6M5 series, the Nakajima company developed the A6M2–N central-float seaplane version, for use where there were not yet any Japanese airfields. Basically an A6M2, these 271 mph aircraft served widely and were called Rufe by the Allies. Mitsubishi meanwhile developed the A6M2–K Zero-Rensen tandem dual-control trainer, produced by Sasebo Arsenal and Hitachi. The latter also made a few A6M5–K trainers.

Built in larger numbers than any other version, the A6M5 was intended as a stop-gap until the new A7M Reppu was ready; non-appearance of the Reppu caused the now-outclassed Reisen to remain in production to the end. In fact, the

Thunderbolts in the background confirm that this A6M5 'Zeke 52' is in Allied hands. The date is June 1944, which was just the time that Japanese aircraft began to become plentiful to Allied Tac-Air Intelligence in the Pacific. Not yet messed about by Allied painting, this aircraft has dark (not white) borders to its Hinomarus.

original A6M5 (Model 52) differed little from a Model 32. Wing skins were thicker, allowing a steeper and much faster dive and thus a better chance of catching anything trying to get away. The engine had individual exhaust stacks, giving a little extra thrust so that, despite an initial 416 lb additional weight (more with later sub-types), speed just exceeded 350 mph, but this was not enough. New wing-tips were fitted, making the span equal to the clipped 32 though without folding portions and of a rounded shape. By March 1944 deliveries switched to the A6M5a with Mk 4 cannon fed with 125-round belts instead of 100-round drums, and a few weeks later the A6M5b followed with one of the fuselage guns replaced by a Type 3 of 13·2 mm calibre (not 12·7 mm as often reported) and an armour-glass canopy. Large numbers were ready for the Battle of the Philippines, but their first meeting with the US Navy Hellcats resulted in such a crushing defeat by the Americans that it was called by them 'The Marianas Turkey Shoot'.

By the summer of 1944 the entire Imperial Navy aircraft programme was in tatters, and in an endeavour to keep aircraft flowing to the battle fronts production of the Reisen continued as rapidly as possible. To try to make the aircraft better able to hold its own, Horikoshi's successor, Eitaro Sano, fitted new armament comprising one 13·2 mm gun in the fuselage, two 13·2 mm in the outer wings and two 20 mm cannon further inboard, with provision for a 551 lb bomb on the centreline tank pylon. There was additional fuselage fuel and armour, so that performance suffered severely. In November 1944 this interim A6M5c version was replaced by the A6M6c with a Sakae 31 engine boosted with water-methanol injection to 1560 hp. Sano had wanted the larger Kinsei engine, and this would have powered the A6M8, widely dispersed manufacture of which was planned to yield 6300 aircraft in 1946.

Total production of the Reisen amounted to 3879 by Mitsubishi and 6570 by Nakajima (a total of 10449), plus 327 A6M2–N seaplanes and 515 trainers. Strangely paralleling some of the major types of Hitler's Luftwaffe, the Reisen had been conceived in enthusiasm, used with immense flair and fantastic success in some of the world's largest-ever military campaigns and then, through lack of a follow-up aircraft, kept in the forefront of battle long after it had become outclassed. No A6M, no matter how boldly flown, could expect to win over an F6F or intercept a B–29. Their one effective use in the closing year of the Second World War was as a Kamikaze suicide missile, which was a tacit admission of defeat.

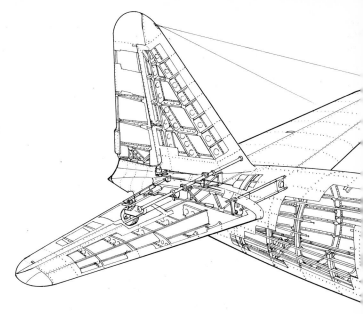

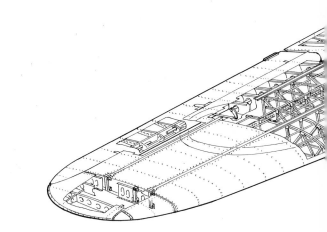

Much of Batchelor's work has been in colour and several of them appear in this book, but his Zeke 52 was done entirely with a pen. Jap cutaways are usually almost as difficult as Russian ones.

SPECIFICATIONS

Types A6M1 to A6M8c

Engine: (A6M1) one 780 hp Mitsubishi MK2 Zuisei 13 14-cylinder two-row radial; (M2) 925 hp Nakajima NK1C Sakae 12 of same layout; (M3) 1 130 hp Sakae 21; (M5) as M3 with individual exhaust stacks; (M6c) Sakae 31 with same rated power but water/methanol boost to 1 210 hp for emergency; (M8c) 1 560 hp Mitsubishi Kinsei 62 of same layout.
Dimensions: span (1, 2) 39 ft 4½ in (12·0 m); (remainder) 36 ft 1 in (11·0 m); length (all) 29 ft 9 in (9·06 m); height (1, 2) 9 ft 7 in (2·92 m); (all later) 9 ft 8 in (2·98 m).
Weights: empty (2) 3 704 lb (1 680 kg); (3) 3 984 lb (1 807 kg); (5) typically 3 920 lb (1 778 kg); (6c) 4 175 lb (1 894 kg); (8c) 4 740 lb (2 150 kg); maximum loaded (2) 5 313 lb (2 410 kg); (3) 5 828 lb (2 644 kg); (5) 6 050 lb (2 733 kg; 2 952 kg as overload); (6c) as 5c; (8c) 6 944 lb (3 149 kg).
Performance: maximum speed (2) 316 mph (509 km/h); (3) 336 mph (541 km/h); (5c, 6c) 354 mph (570 km/h); (8c) 360 mph (580 km/h); initial climb (1, 2, 3) 4 500 ft (1 370 m)/min; (5, 6c) 3 150 ft (960 m)/min; (2–N) not known; service ceiling (1, 2) 33 790 ft (10 300 m); (3) 36 250 ft (11 050 m); (5c, 6c) 37 500 ft (11 500 m); (8c) 39 370 ft (12 000 m); range with drop tank (2) 1 940 miles (3 110 km); (5) 1 200 miles (1 920 km).

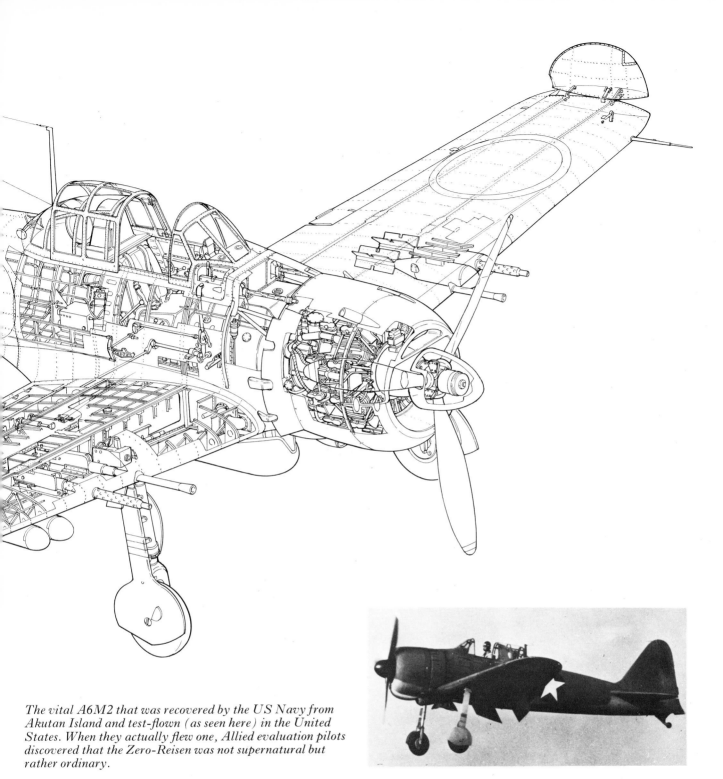

The vital A6M2 that was recovered by the US Navy from Akutan Island and test-flown (as seen here) in the United States. When they actually flew one, Allied evaluation pilots discovered that the Zero-Reisen was not supernatural but rather ordinary.

Right: Known officially as the Mitsubishi A6M Zero-Sen, this single-seat Japanese fighter will always be remembered as the 'Zero'.

Focke-Wulf Fw 190

In July 1941 pilots of RAF fighters engaged in offensive sweeps over northern France began to report that the Luftwaffe was using a fighter with a radial engine. The opinion was expressed by British intelligence that these could only be ex-French Curtiss Mohawks. As a young cadet I discussed the matter with a rather shaken Spitfire V flight commander who had tangled with one. His view was 'That was no Mohawk!' and how very right he was. Had British intelligence taken sufficient interest in German aircraft before the war it would have known about the Fw 190, begun in 1937 and flown three months before the Second World War began. It was a marvellous example of the aircraft designer's art, and one could argue indefinitely about how the Fw 190 shaped up against the P–51D Mustang, or the F4U Corsair. Though they were a close match, nothing could equal the 190 for sheer advanced design and compactness.

The advanced technology of the 190 can be assessed when one realizes when it first appeared, for it was requested by the RLM (German Air Ministry) in the autumn of 1937. At that time the RLM was still planning ahead in a prudent way, and though development was going ahead fast on the Bf 109, it seemed sensible to have a second iron in the fire. By this time monoplane stressed-skin construction, wing-mounted cannon, reflector sights and variable-pitch propellers were taken for granted in Germany. The Focke-Wulf engineering staff under Dipl Ing Kurt Tank pulled out all the stops in trying to produce a design superior to that from the Messerschmitt company, and in doing so it created an aeroplane superior to everything else then in existence. The detail design under R. Blaser was brilliant. The airframe structure was outstandingly simple, divided into easily completed sections which could be rapidly assembled or dismantled, thus facilitating both dispersed mass-production and service repair and maintenance. The radial engine – rather to Focke-Wulf's surprise preferred to the alternative DB 601 by General Udet, head of the RLM technical department – was after preliminary development way ahead of

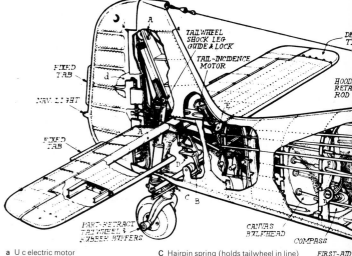

a U c electric motor
b Note split ribs
d Rudder tube construction
e Pilot's seat raising guide and lock
f Rudder pedals with hydraulic wheel-brake operation
g Junction box for electric services each side
h Blister on underside inspection cover (magazine)
j At this point behind spar is another pick-up to fuselage on bulkhead K
k Fuselage bulkhead
l Oxygen bottles
m Angle longeron
n Plug for ground charging

A Tailwheel retracting cable (and see starboard u c radius rod)
B Tailwheel lock (actually on port side) at last part of up travel

C Hairpin spring (holds tailwheel in line)
D Tailwheel lock adjustment screw
E Tailplane radius arm
F Rudder cables in tubes
G Panel
H Bag stowage lid
J Hood frame rods (taper outwards, so toggles J are needed)

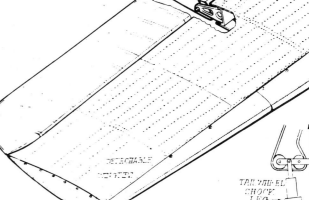

K Reflector sight and ring and bead
L Throttle lever with lamp shining down on press button controls

M Hood racking (with screwdriver opening from outside)
N Throttle lever tightener

Clark's excellent drawing of Arnim Faber's Fw 109, prepared with great speed and showing everything to which access was possible (nobody was going to pull skin off the outer wings). It is odd that he did not identify the two quite different species of cannon. He found he had used key-letter A twice.

SPECIFICATIONS

Types Fw 190A series, D series, F series and Ta 152H

Engine: (A–8, F–8) one 1 700 hp (2 100 hp emergency boost) BMW 801Dg 18-cylinder two-row radial; (D–9) one 1 776 hp (2 240 hp emergency boost) Junkers Jumo 213A–1 12-cylinder inverted-vee liquid-cooled; (Ta 152H–1) one 1 880 hp (2 250 hp) Jumo 213E–1.

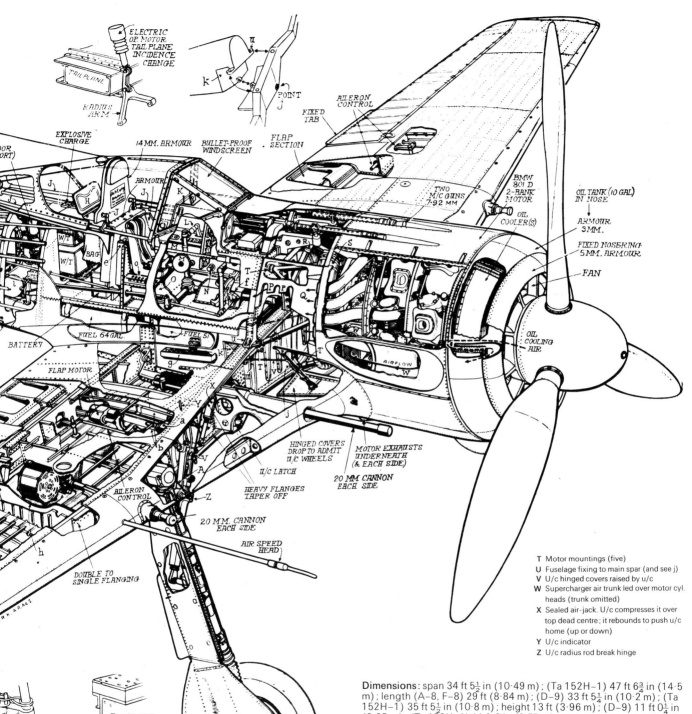

T Motor mountings (five)
U Fuselage fixing to main spar (and see j)
V U/c hinged covers raised by u/c
W Supercharger air trunk led over motor cyl. heads (trunk omitted)
X Sealed air-jack. U/c compresses it over top dead centre; it rebounds to push u/c home (up or down)
Y U/c indicator
Z U/c radius rod break hinge

Dimensions: span 34 ft 5½ in (10·49 m); (Ta 152H–1) 47 ft 6¾ in (14·5 m); length (A–8, F–8) 29 ft (8·84 m); (D–9) 33 ft 5¼ in (10·2 m); (Ta 152H–1) 35 ft 5½ in (10·8 m); height 13 ft (3·96 m); (D–9) 11 ft 0¼ in (3·35 m); (Ta 152H–1) 11 ft 8 in (3·55 m).
Weights: empty (A–8, F–8) 7 055 lb (3 200 kg); (D–9) 7 720 lb (3 500 kg); (Ta 152H–1) 7 940 lb (3 600 kg); loaded (A–8, F–8) 10 800 lb (4 900 kg); (D–9) 10 670 lb (4 840 kg); (Ta 152H–1) 12 125 lb (5 500 kg).
Performance: maximum speed (with boost) (A–8, F–8) 408 mph (653 km/h); (D–9) 440 mph (704 km/h); (Ta 152H–1) 472 mph (755 km/h); initial climb (A–8, F–8) 2 350 ft (720 m)/min; (D–9, Ta 152) about 3 300 ft (1 000 m)/min; service ceiling (A–8, F–8) 37 400 ft (11 410 m); (D–9) 32 810 ft (10 000 m); (Ta 152H–1) 49 215 ft (15 000 m); range on internal fuel (A–8, F–8 and D–9) about 560 miles (900 km); (Ta 152H–1), 745 miles (1 200 km).

O Press button controls on panels (each side)
P Outlet louvres for motor cooling air
Q Exhausts outlet each side
R Cabin heating pipe
S Oil filter

105

Above: *Refuelling one of the first Fw 190s to reach the Luftwaffe. This aircraft, probably SB + IA, is almost certainly an A–2, with MG FF cannon mounted slightly further forward than subsequent aircraft. Initial evaluation at Le Bourget and Maldeghem by II/JG 26 was a disaster, due to the imperfectly developed engine installation.*
Right: A development line-up at Bremen in 1941, with A–1 and A–2 models visible. Most were delivered to the Luftwaffe.
Below: Another early factory model, a late A–0 with MG FF cannon installed in the wings just outboard of the landing gear.

any other radial installation in the world. The landing gear had an exceptionally wide track and was only just behind the propeller, giving outstanding ground stability. The cockpit was roomy, comfortable and equipped like a Cadillac. The clear-view canopy was a wonderfully successful answer to a difficult problem, giving fine all-round visibility in flight. Above all, from stem to stern the 190 was full of new things, about 98 per cent of them electrically operated. This eventually enabled this extremely small and compact aircraft to carry more ordnance, of more assorted varieties, than Allied fighters that were very much larger.

But no amount of cleverness in design is of use if the flight handling is faulty. However, in this respect, partly through luck, the Focke-Wulf was excellent. I once experienced the frustration of sitting in a 190A–3's beautiful and exciting cockpit, knowing that this captured aircraft was allowed to be flown only by a select group of RAF and Ministry test pilots. Such was their enthusiasm for it that, even among that select group, competition to fly it was intense.

Actually, the 190 must have been a winner to fly from the start, because, despite severe overheating of the BMW 139 engine, chief test pilot Hans Sander was little short of ecstatic after the first flight on 1 June 1939. At that time the Fw 190V1 looked like a jet, because its broad-blade VDM propeller had a giant, open-fronted spinner of the same diameter as the engine cowl and serving as a duct for the cooling air. In theory this can give lower drag than a more conventional arrangement, and six years later it was tried on Napier-engined Warwicks and Tempests, but after careful trials with the V1 and V2 prototypes the Focke-Wulf staff decided to drop the idea.

Early development of the 190 was beset by problems. The BMW company abandoned the 139 engine, but in June 1939 offered the 801 as a replacement. The 801 was potentially more powerful, but it was heavier and so different in its installation requirements that the next two prototypes, V3 and V4, were never completed. Then followed two V5 prototypes, the V5k (kleine) with a small wing of 14·9 sq/m, and the V5g (grosse) with 18·3 sq/m. The BMW 801 engine was cowled so neatly it was a revelation to Allied engineers, and cooling was assisted by a fan geared up from the engine, which filled the gap between spinner and cowl lip. To compensate for the increased weight and alleviate unpleasant heat around the pilot's feet the cockpit was moved back, and this allowed two 7·92 mm MG 17 machine guns to be installed in the top decking. Early A–0 development aircraft often had two additional machine guns in the inner wing, but thereafter Fw 190 armament permutations proliferated so rapidly that only a general outline can be given. The fuselage guns remained a pair of MG 17s in most A models, but were often 13 mm MG 131s. The inboard wing position was occupied by two MG 17s, two 20 mm MG FFs or two 20 mm MG 151/20s, the latter being cannon with many times the hitting power of the old FF (Oerlikon). Outboard were two MG 17s, two MG FFs or two more MG

This original Focke-Wulf photograph shows aircraft No 1286 carrying a 2,205-lb bomb (SB 1000). The lower bomb fin had to be removed. The 190G could carry the much larger SC 1800 weighing 3,968 lb, as well as torpedoes and several large missiles.

A Jabo-Rei (long-range fighter/bomber) Fw 190A–5/U8 with an SC 500 (1,102-lb) bomb and two 66-gal tanks on the underwing Messerschmitt pylons.
Usually the inboard MG 151 were the only guns.

151s. Later there were countless combinations with 20 mm MG 151s in single or twin under-wing blisters, 30 mm MK 108s, the much harder-hitting 30 mm MK 103s, or a wide range of recoilless guns, large cannon and rockets.

When the RAF met the new fighter in the summer of 1941 they were dismayed. The new Focke-Wulf was not only a brilliant fighter but it was flown by men of great skill and experience. JG26, under Adolf Galland (later Luftwaffe General der Jagdflieger and in recent years Chief of Staff of the reborn Luftwaffe), was above-average in an above-average service, but the next *gruppe* to fly the 190, JG2, was if anything even better. The Spitfire V had an excellent turning circle if boldly flown and two deadly Hispano cannon; but it was outclassed by the 190. The German fighter was much smaller, and harder to hit. It was notably faster and, if the enemy pilot wished, he could select an over-ride boost throttle setting giving him a further 15 mph. The margin over the Spitfire up to 20000 feet was seldom less than 20 mph and the 190 could dive and climb faster, roll much more rapidly (the margin increasing with indicated airspeed) and appeared to its enemies to have no flight limitations. In combat a 190 was a fearsome opponent. The side exhaust stacks poured thin smoke when the engine was at full power, and a

dense pair of contrails appeared when at high altitude, whilst others formed briefly at the wing tips as the 190 achieved g that would have broken the wings of most other fighters. Even in 1944 when the USAAF fighter pilots wore g-suits, the few remaining *experte* 190 pilots could make tighter turns. The one thing the 190 could not do, even when lightly laden, was equal a Spitfire's radius of turn at lower speeds of around 220 knots, but unlike the Spitfire it could carry a torpedo, a 3970 lb bomb, or four 20 mm cannon plus two 30 mm, to say nothing of the amazing array of futuristic weapons which were fitted in 190s in the final year of the war.

Most of the 20001 Fw 190 production deliveries were used for purposes other than plain air combat. About 8000 served with close support and attack units, some ending their days as the upper, piloted, component of Mistel (Mistletoe) composite aircraft, while others were specially equipped night fighters, tandem-seat trainers or ramming bomber-destroyers with armoured leading edges. Even without the last-named modification the 190 saw wide service in special Sturmstaffel manned by a mixture of volunteers or miscreants, who had to sign a document promising to destroy at least one Allied bomber on each mission, by ramming if necessary. Had this meant a one-for-one ex-

Top: *A superb photograph of CI + XM, the Ta 152 V7, also called a Ta 152C–0/R11. Shown running its DB 603LA engine at Hannover-Langenhagen in December 1944, it was a Zerstörer with an MK 108, two fuselage MG 151s and two wing-root MG 151s.*
Above left: *A most interesting aircraft was CF + OY, the V18 prototype which in the spring of 1942 re-emerged as the first C-series aircraft with DB 603A liquid-cooled engine,*

long exhaust stacks and coolant radiator under the rear fuselage. This led to the Dora–9.
Above right: *One of the last of the whole family, a long-span Ta 152H, probably to H–1/R11 standard, and with Werk Nr 150 167. As numbers normally ran without gaps in any one batch this suggests that at least 167 of this outstanding aircraft were completed at Cottbus. Exhaust stacks for the Jumo 213 are grouped 2–3–1, unlike early units.*

change, one fighter for one bomber, it would have been a bad bargain because, while the Allies had an overwhelming output of bombers and aircrew, the Luftwaffe had hardly any experienced pilots left. In fact the Sturmstaffel did wonders with the 190, and unlike most Luftwaffe units in the final year of the war, set records many times better than one-for-one (once 32 for 2) despite physical and mental exhaustion of the pilots.

In 1939–45 Focke-Wulf managed plants all over central Europe for building or assembling the 190. Meanwhile the development staff at Bremen and Bad Eilsen built at least 80 prototypes – a total which today would be a healthy production run in its own right – to test various improvements. Many of the 1943 prototypes had liquid-cooled engines, and by May 1944 these had led to an example powered by the Jumo 213. Rated at 1776 hp, this excellent inverted V-12 engine could be boosted to 2240 hp for short spells using the highly developed MW 50 (50/50

water/methanol) injection system. By the autumn of 1944 Luftwaffe units were receiving the production offspring, the 190D–9, which was popularly called Dora 9. Previous 190 versions had not received popular names, as had various versions of the 109, and nobody really took to Focke-Wulf's own apellation of Würger (butcher bird). To the RAF, Dora 9 was 'the long-nosed 190', and though by this time the Allies had fighters that could just about outperform the 190, this new model was viewed with some trepidation. It emerged in many forms, and was redesignated Ta 152 in honour of Tank, but inexorably the Luftwaffe had its airfields overrun, its pilots killed and the floods of new fighters were unable to operate through lack of fuel. Of all the Luftwaffe's fighters in the Second World War the Fw 190/Ta 152 was in my view by far the best. It is strange that the thoroughly dislikeable Bf 109G was produced at consistently faster rates and was used by more Luftwaffe units.

Bristol Beaufighter

In the second half of the 1930s the RAF was entirely without any fighter having more than extremely limited range and endurance. Admittedly, for the crucial task of day interception, guided by Watson-Watt's early-warning radar and the new system of radio GCI (ground control of interception), short-endurance fighters could defend adequately the parts of the British Isles reached in strength by the Luftwaffe when war came. But for night defence, when standing patrols were needed, and for almost all operations in the other larger theatres of war, there was a desperate need for bigger long-range aircraft. In the absence of anything better, the RAF put guns under old Blenheim bombers, but these could not even catch a Ju 88, nor shoot enemy raiders down except by sheer luck. Fortunately, back in 1938 the Bristol airframe leader (Barnwell until a tragic accident in 1938 and Leslie Frise thereafter) and their engine king (Roy Fedden) planned a variety of powerful fighters to make good the deficiency. In November 1938 the decision was taken to fit two sleeve-valve Hercules engines into a fighter using for it as many parts and tools as possible of those used in the production of the Beaufort torpedo bomber.

This saved time and reduced risk, and the prototype Type 156 Beaufighter was flown by Cyril Uwins at Filton on 17 July 1939. To develop the most powerful fighter in the world in seven months showed the wisdom of the scheme, but it took twice as much effort, and a further 12 months, to progress from first flight to operational service, though in the context of British performances this was pretty good; the Blackburn Firebrand took so long to produce it missed the war!

A grateful Air Ministry wrote specification F.17/39 to cover the first 300 Beaufighters, and while a wealth of new variations were studied or tested the basic Mk I began to reach operational squadrons from 27 July 1940. It was almost exactly the right aircraft at the right time, thanks entirely to private enterprise.

I was fortunate enough to acquire a little practical experience of what was surely the beefiest, and almost the biggest, of all Allied fighters. The RAF had been worried by the size and weight, and was disappointed that the maximum speed of early 'Beaus' was only about 309 mph when loaded with full equipment; but it was not intended for dog-fighting by day. It was precisely what the night fighting units so urgently needed, for it had a fair performance and

One of the first 50 Beaufighter IFs (R2056 et seq) which lacked the machine guns in the wings. Aircraft with full armament began to reach Fighter Command in the first week of 1941.

Another of the first production batch, with neither Brownings nor AI radar. Still in day camouflage, it was serving with 252 Sqn, code-letters PN.

NAV. LIGHTS
TRIM TAB
BALANCED AILERONS
FLAP
M/c GUNS
SUPERCHARGER AIR INTAKE
FUEL TANK
FUEL JETTISON PIPES
OIL TANK
OIL COOLER & AIR TO CABIN
DE HAVILLAND HYDROMATIC AIRSCREWS
MOTOR OFFERED UP AS COMPLETE UNIT
LEADING-EDGE HINGED SECTIONS
BRISTOL 'HERCULES' MOTORS
TWO EACH
NOSE UNIT OFFERED COMPLETE WITH FIT

yet had carrying capacity for airborne radar, heavy armament and, later, bombs, rockets and a torpedo, together with 550 gallons of fuel. It was one of a minority of combat aircraft which engendered a great feeling of confidence and power.

Sadly, Bristol never got round to building the Type 158, which they called the 'Sports Model'. This would have had a slim body, higher speed and almost certainly a sensible means of entry from the outside. The Beau had a fine cockpit, forming the front of the fat fuselage, but it was no joke reaching it. You pulled open a hatch in the belly, climbed a ladder, stooped low and climbed along a cluttered interior and over the folded back of the seat, where the parachute would be ready in place. Raising the seat and getting harnesses on and other connections made was less of a problem, and once settled one became aware of the great engines looming on either side. Even when cropped to 12 ft 9 in to give safe ground clearance the DH Hydromatic propellers were impressively close.

The general atmosphere of a 'Beau' cockpit was unique. There was nothing in front of the pilot but a sheet of optically flat bullet-proof glass, and the extremely short nose was just long enough to accommodate the pilot's legs. The view was outstanding, except laterally, when the engines got in the way, and the old-timers who had been on Blenheim fighters were glad of the change from the multitude of small Perspex panels which caused annoying internal reflections at night. Instruments and controls were impressive in number, if perhaps in inconvenient places, but in my opinion flying one of these aircraft must have been the most satisfying thing since the Sopwith Camel, and the temptation to do aerobatics irresistible. There was a wheel for the ailerons, but, unlike the P–38, the massive control column was between the pilot's legs on the centreline. The right thumb could readily reach either the lever for the differential brakes or the button that fired the guns.

Armament was heavier than on any previous fighter. The first 50 Beaufighters, delivered by the end of October 1940, had four 20 mm Hispano cannon in the bottom of the centre fuselage and subsequent aircraft added six 0·303 in Brownings in the wings, two on the left and four on the right. There were only two on the left because the landing lights occupied the bay where the other two would have been, though I suppose there must have been a better reason than that the lights were in the same place on the Beaufort. The cannon were great; they could be used at night without causing any bothersome flash, though one had to pull gently on the yoke to stop the aircraft veering off-target. The Ministry of Aircraft Production rejected Bristol's scheme for continuous 20 mm belt feed, and the second

The 'Clark drawing' of the Beaufighter dated from August 1941. As no Beau had at that time fallen into enemy hands (in fact hardly any did) the drawing may have been of some intelligence help, though of course Clark was not allowed to hint at AI radar. Today an artist would probably make at least one propeller blade full length; one ought not to assume too much on the part of the reader!

SPECIFICATIONS

Types I to TF.X (data mainly Mk X)
Engines: two 1 770 hp Bristol Hercules XVII 14-cylinder sleeve-valve radials; (Mk II) 1 250 hp R-R Merlin XX; (other marks) different Hercules; (one-offs had R-R Griffons and Wright GR-2600 Cyclones).
Dimensions: span 57 ft 10 in (17·63 m); length 41 ft 8 in (12·6 m) (II, 42 ft 9 in); height 15 ft 10 in (4·84 m).
Weights: empty 15 600 lb (7 100 kg) (I, II, 13 800 lb; VI, XI, 14 900 lb); loaded 25 400 lb (11 530 kg) (most other marks, 21 000 lb, 9 525 kg).
Performance: maximum speed 312 mph (502 km/h) (fighter marks, 330 mph, 528 km/h); initial climb 1 850 ft (564 m)/min; service ceiling 26 500 ft (8 077 m) (fighters, 30 000 ft, 9 144 m); range 1 540 miles (2 478 km).

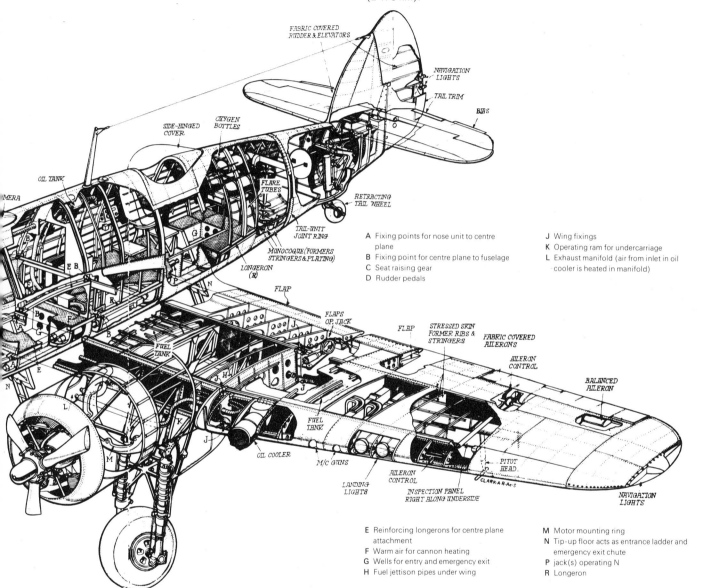

A Fixing points for nose unit to centre plane
B Fixing point for centre plane to fuselage
C Seat raising gear
D Rudder pedals

J Wing fixings
K Operating ram for undercarriage
L Exhaust manifold (air from inlet in oil cooler is heated in manifold)

E Reinforcing longerons for centre plane attachment
F Warm air for cannon heating
G Wells for entry and emergency exit
H Fuel jettison pipes under wing

M Motor mounting ring
N Tip-up floor acts as entrance ladder and emergency exit chute
P jack(s) operating N
R Longeron

crew-member, who was usually called the observer, had to swivel his seat round to the front to undertake the extremely tiring task of reloading all four guns with heavy 60-round drums. On the 401st Beaufighter a continuous feed for the guns, identical to the rejected type, was at last permitted. Firing all guns was exciting, though cordite fumes from the cannon did get into the cockpit.

Thanks to Bristol's initiative the Beaufighter reached the RAF in the nick of time. It was the ideal carrier for AI (airborne interception) radar, and virtually all the first production AI.IV sets were reserved for it. In the hands of such men as Rory Chisholm and John Cunningham the radar-equipped Beaufighter gradually began to make the Luftwaffe's previously immune night raiders suffer severe casualties. Though the termination of the winterlong Blitz on England at the end of May 1941 was due chiefly to the

Above: *A fully operational F–86F (52–4850). The nose-gear door looks enormous. Ground crew invariably headed for the nose-gear bay, activated the emergency hydraulics and opened the main-gear doors to get at system components. If the aircraft was urgently scrambled it was not unknown for the emergency system to be left on, thereby making it impossible to raise the gear after take-off.*
Right: *One of the best air/air portraits of an F–86D, showing USAF 50–518, the 64th to come off the assembly line. At that time practically nothing worked properly – not even the engine, the new D-series J47–17 with afterburner.*

Top: *Fully fledged night-fighter Mk IF Beaus, with matt night finish, ten guns and, by far the most important, AI. Mk IV radar. They were pictured on 23 May 1941, at the climax of the Night Blitz on England, serving with 600 (City of London) Sqn, based at Colerne.*
Below left: *The two entrance hatches can be seen in this picture of* The Benghazi Bus, *a war-weary Mk IF (T5273) of 46 Sqn, at Idku, Alexandria.*
Below right: *A Beau of 272 Sqn based at Idku. The observer's blister has been cut away as a field modification for a rear gun, in the way made standard with some other variants.*

transfer of bombers to the Eastern Front, it was also certainly influenced by the losses the Beaufighters inflicted. In the past, nothing had been more frustrating for the AA guns and night fighters to go into action each night – and the fighters to suffer sorely from accidents – with hardly any success against the enemy. The Beaufighter I can fairly claim to have been the world's first night fighter to combine all the equipment necessary – radio, radar, armament and performance (including a ten-hour endurance when needed) – to hunt down and kill enemies on something better than a hit-and-miss basis.

This in itself was of immense importance to the war, and the Luftwaffe never again dared mount raids on Britain except with scattered high-speed bombers that came across in a great arching dive, let their bombs go blindly and fled for home. These later raids were difficult for the few remaining Beaufighters to cope with, as they

put on a lot of middle-aged weight, the gross rising from 15840 lb on its first flight to 20800 lb for the radar-equipped Mk IF and 25400 lb for the final sub-type in 1945. For this reason Fedden's estimate of 360 mph once the 1615 hp Hercules VI became available was never realised and typical top speeds were always nearer 320 mph.

Some of the many variants were not improvements. In the first year of deliveries from Filton 450 aircraft were fitted with the Morris Motors manufactured standard Merlin XX power unit, as later used on the Lancaster, and with the Rotol non-feathering propeller. These Mk IIs matched the speed of the Hercules aircraft, but had poorer takeoff and climb and such doubtful stability in pitch and yaw as to be only just acceptable. All Beaufighters suffered to some degree from directional instability, and from a proneness to swing on takeoff or landing. After trying the effect of a taller tail, twin fins, dihedralled tailplane and a long dorsal fin, the last two changes were made standard on all marks. Some more experienced pilots were against any change, claiming that a competent pilot never had any trouble; they preferred the greater manoeuvrability with the original tail. One aircraft had Griffon engines with four-bladed propellers, and was probably the fastest of all. Two, called Mk Vs, had most of the fixed guns removed and a four–0·303 in gun turret added, an idea known to be of doubtful use even as it was being carried out. Plans for high-altitude versions were thwarted by poor lateral control at height and the difficulty of pressurizing the interior. One aircraft had Merlin 61s in installations similar to those on the first Merlin Mustang. Other trials included the use of 40 mm guns, one in place of each Hispano, but oddly enough the only carriers of big guns in RAF service were the Mosquito and Hurricane. The tough Beaufighter would have been ideal as a piercer of tanks and U-boats.

By 1941 suffix letters F and C differentiated aircraft for Fighter and Coastal Commands, and though the latter had no radar, the observer was kept busy with extra radio, navaids and a chart

were a bit slow for the Fw 190 and Ju 188, and by 1943 they had mainly been replaced by NF (night fighter) Mosquitoes. But throughout the war later and increasingly effective Beaufighters continued to pour off the assembly lines, not only at Filton but also at the shadow factory at Weston-super-Mare and from Fairey Aviation at Stockport.

Like nearly all combat aircraft the Beaufighter

One of the 38 Mirage 5PA ground-attack aircraft supplied to the Pakistan Air Force. The most obvious difference between this simplified clear-weather bomber and the Mirage III series lies in the slim conical nose, which does not have to accommodate a large radar dish.

table. By the end of the year the Mk VIC and VIF were at last being delivered with the Hercules VI engine, and the VIC gave the observer a Vickers K machine gun firing aft. Both sub-types could carry two 500 lb bombs or eight 60 lb rockets, and the VIF was the first aircraft in the world to become operational with centimetric AI radar. The test flying of AI.VII and AI.VIII was done with a Mk IF, X7579, the first aircraft to have a radome (of the kind called a 'thimble' nose). As often happens with highly-blown engines, the Mk VI Hercules actually gave slightly less power than the Hercules XI (the 100-octane model of the original Hercules III) at altitudes below 10000 feet. The upshot was that Bristol rushed through the Hercules XVII with a cropped supercharger blower giving 1735 hp at low level. The fighter pilots wanted this engine, but were told their business was at 20000 feet or so. The low-blown engine therefore went into the Coastal aircraft, which soon appeared carrying a torpedo as the TF.X. On 4 April 1943 torpedo-carrying Beaufighters sank two ships off Norway, and thenceforward this aircraft did great work with guns, torpedoes and rockets throughout Europe and the Mediterranean and Far East. As for the VIF, this was not only a mainstay of the RAF in the Mediterranean and Italy but, until the summer of 1944, it was also the standard night fighter of the USAAF in the European theatre, hundreds serving with the 1st Tactical AF in Italy and southern France. Others served with the SAAF and the Balkan AF, operating in support of Marshal Tito.

The TF.X was the final mainstream variant, and built in the largest numbers of all (2205); after the war it became the T.T.10 and was relegated to target towing. Though it began simply as a VIC with the 1735 hp engine, it soon acquired Fairey-Youngman bellows-type flap/airbrake units, underwing racks and, in 1944, additional racks under the centre fuselage

Above: *EL223/G was a Mk VIC used for early torpedo trials in August 1942. Curiously, this official photograph carefully identifies it as a Mk IC with Hercules III engines. Underwing roundels are to an earlier specification; this was one of the first Beaus to have a dihedralled tailplane.*
Below: *Taken by the observer of another Beau, this Mk VIF is setting out from Malta in 1942. It is believed to be an aircraft of 252 Sqn, one of the original customers in Fighter Command. Note Vickers G0 rear gun.*

for two 500 lb bombs. Production was swelled by Roots at Blythe Bridge, and when production ceased on 21 September 1945, a total of 5562 Beaufighters had been built in Britain. They were in the front-line to the end, one of their most striking accomplishments being the sinking of the 51000-ton *Rex* by 55 rocket hits just below the water-line!

From 1941 Beaufighters had been supplied to the RAAF, and after much discussion (mainly about which engine should be used) the Mk 21 went into production in Australia in 1944 at Fishermen's Bend, Melbourne, as a follow-on to the Beaufort programme. By late 1945 a total of 364 had been built, with Hercules XVIII engines, four 0·5 in wing guns and a Sperry autopilot in a bulge above the nose. They saw action alongside the British-built Beaufighters in south-east Asia, earning the name 'Whispering Death' among the Japanese, who preferred aircraft that gave some warning of their approach.

Above: *One from the final production batch in 1945, SR914 was a TF.X converted after the war to TT.10 standard, as seen here. Someone is (crouching) looking over the pilot's left shoulder.*

Above: *A pleasing portrait of the 91st IIIC interceptor in service with the Armée de l' Air in the early 1960s. The unit is I/2 Cicogne, and the missile the R 530, replacing the R 511 used when the Mirage IIIC entered service.*

Left: *Flight-refuelling a Phantom FGR.2 of No 111 Sqn RAF. The old Victor K.1 tanker belonged to 57 Sqn, since re-equipped with the completely rebuilt K.2. The Phantom was one of the first aircraft to incorporate a neat retractable FR probe.*

Below: *Recovery of a Phantom aboard USS America. The Phantom – surely the king of modern fighters – has an exceptional record of versatility and improvement. This one, an F–4B, appears to belong to VF–101, which in 1961 was the second outfit to receive Phantoms.*

North American P-51 Mustang

Today, more than 30 years after the Second World War ended, the general consensus of opinion is that, if one had to name the best all-round fighter on either side, the choice would fall on the Mustang. While it is true that the Mustang, in its different versions, was never wholly free from faults, it played probably the biggest part in the most crucial battle of the entire air war. This was the sustained day-by-day offensive by the US 8th Air Force which eventually not only devastated German ground targets but achieved air supremacy over the German heartland. From that time, Germany had lost the war. The Luftwaffe could not make good the resulting attrition in skilled pilots, and by 1945 the air war over Central Europe had degenerated into a mopping-up process, with individual P-51 pilots shooting down as many as six of the enemy during a single mission. Thus, while the Hurricane and Spitfire in 1940 ensured that the war was not lost, the Mustang in 1944–45 ensured that it was won.

But the Mustang of 1944–45 was a considerably more refined aircraft than the original. And, like nearly all the most famous Allied combat aircraft of the Second World War, it was not designed to meet an official requirement but arose solely through the initiative of private industry. North American Aviation, at Inglewood, in Los Angeles, was a latecomer to the US manufacturing scene but from the start, in 1934, it had established a great reputation for clean and efficient structural design of the then-new all-metal stressed-skin type. In 1938 the British Purchasing Commission, set up to investigate the possibility of buying military aircraft from the United States, signed its first contract with NAA, for a trainer that became famous as the Harvard. NAA's board chairman, 'Dutch' Kindelberger, wondered if the British might be the key to his company building a fighter. The US Army Air Corps was over-whelmed with new pursuit designs. The NAA engineering team were not impressed by most of them, but could see no market opening until Sir Henry Self, head of the British commission, asked whether NAA would consider making the Curtiss P–40 (Tomahawk) to augment output for Britain. But between January and April 1940 Kindelberger managed to persuade the British that his company could build a fighter superior to the P–40. On 29 May, as the German Blitzkrieg swept across France, the British commission ordered 320 non-existent fighters known only as the NA–73.

Perhaps the best way to ensure a good result in almost any activity to do with aircraft is to have an outstanding team and then put them under pressure. NAA had no experience of pursuit aircraft, but had undertaken to have the NA–73 prototype ready in four months. Work went on round the clock, and the company was still small and personal enough for the men who did the day shift often to do the night shift also. From the start the only engine considered had been the Allison V–1710–F3R liquid-cooled V–12, which appeared to offer the minimum drag when installed which the team was seeking to achieve.

When the Allied Fifth Army established an airstrip in the Anzio beach head it made protective revetments out of Italian wine casks filled with earth, topped by sandbags. Betty Jean was an Allison-engined P–51, first production model for the USAAF, with four 20 mm cannon.

Despite the vulnerability in battle of long coolant piping, the radiator was placed under the rear fuselage, and to turn drag into thrust the core matrix was installed in a profiled duct with a variable exit shutter, so that the heated air gave a modest propulsive jet which in other fighters was wasted. To achieve high performance NAA could have made the NA–73 small, like a Bf 109

Above: The first version to see combat with the USAAF was the A–36A, in Sicily in August 1943. Originally intended as a dive-bomber, with six 0·5-in guns and two 500-lb bombs, it soon became a general-purpose attack aircraft.

Left: *A McDonnell Aircraft (MAIR) photograph of an early F–4E on test from St Louis. The two new changes, the slatted high-lift wing and the under-nose 'Gatling gun', are clearly evident, the slats having opened in this zoom climb. The white EROS (Eliminate Range-Zero System) pod under the belly is the MCAIR-developed anti-collision device, clipped to all St Louis fighters on flight test.*
Below: *Today's RAF has little time or finance for publicity, but RAF Coningsby did put together this static display of a 6 Sqn Phantom FGR.2 and assortment of stores (which did not include reconnaissance or ECM pods).*

Weal's drawing of the Mustang, a Mustang III with Malcolm bulged hood corresponding to the USAAF P–51B–15 and some C-models. This time the propeller is much better, and two blades almost perfect.

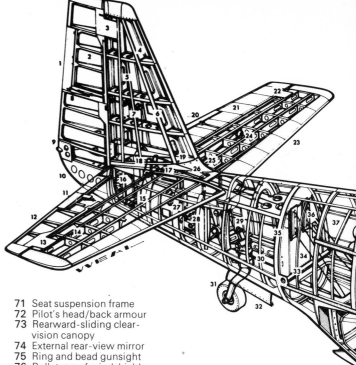

1 Rudder plastic trim tab
2 Rudder frame (fabric covered)
3 Rudder balance
4 Tailfin front spar
5 Tailfin structure
6 Access panel
7 Rudder trim tab actuating drum
8 Rudder trim tab control link
9 Rear navigation light
10 Rudder metal bottom section
11 Elevator plywood trim tab
12 Starboard elevator frame
13 Elevator balance weight
14 Starboard tailplane structure
15 Reinforced bracket (rear steering stresses)
16 Rudder operating horn forging
17 Elevator operating horns
18 Tab control turnbuckles
19 Tailfin front spar/fuselage attachment
20 Port elevator tab
21 Fabric covered elevator
22 Elevator balance weight
23 Port tailplane
24 Tab control drum
25 Finroot fairing
26 Elevator cables
27 Tab control access panels
28 Tailwheel steering mechanism
29 Tailwheel retraction mechanism
30 Tailwheel leg assembly
31 Forward-retracting steerable tailwheel
32 Tailwheel doors
33 Lifting tube
34 Fuselage aft bulkhead/breakpoint
35 Fuselage break point

36 Control cable pulley brackets
37 Fuselage frames
38 Oxygen bottles
39 Cooling air exit flap actuating mechanism
40 Rudder cables
41 Fuselage lower longeron
42 Rear tunnel
43 Cooling air exit flap
44 Coolant radiator assembly
45 Radio and equipment shelf
46 Power supply pack
47 Fuselage upper longeron
48 Radio bay aft bulkhead (plywood)
49 Fuselage stringers
50 SCR–695 radio transmitter-receiver (on upper sliding shelf)
51 Whip aerial
52 Junction box
53 Cockpit aft glazing
54 Canopy track
55 SCR–522 radio transmitter-receiver
56 Battery installation
57 Radiator/supercharger coolant pipes
58 Radiator forward air duct
59 Coolant header tank/radiator pipe
60 Coolant radiator ventral access cover
61 Oil cooler air inlet door
62 Oil radiator
63 Oil pipes
64 Flap control linkage
65 Wing rear spar/fuselage attachment bracket
66 Crash pylon structure
67 Aileron control linkage
68 Hydraulic hand pump
69 Radio control boxes
70 Pilot's seat

71 Seat suspension frame
72 Pilot's head/back armour
73 Rearward-sliding clear-vision canopy
74 External rear-view mirror
75 Ring and bead gunsight
76 Bullet-proof windshield
77 Gyroscopic gunsight
78 Engine controls
79 Signal pistol discharge tube
80 Circuit-breaker panel
81 Oxygen regulator
82 Pilot's foot-rest and seat mounting bracket
83 Control linkage
84 Rudder pedal
85 Tailwheel lock control
86 Wing centre-section
87 Hydraulic reservoir
88 Port wing fuel tank filler point
89 Port 0·5-in (12·7-mm) cal machine-guns
90 Ammunition feed chutes
91 Gun bay access door (raised)
92 Ammunition box troughs
93 Aileron control cables
94 Flap lower skin (Alclad)
95 Aileron profile (internal aerodynamic balance diaphragm)
96 Aileron control drum and mounting bracket
97 Aileron trim tab control drum
98 Aileron plastic (Phenol fibre) trim tab
99 Port aileron assembly
100 Wing skinning
101 Outer section sub-assembly
102 Port navigation light
103 Port wingtip
104 Leading-edge skin
105 Landing lamp
106 Weapons/stores pylon
107 500-lb bomb
108 Gun ports
109 Machine-gun barrels
110 Detachable cowling panels
111 Firewall/integral armour
112 Oil tank
113 Oil pipes
114 Upper longeron/engine mount attachment
115 Oil tank metal retaining straps
116 Carburettor
117 Engine bearer assembly
118 Cowling panel frames
119 Engine aftercooler
120 Engine leads

121 Packard-Rolls-Royce Merlin V–1650 engine
122 Exhaust fairing panel
123 Stub exhausts
124 Magneto
125 Coolant pipes
126 Cowling forward frame
127 Coolant header tank
128 Armour plate
129 Propeller hub
130 Spinner

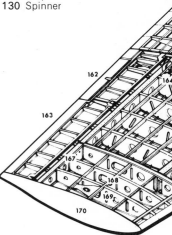

131 Four-blade Hamilton Standard Hydromatic propeller
132 Carburettor air intake, integral with (133)
133 Engine mount front frame assembly
134 Intake trunking
135 Engine mount reinforcing tie
136 Hand crank starter
137 Carburettor/trunking vibration-absorbing connection
138 Wing centre-section front bulkhead
139 Wing centre-section end rib
140 Starboard mainwheel well
141 Wing front spar/fuselage attachment bracket

SPECIFICATIONS

Types P-51 to P-51L, A-36, F-6, Cavalier 750 to 2500, Piper Enforcer and F-82 Twin Mustang

Engine: (P-51, A, A-36, F-6A) one 1 150 hp Allison V-1710-F3R or 1 125 hp V-1710-81 vee-12 liquid-cooled; (P-51B, C, D and K, F-6C) one Packard V-1650 (licence-built R-R Merlin 61-series), originally 1 520 hp V-1650-3 followed during P-51D run by 1 590 hp V-1650-7; (P-51H) 2 218 hp V-1650-9; (Cavalier) mainly V-1650-7; (Turbo-Mustang III) 1 740 hp Rolls-Royce Dart 510 turboprop; (Enforcer) 2 535 hp Lycoming T55-9 turboprop; (F-82F, G, H) two 2 300 hp (wet rating) Allison V-1710-143/145.
Dimensions: span 37 ft 0½ in (11·29 m) (tip-tanked Cavalier models, 40 ft 1 in); (F-82) 51 ft 3 in (15·61 m); length 32 ft 2½ in (9·81 m); (P-51H) 33 ft 4 in; (Turbo-Mustang and Enforcer) 38 ft 6 in; (F-82E) 39 ft 1 in (11·88 m); (F-82F) 42 ft 2 in; height (P-51, A, A-36, F-6) 12 ft 2 in (3·72 m); (other P-51) 13 ft 8 in (4·1 m); (F-82) 13 ft 10 in (4·2 m).
Weights: empty (P-51 early V-1710 models, typical) 6 300 lb (2 858 kg); (P-51D) 7 125 lb (3 230 kg); (Cavalier 2500) 7 500 lb (3 402 kg); (Turbo-Mustang/Enforcer) 6 696 lb (3 037 kg); (F-82E) 14 350 lb (6 509 kg); maximum loaded (P-51 early) 8 600 lb (3 901 kg); (P-51D) 11 600 lb (5 260 kg); (Cavalier) 10 500 lb (4 763 kg); (Turbo) 14 000 lb (6 350 kg); (F-82E) 24 864 lb (11 276 kg); (F-82F) 26 208 lb (11 880 kg).
Performance: maximum speed (early P-51) 390 mph (628 km/h); (P-51D) 437 mph (703 km/h), (Cavalier, typical) 457 mph (735 km/h); (F-82, typical) 465 mph (750 km/h); initial climb (early) 2 600 ft (792 m)/min, (P-51D) 3 475 ft (1 060 m)/min; service ceiling (early) 30 000 ft (9 144 m); (P-51D) 41 900 ft (12 770 m), (also typical for Cavaliers and F-82s); range with maximum fuel (early) 450 miles (724 km); (P-51D) combat range 950 miles, operational range 1 300 miles with drop tanks and absolute range to dry tanks of 2 080 miles; (Cavaliers) 750-2 500 miles depending on customer choice; (Turbo) 2 300 miles; (F-82E) 2 504 miles; (F-82F) 2 200 miles.

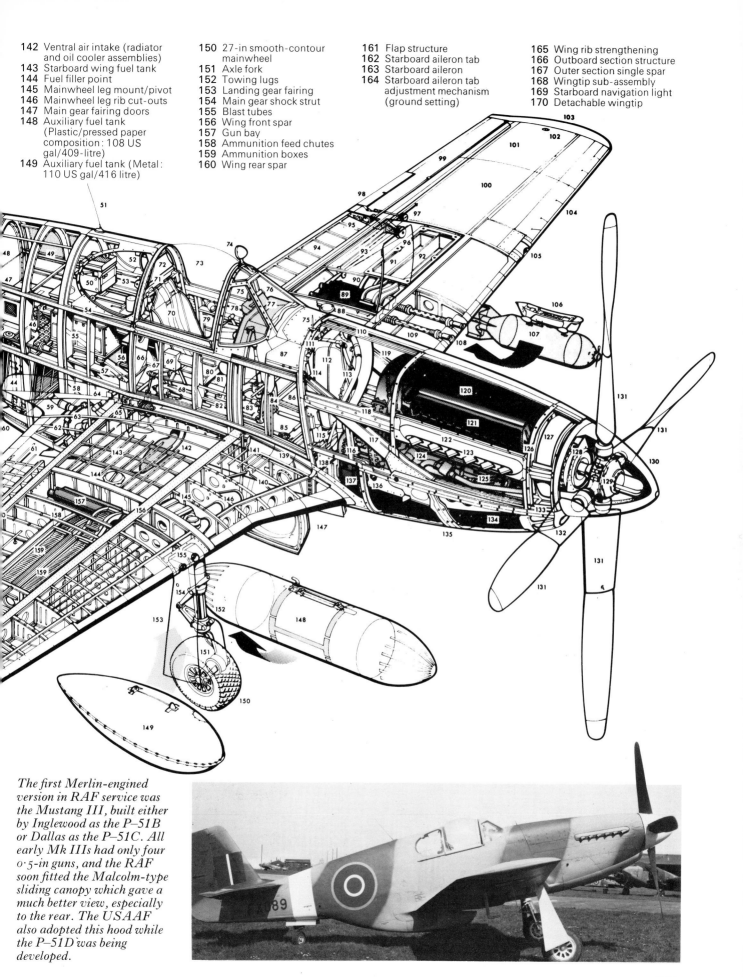

142 Ventral air intake (radiator and oil cooler assemblies)
143 Starboard wing fuel tank
144 Fuel filler point
145 Mainwheel leg mount/pivot
146 Mainwheel leg rib cut-outs
147 Main gear fairing doors
148 Auxiliary fuel tank (Plastic/pressed paper composition: 108 US gal/409-litre)
149 Auxiliary fuel tank (Metal: 110 US gal/416 litre)

150 27-in smooth-contour mainwheel
151 Axle fork
152 Towing lugs
153 Landing gear fairing
154 Main gear shock strut
155 Blast tubes
156 Wing front spar
157 Gun bay
158 Ammunition feed chutes
159 Ammunition boxes
160 Wing rear spar

161 Flap structure
162 Starboard aileron tab
163 Starboard aileron
164 Starboard aileron tab adjustment mechanism (ground setting)

165 Wing rib strengthening
166 Outboard section structure
167 Outer section single spar
168 Wingtip sub-assembly
169 Starboard navigation light
170 Detachable wingtip

The first Merlin-engined version in RAF service was the Mustang III, built either by Inglewood as the P–51B or Dallas as the P–51C. All early Mk IIIs had only four 0·5-in guns, and the RAF soon fitted the Malcolm-type sliding canopy which gave a much better view, especially to the rear. The USAAF also adopted this hood while the P–51D was being developed.

First of the many : some of the first V–1650-powered P–51B Mustangs to join the embattled US Army Air Force in England in the winter of 1943–44.

EW998 was an A–36A dive bomber (ex-USAAF 42–83685) supplied to the RAF for evaluation. The type was not adopted by the RAF.

or Spitfire; instead they chose to achieve it by refinement. The NA–73 was, by a mixture of brilliance and luck, exactly the right compromise between big and small, with a profusion of advanced design features thrown in as a bonus.

By September the NA–73X was structurally complete, but no engine had been delivered. The British, who had thought of the name Apache, finally settled for Mustang, and upped their order from 320 to 620. In October the first engine arrived, was fitted in 24 hours and almost at once Vance Breeze began taxiing trials. Flight testing started on 26 October, and went well until Paul Balfour, the pilot on flight No 5, inadvertently cut off the fuel at low level and caused a write-off. But by this time the Mustang was known to be a winner. On 24 October 1941 the first production Mustang I to reach Britain was unloaded at Liverpool docks.

However, by this time RAF Fighter Command was no longer short of fighters, and the extremely poor performance of the Allison F3R engine

above 15000 feet made the Mustang unacceptable to it. Low down, though, the new American fighter was outstanding, and the recently formed (December 1940) Army Co-operation Command gladly took all the Mustangs it could get, to replace the Tomahawk. Up to the middle altitude range the newcomer was markedly faster than any other aircraft in service, and about as fast as the much smaller Bf 109F and Fw 190A on the other side of the Channel. This speed, around 380 mph, was attained by sheer aerodynamic efficiency, and especially by using a wing with a very accurate profile, having the maximum thickness well back – the so-called 'laminar flow' section – which resulted in the NAA fighter having profile drag significantly lower than any other fighter. On top of this its large fuel capacity enabled it to fly twice as far as most of its contemporaries, about 1050 miles in four hours compared with 470 miles in two hours for a Spitfire V. Despite its weight of 8600 lb, compared with a little over 6000 lb for a 109F or

One of the many, a Mustang IV with every desirable feature. It was one of a batch of ex-USAAF-account P–51K with Aeroproducts propeller, built at Dallas. Total K production was 1,337, of which 594 became RAF Mustang IVs.

Steel matting covered many Allied airfields by late 1944.
This one is in the Philippines, where P–51Ds of the 5th Air Force 35th FG are taxiing out on a strike against Japanese pockets in northern Luzon.

Spitfire V, it could hold its own in a dogfight and was very fast in a dive. Armament was more than adequate, because under the nose and in the wings were four of the big '·50-calibre' Brownings, backed up by four 0·303-in Brownings in the wings. Over 800 of these first-generation Mustangs served 23 Army Co-operation Command squadrons and the Combined Ops unit, and its work was outstanding. Equipped with an oblique camera behind the pilot's head, it penetrated into Germany on hazardous low-level Rhubarb and Ranger armed reconnaissance missions, and also dabbled in night intrusion over Luftwaffe airfields.

NAA had undertaken freely to supply the US Army Air Corps with two of the first batch of NA–73s, and these were found to be so good that – much to the maker's suprise, because the AAC did not really want more types of pursuit aircraft, and certainly not a 'foreign' one – the Army bought 310 as the P–51A, plus 500 dive-bomber A–36 versions and a further 150 were bought under the Lend-Lease programme for the RAF, these with four 20 mm cannon. Many early Army P–51s were fitted with two K–24 cameras to fly as F–6A photo-reconnaissance aircraft. Hundreds of P–51 and A–36 models saw action in North Africa, Sicily and Italy, as well as north-west Europe.

But the Mustang remained a low-level aircraft. It must have occurred to many in 1940–41 that it might become a better high-altitude performer if fitted with a Merlin engine, but the serious proposal to try this out was triggered by Rolls-Royce test pilot Flt Lt Ron Harker, who flew a Mustang in April 1942. So outstanding were the Rolls performance calculations for the superb Mustang airframe if re-engined with the 60-series Merlin with two-stage supercharger, that Air Ministry sanction to convert five aircraft was obtained very quickly, and the first 'Mustang X' flew on 13 October 1942. It looked totally different, because there was now a second air intake just below and behind the spinner, serving

the fuel-injection carburettor (which in the Allison had a small inlet on top) and a new charge-intercooler. Performance was all the engine experts had predicted; speed jumped from 380 to well over 430 mph, and the time to climb to 20000 feet was reduced from 11 minutes to just over 6. But the main objective of NAA had been to persuade the US Army Air Force that NAA's own production should switch to the Packard V-1650-7, the American-made Merlin. This was a hard task, because the P–38 and P–47 were thought to meet all US needs at high-altitude. However, once a V-1650 had been tested in a much neater installation in the first XP–51B, in the final month of 1942, the war-winning Merlin-Mustang became inevitable.

Compared with the 'X' model the P–51B was dramatically faster, more manoeuvrable and far better in all aspects of air combat. Its shortcomings were that it was nothing like as sleek externally as the Allison-Mustang, needed more care and attention, and tended to have even more unpleasant stalling characteristics. On the sole occasion when I stalled a Mustang, in a deliberate dive pull-out at about 300 knots, the wing-drop was vicious enough to bang the canopy very hard against my head, and this was long before bonedomes had been invented! There was no advance warning as to when this would happen, and ground attack, especially with long-range tanks and bombs, must have needed careful judgement. The other fault of the P–51B was that it had only four 0·50 in guns (all now in the wings), half as many as in the monster P–47.

By this time NAA's plants at Inglewood (P–51B) and Dallas (P–51C) were building so fast that a thousand machines could be through the plants before the next modification could be introduced. With the P–51C (RAF Mustang III) there arrived a bulged frameless cockpit canopy giving a much better view, and like a few late P–51B models the internal fuel capacity was increased and the wing was redesigned to house six 0·50 in guns and carry 2000 lb of drop tanks,

Above: *The second prototype XP–82 Twin Mustang, flown at the very end of the war. Most Twins were post-war, with Allison engines.*

Below: *Dated 17 December 1950, this fine action picture shows Capt G. B. Lipawsky, of Randfontein, departing on a mission against the invading North Koreans amidst winter desolation.*

bombs or rockets. In February 1944 came the first P–51D, made in much greater numbers (7956, plus 1337 P–51K with an Aeroproducts propeller instead of the usual Hamilton) than all others combined. The D had a teardrop canopy, giving perfect all-round view, and a dorsal fin, giving better directional stability, which had been impaired by the high-altitude propellers for the V-1650, with four 'paddle' blades. Pilots often complained that the six-gun Mustangs, especially the heavier D, were poorer performers than the B. This was true, though the difference was slight, and in 1943–44 NAA built completely redesigned 'lightweight' P–51F, G and J Mustangs, offering fantastic near-500 mph performance. These led to the best Mustang of all, the 487 mph P–51H with a 2218 hp V-1650-9 engine, taller fin and redesigned fuselage, of

which 555 were delivered and just saw combat in the Second World War.

Since the end of the war Mustangs have been made in Australia, and hundreds have been built from new, or remanufactured for fresh duty with many air forces. Cavalier Aircraft produced numerous updated light tactical versions, some having Rolls-Royce Dart turboprops. From one of these, Piper produced a Lycoming-turboprop version called the Enforcer, while as far back as 1944 NAA made the most startling change of all by developing the Twin Mustang. This hard-hitting night fighter and long-range attack aircraft was one of the most potent piston-engined warplanes ever built. Altogether it is a good thing NAA did not agree in 1940 simply to build a few P–40s.

Republic P-47 Thunderbolt

One of the largest and heaviest of all fighters with a single piston engine, the P–47 was a real thoroughbred. Back in the spring of 1935 the chief engineer of Seversky Aircraft, Alex Kartveli, had in an amazingly short time designed and built a fighter to compete in the June 1935 US Army Air Corps competition for a fighter (pursuit) to succeed the P–26. This was the start of an outstanding line of fighters he produced that terminated with the last P–47 at the end of the Second World War. Of course,

from Tiflis, Maj Alexander P. de Seversky. The two men got on well together and led a technical team that conjured up a new fighter out of nothing in a matter of four weeks, and made it good enough to be adopted as a standard Air Corps type. This was the Seversky P–35, and Kartveli strongly denied being in the least influenced in its design by the P–26, though the P–36 also had an elliptical wing, a tubby fuselage, and the shape of the tails was almost identical. However, there the similarity stopped, because

Two early P–47C Thunderbolts, with lengthened fuselage. Pictured over East Anglia, they have yet to receive unit codes but are wearing the white markings thought necessary to prevent confusion with the Fw 190.

some great fighters have had no obvious ancestors and no successors, but good breeding is said to be of as much importance in aircraft as it is with people and horses. But that did not stop pilots making rude remarks when they first encountered the P–47.

Kartveli was born in Tiflis, but at the age of 21 left Russia after the revolution, studied in Paris and eventually became top designer in America for an even more famous and flamboyant emigré

the P–35 was a completely unbraced stressed-skin machine, with a landing gear which folded backwards inside large 'bathtub' fairings. The US Army bought 77, and Sweden a further 120 with double the armament (two 0·3 in and two 0·5 in guns instead of one of each), but the second 60 for Sweden were commandeered by the US Army in October 1938 and eventually saw combat defending the Philippines, when they were no match for the A6M and Ki-43.

Above: *While the limelight focussed on the Jugs of the 8th Air Force, and especially the 56th Fighter Group, thousands were hammering away at the Japanese with several Allied air forces. These early D-models are seen undergoing open-air major overhaul at a US 7th Air Force base in the Marianas.*

Below: *The way to win a war: millions of rounds of 'fifty-caliber' and serried rows of Jerricans support invasion-striped P-47D fighter-bombers at a 9th Air Force advanced base in France in the summer of 1944. The ammunition feeds explain why the guns were staggered.*

In March 1939 the last production P–35 of the original batch was completed as a markedly more advanced machine, the XP–41, with a longer and fatter fuselage, inward-retracting landing gear and a 1200 hp Pratt & Whitney Twin Wasp. In the same month the Army ordered 13 YP–43 test aircraft based on an even later privately built prototype, the AP–4, with a turbosupercharger under the rear fuselage. The first YP–43 was delivered in September 1940, by which time the company had been reconstituted as the Republic Aviation Corporation.

Back in September 1939 the Army Air Corps had ordered 80 aircraft designated P–44, but the fighting in Europe made it obvious that no fighter with a 1200 hp Twin Wasp engine was going to be capable enough. By September 1940 no fewer than 827 more P–44s had been ordered, but Kartveli convinced the Army of the vital need for a still later and more formidable fighter, and all P–44 contracts were cancelled. His courage and foresight caused a problem and to keep the plant at Farmingdale, Long Island, busy a further 54 Republic P–43 Lancers were ordered, plus 80 P–43As, and later 108 similar Lancers were supplied to China. The Lancer had four 0·5 in guns, bomb racks and a speed of 356 mph. It was probably better than the Curtiss Hawk 75 family, which were made in vast numbers, but it was not good enough for Kartveli and Republic.

It is strange that, while some of the greatest fighter designers insisted on the need for small size and light weight, Kartveli deliberately went far in the other direction. In this he followed in the footsteps of Rex Beisel and his team at Vought, then at Stratford, Connecticut and a division of United Aircraft, Pratt & Whitney being another. As early as 1938 Beisel had planned the great fighter which was to become the F4U Corsair, building it round the promising 2000 hp Pratt & Whitney R–2800 Double Wasp engine, turning a propeller larger than any previously fitted to a fighter. In October 1940 the prototype Corsair had exceeded 400 mph in level flight, making it possibly the fastest military aircraft in the world at that time. After studying the Corsair and many other alternatives, Kartveli concluded that the R–2800 engine was the only answer for the kind of fighter that would be needed. He felt that brute power and strength in an aircraft would more than make up in armament carried, and in ability to accommodate extra equipment and fuel, for what it might lose in reduced manoeuvrability.

On 12 June 1940 Kartveli completed general-arrangement drawings and specifications for a development of his AP–4L project which, in all essentials, was the Thunderbolt. He had pre-

viously studied XP–47 and XP–47A projects with an Allison engine, and the Army allotted the new machine the number XP–47B despite the fact that it was considerably larger and twice as heavy. The prototype was ordered on 6 September 1940, and flew after the amazingly short time of eight months, on 6 May 1941.

Eight months would have been good development time for any advanced fighter in 1941, but the XP–47B almost certainly posed more technical problems than any previous combat aircraft. This was partly because it had more things in it to pose problems. In designing it, Kartveli and his engineers first drew the Double Wasp engine, the propeller, and the best possible arrangement of air ducts under the engine, leading through or past the oil coolers to the turbocharger in the bottom of the rear fuselage. The turbo could have been adjacent to the engine but the rear fuselage had proved a good location in the Lancer and Kartveli stuck to it, despite the need for about 40 feet of large-diameter piping for cold air and hot exhaust gases. Having got an ideal engine installation, the team then decided where to put

Olive-drab and natural-metal T-bolts on another forward airstrip in France, this time enjoying the luxury of bowser refuelling. Note the steel helmets, and M–1 carbines propped against the left mainwheel.

the rest of the parts. The air entered under the engine in an elliptical cowl, as on the Lancer, and the wing was eventually placed above the ducts. This brought the 12 ft 2 in four-blade Curtiss Electric propeller too close to the ground. The answer seemed to be longer undercarriage legs, but when they were retracted there would be no room in the outer wings for the devastating armament of eight 0·5 in guns and their magazines. Eventually a leg was devised which extended nine inches whilst the gear was being lowered, and gave both room for the armament and good ground clearance for the propeller.

Weal's P–47D–10 is completely satisfying, and markedly higher in standard than any of the wartime cutaways. Many of the fighter buffs who relive the great days of the 'Jug' may not have known just how much hot gas and cold air was ducted up and down the fat fuselage.

1 Rudder upper hinge
2 Aerial attachment
3 Tailfin flanged ribs
4 Rudder post/tailfin aft spar
5 Tailfin front spar
6 Rudder trim tab worm and screw actuating mechanism (chain driven)
7 Rudder centre hinge
8 Rudder trim tab
9 Rudder structure
10 Tail navigation light
11 Elevator fixed tab
12 Elevator trim tab
13 Starboard elevator structure
14 Elevator outboard hinge
15 Elevator torque tube
16 Elevator trim tab worm and screw actuating mechanism
17 Chain drive
18 Starboard tailplane
19 Tail jacking point
20 Rudder control cables
21 Elevator control rod and linkage
22 Tailfin spar/fuselage attachment points
23 Port elevator
24 Aerial
25 Port tailplane structure (two spar with flanged ribs)
26 Tailwheel retraction worm gear
27 Tailwheel anti-shimmy damper
28 Tailwheel oleo
29 Tailwheel doors
30 Retractable and steerable tailwheel
31 Tailwheel fork
32 Tailwheel mount and pivot
33 Rudder cables
34 Rudder and elevator trim control cables
35 Lifting tube
36 Elevator rod linkage
37 Semi-monocoque all-metal fuselage construction
38 Fuselage dorsal 'Razorback' profile
39 Aerial lead-in
40 Fuselage stringers
41 Supercharger air filter
42 Supercharger
43 Turbine casing
44 Turbo-supercharger compartment air vent
45 Turbo-supercharger exhaust flight hood fairing (stainless steel)
46 Outlet louvres
47 Intercooler exhaust doors (port and starboard)
48 Exhaust pipes
49 Cooling air ducts
50 Intercooler unit (cooling and supercharged air)
51 Radio transmitter and receiver packs (Detrola)
52 Canopy track
53 Elevator rod linkage
54 Aerial mast
55 Formation light
56 Rearward-vision frame cut-out and glazing
57 Oxygen bottles
58 Supercharged and cooling air pipe (supercharger to carburettor) port

59 Elevator linkage
60 Supercharged and cooling air pipe (supercharger to carburettor) starboard
61 Central duct (to intercooler unit)
62 Wingroot air louvres
63 Wingroot fillet
64 Auxiliary fuel tank (100 US gal/379 litre)
65 Auxiliary fuel filler point
66 Rudder cable turnbuckle
67 Cockpit floor support
68 Seat adjustment lever
69 Pilot's seat
70 Canopy emergency release (port and starboard)
71 Trim tab controls
72 Back and head armour
73 Headrest
74 Rearward-sliding canopy
75 Rear-view mirror fairing
76 'Vee' windshields with central pillar
77 Internal bulletproof glass screen
78 Gunsight
79 Engine control quadrant (cockpit port wall)
80 Control column
81 Rudder pedals
82 Oxygen regulator
83 Underfloor elevator control quadrant
84 Rudder cable linkage
85 Wing rear spar/fuselage attachment (tapered bolts/bushings)
86 Wing supporting lower bulkhead section
87 Main fuel tank (205 US gal/776 litres)
88 Fuselage forward structure
89 Stainless steel/Alclad firewall bulkhead
90 Cowl flap valve
91 Main fuel filler point
92 Anti-freeze fluid tank
93 Hydraulic reservoir
94 Aileron control rod
95 Aileron trim tab control cables
96 Aileron hinge access penels
97 Aileron and tab control linkage
98 Aileron trim tab (port wing only)
99 Frise-type aileron
100 Wing rear (No. 2) spar
101 Port navigation light
102 Pitot head
103 Wing front (No. 1) spar
104 Wing stressed skin
105 Four-gun ammunition troughs (individual bays)
106 Staggered gun barrels
107 Removable panel
108 Inter-spar gun bay access panel
109 Forward gunsight bead
110 Oil feed pipes
111 Oil tank (28·6 US gal/108 litres)
112 Hydraulic pressure line
113 Engine upper bearers
114 Engine control correlating cam
115 Eclipse pump (anti-icing)
116 Fuel level transmitter

117 Generator
118 Battery junction box
119 Storage battery
120 Exhaust collector ring
121 Cowl flap actuating cylinder
122 Exhaust outlets to collector ring
123 Cowl flaps
124 Supercharged and cooling air ducts to carburettor (port and starboard)
125 Exhaust upper outlets
126 Cowling frame
127 2 000 hp Pratt & Whitney R-2800-21 eighteen-cylinder twin-row engine
128 Cowling nose panel
129 Magnetos
130 Propeller governor
131 Propeller hub
132 Reduction gear casing
133 Spinner
134 Propeller cuffs
135 12' 2'' dia. four-blade Curtiss constant-speed electric propeller
136 Oil cooler intakes (port and starboard)
137 Supercharger intercooler (central) air intake
138 Ducting
139 Oil cooler feed pipes
140 Starboard oil cooler
141 Engine lower bearers
142 Oil cooler exhaust variable shutter
143 Fixed deflector
144 Excess exhaust gas gate
145 Belly stores/weapons shackles
146 Metal auxiliary drop tank (75 US gal/284 litre)

147 Inboard mainwheel well door
148 Mainwheel well door actuating cylinder
149 Camera gun port
150 Cabin air-conditioning intake (starboard wing only)
151 Wingroot fairing
152 Wing front spar/fuselage attachment (tapered bolts/bushings)
153 Wing inboard rib mainwheel well recess
154 Wing front (No. 1) spar
155 Undercarriage pivot point
156 Hydraulic retraction cylinder

157 Auxiliary (undercarriage mounting) wing spar
158 Gun bay warm air flexible duct
159 Wing rear (No. 2) spar
160 Landing flap inboard hinge

SPECIFICATIONS

Types P-47B, C, D, M and N
Engine: one Pratt & Whitney R-2800 Double Wasp 18-cylinder two-row radial; (B) 2 000 hp R-2800-21; (C, most D) 2 300 hp R-2800-59; (M, N) 2 800 hp R-2800-57 or -77 (emergency wet rating).
Dimensions: span 40 ft $9\frac{1}{4}$ in (12·4 m); length (B) 34 ft 10 in; (C, D, M, N) 36 ft $1\frac{1}{4}$ in (11·03 m); height (B) 12 ft 8 in; (C, D) 14 ft 2 in (4·3 m); (M, N) 14 ft 8 in.
Weights: empty (B) 9 010 lb (4 087 kg); (D) 10 700 lb (4 853 kg); maximum loaded (B) 12 700 lb (5 760 kg); (D) 14 925 lb; (D) 19 400 lb (8 800 kg); (M) 14 700 lb; (N) 21 200 lb (9 616 kg).
Performance: maximum speed (B) 412 mph; (C) 433 mph; (D) 428 mph (690 km/h); (M) 470 mph; (N) 467 mph (751 km/h); initial climb (typical) 2 800 ft (855 m)/min; service ceiling (B) 38 000 ft; (C–N) 42 000–43 000 ft (13 000 m); range on internal fuel (B) 575 miles; (D) 1 000 miles (1 600 km); ultimate range (drop tanks) (D) 1 900 miles (3 060 km); (N) 2 350 miles (3 800 km).

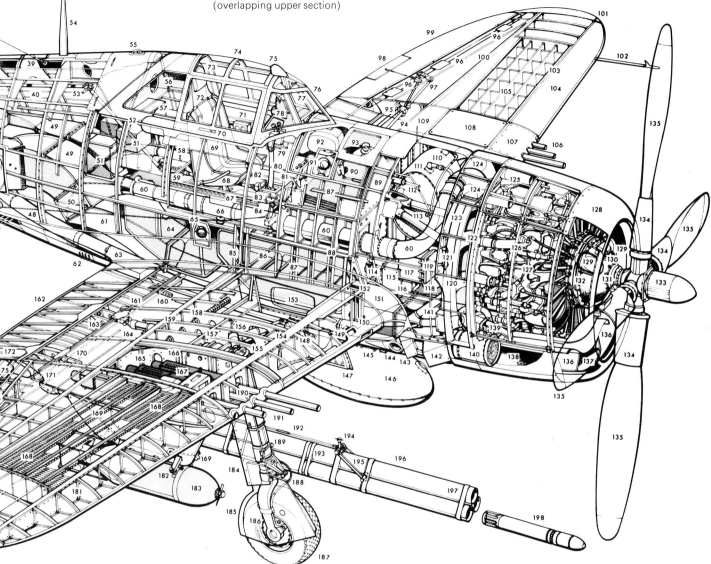

161 Auxiliary (No. 3) wing spar inboard section (flap mounting)
162 NACA slotted trailing-edge landing flaps

179 Wingtip structure
180 Starboard navigation light
181 Leading-edge rib sections
182 Bomb shackles
183 500-lb (227-kg) M-43 demolition bomb
184 Undercarriage leg fairing (overlapping upper section)

185 Mainwheel fairing (lower section)
186 Wheel fork
187 Starboard mainwheel
188 Brake lines
189 Landing gear air-oil shock strut

163 Landing flap centre hinge
164 Landing flap hydraulic cylinder
165 Four 0·5 in (12·7 mm) Browning machine-guns
166 Inter-spar gun bay inboard rib
167 Ammunition feed chutes
168 Individual ammunition troughs (350 + rpg)
169 Underwing stores/weapons pylon
170 Landing flap outboard hinge
171 Flap door
172 Landing flap profile
173 Aileron fixed tab (starboard wing only)
174 Frise-type aileron structure
175 Aileron hinge/steel forging spar attachments
176 Auxiliary (No. 3) wing spar outboard section (aileron mounting)
177 Multi-cellular wing construction
178 Wing outboard ribs

190 Machine-gun barrel blast tubes
191 Staggered gun barrels
192 Rocket-launcher slide bar
193 Centre strap
194 Front mount (attached below front spar between inboard pair of guns)

195 Deflector arms
196 Triple-tube 4·5-in (11·4-cm) rocket-launcher (Type M10)
197 Front retaining band
198 4·5-in (11·4 cm) M8 rocket projectile

While a buddy plugs his ears, a tough armourer of the 19th Fighter Sqn, 318th Fighter Group, speaks into the field telephone as four 'fifties' open up right beside his ear. Boresighting the guns, here being carried out on Saipan island in July 1944, was an essential prerequisite to good shooting.

The Burma Yank was Lt Wharton E. Moller of Los Angeles, who toted two thousand-pounders at a time and could have hung another on the centreline (usual maximum, 2,500 lb total). This aircraft is a D-model.

In 1941 the USAAF ordered 171 P–47B and 602 P–47C Thunderbolts, and, despite serious misgivings concerning the wisdom of so large and weighty a fighter, soon came to rate it priority No 1 in its procurement programmes. However, problems continued to plague development, most centring on the flight controls, canopy, fuel system, engine installation and armament. The growing Republic staff tackled them with energy in what had become characteristic American style, and in March 1942 the first production P–47B came off the line. It looked almost exactly like the prototype but had a sliding (instead of hinged) canopy, metal-skinned control surfaces with aerodynamic balance and balance/trim tabs, and greatly developed armament and equipment.

In June 1942 the monster new fighter began to reach the 56th Fighter Group. The 56th had been activated early the previous year, gaining experience first with the P–40 and P–39 so that they were able to appreciate that the P–47 offered a lot in return for problems still to be resolved with their new mounts. The 56th were a skilled and experienced unit and, throughout the second half of 1942, not only became ready for combat in Europe, but also worked the bugs out of the Thunderbolt. There were plenty. Not all their aircraft had metal-skinned controls, and frequent failure of the original surfaces was rated second only in seriousness to the repeated tyre-bursts. On the plus side the P–47 was reckoned the toughest fighter ever, and many pilots walked away from crashes and belly landings on rough ground which in other machines would have been fatal. Not for nothing did they call the Thunderbolt the Juggernaut, and soon this was

shortened to Jug, the name that has been associated with the P–47 ever since.

In January 1943 the 56th arrived in England, and set up business at Kings Cliffe, Northants. A few weeks later they were joined by the 4th FG, the famed unit formed from the RAF Eagle squadrons, which became operational at Debden. For the remainder of the Second World War the 56th and 4th were to vie with each other as the top-scoring outfits of the whole Army Air Force. The final result was that the 56th had the top air combat score ($674\frac{1}{2}$) but the 4th had the greatest for air combat plus ground strafing ($583\frac{1}{2} + 469$). The comparison, however, is not completely valid as, early in 1944, the 4th re-equipped with the P–51 and flew most of its missions with the rival fighter.

Flying a red-nosed Mustang of the 4th FG was the pinnacle for some Second World War pilots, but one cannot lightly pass over its monster rival. When the P–47C Thunderbolt arrived in England in the final days of 1942 the first ones were painted with white stripes to avoid confusion in the air with the Fw 190. In fact they were utterly unlike each other, and mock combat with the RAF's captured 190A–3 highlighted some further hidden differences. At first these mostly seemed to favour the nimble German fighter, which could climb faster and turn more tightly, and the only thing the Jug seemed to be able to do at least as well as anything in the sky was dive away, though the tactless RAF said that P–47 pilots could avoid enemy cannon shells just as well by running about inside the cockpit.

It was only later, in the thick of battle, that the full worth of this great fighter gradually emerged, and its best quality continued to be survivability. Not only could the pilot walk away from a horrific crash but the Jug could take more punishment than any other fighter and still fly home. Most of the USAAF's giant total of 15 660 P–47s – more than any other American fighter – were C and D models, the former having a drop tank or bomb racks, a longer fuselage and many other changes, and the first D-models a better turbo installation, water-injection as standard to give 2 300 hp (later 2 500) at 27 000 feet, and more armour. With two 1 000 lb bombs and a centreline tank, the D weighed 17 500 lb, about $2\frac{1}{2}$ tons more than the XP–47B, but the improved multi-ply tyres which were now fitted stayed intact even on rough airstrips. Some aircraft had only six guns, and the eight-gun Jugs had reduced ammunition for each gun. In 1943 an experimental prototype (one of scores) flew with a cut-down rear fuselage and teardrop hood, and this was so good that it was promptly put into production on the P–47D–25. Later D-models had paddle-blade propellers,

A pair of the ultimate model, the new-winged P–47N–5–RE, with exceptional range for the Pacific theatre. Suffixes for P–47 production were : RE, Republic Farmingdale ; RA, Republic Evansville ; CU, Curtiss-Wright at Buffalo.

bigger drop tanks, a dorsal fin and new armament options, including 4·5 in rocket tubes or zero-length launchers for the 5 in rocket. Total production of the P–47D reached the staggering figure of 12602, by Farmingdale, Evansville and, by Curtiss, at Buffalo.

The combat record of the Jug stands alongside that of any other fighter in history. Its toughness and firepower more than made up for deficiencies in climb, turn radius and, compared with the P–51D, range. Most of the greatest American aces flew Jugs, among them Hubert Zemke (original CO of the 56th), Gabby Gabreski, Bob Johnson, John C. Meyer (later Chief of Staff of the USAF), Dave Schilling, Walker Mahurin, Glenn Duncan and Walter Beckham. Notable Thunderbolt actions are countless – some were carried out by the 852 supplied to the RAF, mainly in Burma – but perhaps the most

remarkable was on 23 December 1944, when a watery Sun at last let Allied airpower help the hard-pressed troops in the Ardennes. Dave Schilling led the 56th into a tangle with a top-ranking Luftwaffe unit, a gruppe of the famed JG 27 flying a motley gaggle of 109Gs and short-nose Dora–9 190s. The final tally was 37 of the enemy downed at the cost of four Jugs, one of which struggled to Allied territory in Belgium.

It only remains to comment briefly on the wealth of experimental versions (one of which reputedly reached 504 mph on the level), and the 'hot-rod' 470 mph P–47M, produced in a matter of days to chase flying bombs, and the P–47N for the Pacific War. This was bigger and heavier even than earlier versions, carrying an amazing 954 gallons of fuel for a range of 2350 miles. It was a long while before Kartveli could equal such a range with his post-war Thunderjet.

Messerschmitt Me 262

I do not want to insist that the 262 was (or was not) the world's first jet fighter. Such an assertion is meaningless unless qualified carefully. The first jet, defined as the first aircraft to fly with a turbojet engine, was the Heinkel He 178, flown on 27 August 1939. The first jet fighter to fly was the Heinkel He 280 on 2 April 1941. The first jet fighter delivered to a customer was the USAAF's Bell YP–59 Airacomet, in June 1943. The first jet fighter delivered to a regular squadron for combat duty was the Gloster Meteor I, equipping 616 Squadron of the RAF from 12 July 1944. The first jet fighter to meet the enemy and fire its guns in anger was the Me 262, on an unknown day around 20 July 1944, though it was with a test unit, not a regular squadron. So there is no simple answer to what is a rather pointless question. What is beyond dispute is that, of all Second World War jets, the Me 262 was by far the most important.

It did not appear overnight. Politicians love to take refuge in the belief that a nation's defence expenditure can safely be pared to the bone and, in a sudden emergency, raised sky-high with instant results in new equipment. This is nonsense. Modern aircraft are infinitely more complex than the Me 262, and the Me 262 programme was started in the autumn of 1938, too late for it to be used extensively in the war. The Nazi leaders did not help the programme, by continually changing their thinking, and there was no way Junkers could get the new engines into production before the late summer of 1944. By that time no fighter, however revolutionary, could influence the outcome of the conflict.

Forty years ago there was a marked contrast between the British and German approach to jet fighters. In Britain there was a handful of enthusiastic engineers working on a single engine, motivated entirely by a man so famous he need hardly be named. In 1941, when a second engine at last took over (the original having gradually become 'a running heap of scrap'), the top Air Ministry scientist, Sir Henry Tizard, said 'We're either spending a lot of money on a flop, or not nearly enough on a most valuable invention'.

Most of the official establishment, having poured scorn on Whittle and his ideas in the past, were careful not to become enthusiastic all of a sudden; Tizard, a bigger man than most, was more open-minded. But in Germany there were major turbojet development programmes at Heinkel, BMW and Junkers, soon to be joined by others, and a real desire to create combat aircraft using the radical new form of propulsion. There followed a proliferation of jet-aircraft programmes – too many, in fact, and none influenced the war. In Britain, not only were there too few but there was no attempt to look ahead and make long-term plans for jets, using them perhaps for long-range bombers. A fixation on aircraft that could be important only in the short term was to result in the RAF having no modern bomber after the war (except for old ex-USAAF B–29 Superfortresses loaned by the United States) and no counterpart to US bombers such as the B–45 or B–47, both first flown in 1947.

The jet fighter proposal from Messerschmitt, which was totally separate from the Lippisch-inspired tailless rocket interceptor (Me 163) programme, went through various metamorphoses and crystallized in May 1940. The first prototype flew on 1 April 1941 with a Jumo 210 driving a propeller in the nose. Though this was two weeks after the He 280 had flown on its jets, the BMW 003 axial engines for the Me 262 were not ready, and its 700 hp piston engine could only just get the thin-winged machine off the ground. This Me 262 V1 (first prototype) looked like some late-war Japanese machines, with rather severe lines, a wide-track tailwheel landing gear and laminar-flow high-speed wings with slightly swept outer panels. It could not exceed 260 mph on the level, but flew beautifully.

On 25 March 1942 a flight was made with the turbojets installed, but the takeoff was hair-raising; the jets flamed out, and pilot Fritz Wendel only just managed to complete the circuit. BMW still had a long way to go with the 003, but the rival 004 engine by the new Junkers jet team under Anselm Franz had overtaken it and was ready to fly. More conservatively

An apparently standard but rather tatty Me 262A–1a pictured in a line-up of German and Japanese aircraft in the United States (probably at Wright Field) after the war.
Below: *Messerschmitt AG took this photograph of an A–1a with only the outer pair of 30 mm guns. Apparently Werk-Nr 170 056, it is not an A–1a/U3 reconnaissance model, which often had no guns at all, nor does it have bomb racks. Several pure fighter versions serving with KG(J) 54 and JV 44 in 1945 had only two guns.*

Photographed at Farnborough in 1945, this apparently standard A–1a had seen operational service with JG 7.

designed, it was bigger than the 003 and the Me 262 V3 accordingly emerged with longer nacelles and a larger vertical tail to maintain directional stability. On 18 July 1942 Wendel tried to fly V3 off the paved runway at Leipheim, but could not get the tail up. Someone suggested a brief application of the brakes as take-off speed was reached. This did the trick; the tail lifted, the elevators became instantly effective, and the twin-jet climbed away. Subsequently there were still to be countless disasters and technical problems, but the stage was set for what was technically the outstanding fighter of the Second World War.

It was outstanding because of its combination of qualities. In flight performance it was virtually in a class by itself. The only wartime aircraft that came near it – apart from later German jets which hardly got into service – was the Me 163, and this was a specialized target-defence interceptor with extremely short range and endurance. Other contemporary jets, such as the Ar 234, the British Meteor and American P–59A, had much poorer performance, comparable only with the best piston-engined machines. The 262, however, could reach level speeds of around 540 mph, climb at about 4000 feet per minute and fly over

600 miles without drop tanks. Its handling qualities were outstandingly good, and a welcome contrast to the Bf 109G. The main shortcomings were the unreliability and short life of the 1980 lb-thrust Jumo 004B engines, a proneness of the landing gears (which from V5 were of the nosewheel type) to jam or collapse, poor view downwards because of the roughly triangular cross-section of the broad fuselage, and the difficulty of adjusting engine settings in flight, especially at altitude. Though the German axial engines were of more advanced concept than the British centrifugal turbojets, they were nothing like so well developed, so flexible in operation or so durable, and if possible the 262 pilots set them for a good high-speed cruise and thereafter left them alone. Obviously, inability to juggle with the throttles was a handicap in combat, and made it doubly difficult to operate a number of aircraft in any kind of close formation.

During development the inner wing of the 262 was extended at the leading edge to give greater root chord, a swept leading edge throughout and better airflow, while the slats were continued inboard of the engines. The control surfaces were fitted with geared tabs, and though on early production aircraft they were fabric-covered they were soon changed to metal. About 570 gallons of diesel oil were accommodated in self-sealing bladders in front of, beneath and behind the cockpit, and most aircraft could carry two 66 gal or one 132 gal drop tank.

From the start the 262 had been recognised as large enough to carry devastating armament. One of the early schemes envisaged six cannon: two MG 151/20s, two stubby MK 108s and two of the tremendous MK 103s. Soon attention concentrated on the two MK weapons, each of 30 mm calibre, and by December 1943 the standard armament for the Me 262A–0 (and subsequent production versions) was settled as four MK 108s in the upper part of the nose.

By this time Messerschmitt's enormous technical staff had acquired extensive experience of transonic flight, both in the air and in wind tunnels, studying shockwaves, swept surfaces, and stability and control problems at Mach numbers exceeding 0·9. Britain did nothing comparable for several years after the Second World War, with the notable exception of courageous steep test dives made by Sqn Ldr Martindale and a handful of other pilots in Spitfires, which reached similar Mach numbers and could have been put to practical use. One Me 262 was timed at 624 mph on the level in 6 July 1944, but the machine had special low-drag features.

Though the first 262 test-flight in 1942 by an official from Rechlin ended in a manure-heap, things were better in 1943. On 22 May of that year General of Fighters Adolf Galland flew V4 and came away brimming with enthusiasm. There followed months of heated discussion, much of it in the circumlocutory vein that characterised the Nazi leaders, until on 2 November Goering told Messerschmitt that the Führer wanted to know only one thing about the new jet: could it carry bombs? Messerschmitt foolishly suggested the conversion could almost be done while Goering waited, and from that point on Hitler flew into a rage at any suggestion of the 262 being used as a fighter. The upshot was that the production programme was disrupted to make the standard version into the A–2a Sturmvogel (Stormbird) with two pylons under the fuselage to carry a great variety of weapons with a total weight of 2205 lb. However, though a nuisance to all concerned, Hitler's polarization on his *Blitz-bomber* did not really delay the programme, which was held back in any case by poor engine deliveries.

Early production Me 262A–1a Schwalbe (Swallow) fighters were delivered in April 1944 to EKdo (test unit) 262 at Lechfeld, where company pilots began to train Luftwaffe instructors. By July sorties were being flown with loaded guns, and in the course of the month the unit claimed two F–5 Lightnings and a photographic Mosquito. In August another special unit, the Kommando Schenck, began operations over north-west Europe, and on the 28th two Thunderbolts managed to shoot down an unwary pilot near Brussels, probably the first piloted jet ever downed in combat. On 3 October 1944 EKdo 262 became the Kommando Nowotny, and though it claimed 22 Allied aircraft in its first month, its average strength of 30 Schwalbes suffered numerous accidents and also several unexpected losses from P–51s and other Allied fighters who pounced on the Kommando's bases at Achmer and Hesepe. In October the Sturmvogel became operational with the 3/KG 51 at Hopsten, which devoted most of its efforts to trying to wreck the Remagen bridge over the Rhine, finally demolished by Ar 234Bs. The first regular Schwalbe unit was III/JG 7, formed at Parchim in November, which with the geschwader's staff unit claimed the remarkable total of 427 aircraft downed, including 300 four-engined bombers. The final, and élite, unit was Galland's own JV 44 at the end of the war.

Many special armament schemes were flown on the 262, some of them in combat. The most important was the underwing array of 24 R4/M air-to-air spin-stabilized rockets, which proved most effective against USAAF bombers and led to the post-war Mighty Mouse FFAR folding-fin aircraft rocket. One aircraft had a 5 cm BK 5 cannon, another was an unarmed lead-ship with bombardier, some had booster rockets giving them a fantastic climb performance and several carried radar and led to the Me 262B tandem-seat night-fighter series. At the end of the war such futuristic weapons as the MG 213 revolver cannon, the SG 117 multi-barrel gun and the X–4 guided air-to-air missile were all about to undergo trials in Me 262s. These weapons would still not have postponed the defeat of Nazi Germany, but they were far in advance of anything being developed by the Allies.

Altogether about 1433 Me 262s were completed. Of these 865 were built in 1945, in hidden forest assembly sheds to which came parts – by truck, horse-cart and bicycle, from tiny manufacturing groups throughout Germany. There was also a gigantic underground plant in Thuringia which never went into production but was planned to add 1000 aircraft per month to the number. What a contrast to British industry which, through lack of motivation, delivered barely 50 Meteors by VE Day, even though it could build them in unbombed factories.

North American F-86 Sabre

Since the Second World War the business of providing fighters for the world's air forces, far from dwindling, has forged ahead at breakneck pace, though modern fighters tend to be produced in scores or hundreds rather than in the tens of thousands of the war years. Very few military aircraft since 1945 have had a production programme remotely resembling those of the great fighters of history, such as feature in the preceding 15 chapters. Those which come nearest to it include the American F–86 Sabre and F–4 Phantom. Very large numbers have also been made of a long succession of MiG fighters, but these are absent from this book. There are several reasons for this, not the least of which is that, like most people outside the MiG bureau and the Kremlin, I do not know enough about their background. Suffice to say that the second post-war MiG, the MiG–15, was so good that only one Western fighter could tangle with it, and that fighter is the subject of this chapter.

It was fortunate for the United Nations forces in Korea that the F–86 happened when it did, and in the way it did. North American Aviation had once before refused the easy way, and instead of simply making a profit building the P–40 for Britain, had stuck out for producing something better. Even as late as 1943 the engineering project staff under Lee Atwood and Ray Rice were studying jet fighters still based on the same P–51 airframe, but NAA was never a company to accept compromise. By the summer of 1944 it had started with a clean sheet of paper and produced drawings for two wholly new jet fighters, the NA–134 for the Navy and NA–140 for the USAAF (USAF from 1947). There was then no pressure for any similarity between the two designs to reduce costs. Both had wings rather like those of a P–51, a straight-through duct from the nose to an axial turbojet in the rear fuselage, a long teardrop canopy over a pressurized cockpit placed well forward, and nosewheel-type landing gear. All guns were grouped in the nose, and fuel was housed in the fuselage and wings, as well as in the newly fashionable wingtip tanks, but apart from this there was little in the two designs that was similar. In general the Navy aircraft was more compact for carrier stowage while the landbased machine was longer, slimmer, more rakish and heavier. Though started later as a development of the NA–134 the NA–140 was placed under contract first, the AAF ordering prototypes on 30 August 1944 with the designation XP–86.

Work went ahead fast on what looked like being a naturally attractive fighter, and on the first day of 1945 the Navy ordered the NA–134 as the XFJ–1, so the future looked good. A few weeks later Republic was given a contract for the XP–84 Thunderjet, and, as this was extremely like the XP–86 and probably to be powered by the same TG–180 engine, North American Aviation saw possible trouble ahead. In the days of peace that would follow victory, orders might be hard to come by, and everything would depend on technical superiority. NAA was used to this situation, and believed in its ability to beat Republic. Had it just continued as it was going, it would probably have won limited production orders for the P–86 and held its own alongside the P–84, with further orders going to the somewhat earlier and cheaper Lockheed P–80 Shooting Star. But in June 1945 Atwood and Rice picked up the first really useful reports to be gathered in Germany on the use of swept wings. The idea of sweeping a wing back at an angle to the airflow had been discussed in a paper read by Busemann at the Volta Congress in 1935. Every delegate to that conference had walked off with a copy of the text, which explained how the swept wing could reduce the wing's effective thickness and almost convince the airflow at low supersonic speeds into thinking it was subsonic, thus giving reduced force coefficients and higher efficiency.

Above: *Vivid white camera markings on the Midnight Blue finish made it easier to evaluate the precise behaviour of an FJ–1 Fury on carrier evaluation in March 1948.*
Below: *Twenty-four Mighty Mice ripple away in the twinkling of an eye from an F–86D–60, the final production version of the semi-automatic all-weather interceptor. More were made of this version than any other Sabre variant, a total of 2,504.*

Nobody at the time had appreciated the tremendous importance of this, and as the fighters then at readiness were 200-mph biplanes this is not surprising. Sweepback was to come into the world with amazing slowness. In 1937 Busemann read a second paper, which triggered Albert Betz at the DVL (the German aviation research establishment) to begin wind-tunnel research. This in turn came to the notice of Waldemar Voigt, chief project engineer at Messerschmitt AG who, in 1941, launched a major research programme. Meanwhile Lippisch had recognised the drawback of acute sweepback at take-off and landing, and in 1942 filed a patent for a variable-sweep 'swing-wing' aircraft. Subsequently dozens of swept-wing projects mushroomed in Germany, and, when Allied intelligence teams began combing through the rubble, swept wings were thick upon the ground.

In Britain, Sir Roy Fedden took a package of swept-wing documents to Sydney Camm at Hawker Aircraft, but the famed chief engineer simply laughed. The general consensus of opinion among the British establishment was that the war had been won; swept wings, like rockets, guided missiles and all the other new German ideas, were Wellsian fantasies which could be ignored, but in distant California

Atwood and Rice took a different view, and at once began discussing swept wings with their Service customers. The Navy, apprehensive about carrier compatibility, decided to carry on with the original machine, which became the FJ–1 Fury. Though perfectly satisfactory, it was no better than rival aircraft and only 30 production examples were built. However, the Army Air Force agreed to up to a year's delay in the P–86 programme so that NAA could try out swept surfaces and see if they might prove beneficial. It was probably the most profitable delay in aviation history.

Most of the company's research centred on surfaces swept at 35°. Similar experiments were conducted by the National Advisory Committee for Aeronautics and, to provide full-scale confirmation, Bell flew a P–63 rebuilt with AAF funds with a 35° wing. On 1 November 1945 the AAF approved the radically revised XP–86, the NA–140 number being retained. On 20 December 1946 the AAF ordered 33 production P–86 Sabres, and the Los Angeles plant was tooling-up for production when George Welch flew the first XP–86 at Lake Muroc on 1 October 1947. Like the monster six-jet Boeing XB–47, flown a few weeks later, all its wing and tail surfaces were raked back at 35°. This was to

Arthur (Art) Bowbeer's cutaway of the F–86E Sabre was a considerable scoop, accomplished chiefly with the collaboration of Canadair, the licensee of North American Aviation, and the RCAF in England. No drawing of any modern jet fighter had previously been published in anything like such detail.

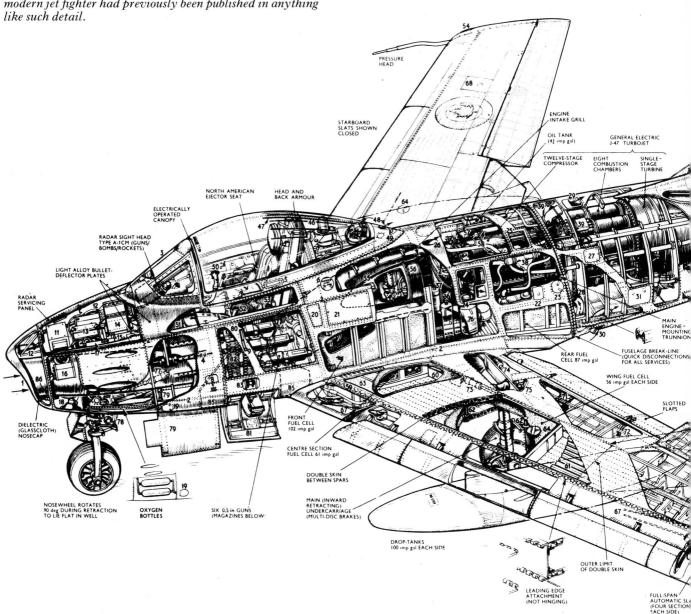

SPECIFICATIONS

Types NA–134 (XFJ–1), NA–140 (XP–86), F–86A to L, FJ–1 to 4B (F–1A to AF–1E), CL–13 (and Orenda-Sabre), CA–26 (and Avon-Sabre).

Engine: (FJ–1) one 4 000 lb (1 814 kg) thrust Allison J35–2 single-shaft axial turbojet; (F–86A) one 4 850 lb (2 200 kg) General Electric J47–1 of same layout; (F–86D) one J47–17 or –33 rated at 7 650 lb (3 470 kg with afterburner); (F–86E) one 5 200 lb (2 358 kg) J47–13; (F–86F) one 5 970 lb (2 710 kg) J47–27; (F–86H) one 8 920 lb (4 046 kg) GE J73–3E of same layout; (F–86K) one J47–17B rated at 7 500 lb (3 402 kg) with afterburner; (FJ–2) one 6 100 lb (2 767 kg) J47–27A; (FJ–3, (F–1C)) one 7 200 lb (3 266 kg) Wright J65–2 (Sapphire) single-shaft turbojet; (FJ–4, (F–1E)) one 7 800 lb (3 538 kg) J65–4; (FJ–4B, (AF–1E)) one 7 700 lb J65–16A; (CL–13A Sabre 5) one 6 355 lb (2 883 kg) Orenda 10 single-shaft turbojet; (CL–13B Sabre 6) one 7 275 lb (3 300 kg) Orenda 14; (CA–27 Sabre 32) one 7 500 lb (3 402 kg) CAC-built Rolls-Royce Avon 26 single-shaft turbojet.

Dimensions: span (most) 37 ft 1½ in (11·31 m); (F–86F–40 and later blocks, F–86H, K. L, CL–13 Sabre 5 (not 6), F–1E, AF–1E) all 39 ft 1 in or 39 ft 1½ in (11·9 m); length (most) 37 ft 6 in (11·43 m); (D) 40 ft 3¼ in, (H) 38 ft 10 in; (K) 40 ft 11 in; (F–1C) 37 ft 7½ in; (F–1E, AF–1E) 36 ft 4 in; height (typical) 14 ft 8¾ in (4·47 m).

Weights: empty (A) 10 606 lb; (F) 11 125 lb (5 045 kg); (H) 13 836 lb; (D) 13 498 lb; (K) 13 367 lb; (AF–1E) 13 990 lb; (Sabre 32) 12 120 lb; maximum loaded (A) 16 223 lb; (F) 20 611 (9 350 kg); (H) 24 296 lb; (D) 18 483 lb; (K) 20 171 lb; (AF–1E) 26 000 lb; (Sabre 32) 18 650 lb.

Performance: maximum speed (A) 675 mph; (F) 678 mph (1 091 km/h); (H, D, K) 692 mph; (AF–1E) 680 mph; (Sabre 6, 32) both about 705 mph (peak Mach of all versions, usually 0·92); initial climb (clean) typically 8 000 ft (2 440 m)/min, with D, H, K and Sabre 6 and 32 at 12 000 ft/min; service ceiling (clean) typically 50 000 ft (15 240 m); range, with external fuel, high, typically 850 miles (1 368 km), except (F–1E) 2 020 miles and (AF–1E) 2 700 miles.

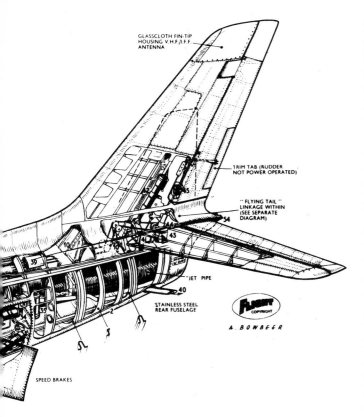

GLASSCLOTH FIN-TIP
HOUSING V.H.F./I.F.F.
ANTENNA

TRIM TAB (RUDDER
NOT POWER OPERATED)

"FLYING TAIL"
LINKAGE WITHIN
(SEE SEPARATE
DIAGRAM)

JET PIPE

STAINLESS STEEL
REAR FUSELAGE

FLIGHT
COPYRIGHT

A. BOWBEER

SPEED BRAKES

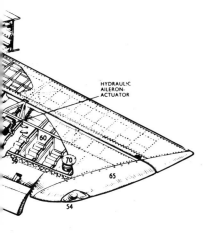

HYDRAULIC
AILERON-
ACTUATOR

Probably taken in 1953, when many hundreds of Dogships had been built, this shows cold-weather testing in Alaska. The unfortunate F–86D is parked in mid-winter at Eielson AFB and will then be suddenly scrambled. It has to work.

prove of tremendous significance. Though it was quite heavy, with a design gross weight of 13311 lb without tanks or bombs, and underpowered by an early Chevrolet-built TG–180 engine rated at only 3750 lb thrust, the XP–86 proved to be faster than predicted. Instead of 585 mph it clocked 613, and its handling was a dream.

Pilot view from the cockpit could fairly be described as unsurpassed, and equalled by few other fighters before or since. Technically, the canopy was a tour de force, and eight years later British industry still could not quite equal it. The wing was a neat blend of traditional structures and new ones, with thick tapered skins to give the great strength needed by a wing of a thickness only 10 per cent of the chord, yet avoiding any extensive internal structure machined from solid. Along the leading edge was a large slat, which could be unlocked at low speed to improve safety and handling, at which time the new prototype rode the air with its nose at the grotesquely high angles typical of all swept-wing aircraft. The control surfaces operated with an hydraulic boost, and from the start this gave superlative and instantaneous control that at first disconcerted pilots and then delighted them. During its 30 years of life the all-round handling of this classic fighter has been something remembered with pleasure by all who flew it. In fact one very experienced pilot wrote in *Flying Combat Aicraft* (Iowa University Press), 'The F–86 was the only aircraft I have flown that gave the pilot confidence that he could do any maneuver he desired, at any time, with full assurance of safety throughout.' From April 1948 the possible manoeuvres included one that no fighter had ever done before. By opening the throttle, half-rolling into a dive and finally pulling out at lower level (rolling in the dive to set up the desired exit heading) it was possible to exceed Mach 1, the speed of sound, with no bother at all. In the spring of 1948 residents of Los Angeles wondered at what seemed to be powerful explosions coming from nowhere, and soon learned about the sonic bang.

On 20 May 1948 the first of what had grown to be a batch of 221 P–86As flew in the insignia of

the new US Air Force, and a month later the old terminology of 'pursuit' was changed to 'fighter', leading to the designation F–86A for the aircraft. In 1949 the F–86 was named Sabre, and by this time the 1st and 4th Fighter Groups were operational, with the 81st converting to the new machine. Pilots wore new flying clothing including a g-suit and bonedome, sat in an ejection seat, and had to master such equipment as a Machmeter, operate nosewheeel steering, a speed-brake switch, uhf radio and the Mk 18 lead-computing gunsight. Almost the only thing that was not new was the armament of six 0·5 in guns in the sides of the nose, converging at a point 1000 feet ahead. In full combat trim an F–86A broke the world speed record on 15 September 1948 at 671 mph, the first time this had ever been done by an absolutely standard fighter, though the record-breaking Meteor of 1945 was modified only to the extent of fairing over the gun ports. Powered by a development of the TG–180 engine, the 5200 lb-thrust General Electric J47, the earliest Sabres could easily outfly all other fighters except one, the MiG–15, then still unknown in the West.

In the Korean war of 1950–53 the F–86 saw action in three forms. The basic F–86A was followed by the E with an 'all-flying' tail, in which the tailplane became the primary control surface with the elevators adding camber and thus control power, and with an artificial-feel system to stop the pilot overcontrolling at high indicated airspeeds. The F had a new leading edge with extended chord, small airflow fences and no slats, and a 5910 lb J47 engine. In many dogfights with the MiG–15, a 'kill ratio' alleged to be $12\frac{1}{2}$:1 in the F–86's favour gives a slightly misleading picture of the merits of the two. Above about 38000 feet the Communist fighter was in many respects superior, and it was always at least the equal of the Sabre in climb, turn radius and ceiling. The edge lay chiefly with the greater skill, experience and some of the equipment of the F–86 pilots, though some of the latter were outspoken in their wish for a lighter, simpler fighter that could get on top of the MiG. One even said that the Mk 18, and the later A–1CM radar-ranging sight, could with advantage be replaced by a 'gum' sight – a piece of well-chewed gum stuck in the middle of the windscreen.

Subsequently Canadair made 1815 Sabres, of

The first YF–86H, the final model of USAF Sabre with much more power and many other changes including (in the production version) four 20 mm M–39 cannon. Photo dated 13 May 1953, first flight at Edwards having been on 30 April that year.

A beautiful picture of one of the most numerous post-war fixed-wing military aircraft in the West. The subject is US Navy serial 141 451, and FJ–4B (AF–1E) fighter-bomber serving with attack squadron VA–14 in 1961. Ultimate model in the entire family, it had virtually nothing in common with land-based Sabres but the maker's name. Ring fins on the noses of the tanks are not standard.

which 430 were supplied in 1952–53 to help the ailing RAF which could get nothing comparable from the home industry until more than two years later. The Sabre 6, the final Canadian model with a 7 275 lb Orenda 14 engine is – so some of my friends insist – the absolute last word in dogfight capability for its generation. The RAAF used a model that ran the Orenda-Sabre very close: the Sabre 32 with a 7 500 lb Rolls-Royce Avon, two 30 mm Adens and Sidewinder missiles. The final US fighter/bomber version was the F–86H with the 8 920 lb General Electric J73 engine, four M39 revolver cannon and a heavy bomb load.

The most numerous of all Sabre types was a totally different machine, the F–86D 'Dogship' all-weather interceptor. Much heavier and more complex, this had an extremely advanced radar fire-control system developed by the new Hughes company, with the scanner in a large radome above the air inlet. In the belly was a retractable pack of 24 Mighty Mouse rockets, which were salvoed automatically into the airspace where a moving target would be in a few seconds' time. To handle the extra weight, a new J47 engine was fitted, with an afterburner boosting thrust to 7 650 lb, and a Dogship raised

the world speed record to over 715 mph. Later some of the 2 504 built were modified to F–86L standard, with new electronics and an improved long-span wing, while Fiat in Italy assembled for European NATO air forces a simpler F–86K version with radar matched to four-cannon armament.

In Japan Mitsubishi assembled 300 Sabres, many of which remain in second-line use to this day. There are numerous other users of the Sabre, and also a few survivors from the important family of FJ Furies which in 1952–56 were originally supplied to the US Navy and Marines. The FJ–2 was almost a navalised F–86E with four cannon, but the FJ–3 had the 7 200 lb Wright J65 engine (the British Sapphire made under licence), and the FJ–4 had a 7 800 lb J65 and a totally redesigned airframe accommodating 50 per cent more fuel. The final model, the FJ–4B (redesignated AF–1E in 1962) was a potent ground-attack aircraft carrying guided missiles and able to take off at just twice the 1 300 lb of the original XP–86. In between these two aircraft came over 9 500 Sabres and Furies of all types, a figure which underlines the importance of the bold decision made by NAA to delay the programme and sweep back the wings and tail.

Dassault Mirage III/5

In the years following the Second World War the French aircraft industry rebuilt itself and, despite the fact that nearly all its strength was concentrated into nationalized groups, it threatened to proliferate into hundreds of companies such as had existed pre-war. But nearly all of them quickly disappeared as a result of bankruptcies and mergers, and for almost the entire period up to the present there have only been two big-league teams left. One is nationalised, and despite every possible kind of propping up by government funds, it has for many years been in severe trouble because it cannot sell enough aircraft. Its rival is the private-enterprise Dassault firm, and the fantastic success of this company – currently No 4 of all companies in France – has made all who hate private enterprise seethe with anger. Dassault put France on the world map as an exporter of major defence products, and so greatly exceeded the expected output of a company of such a modest size that its methods have been officially dissected and analysed by the US Air Force, which has a vested interest in improving the efficiency of the

industry at home. Just whether the giant American planemakers could learn today, or could have at any time in the past learned much from Dassault, is something I would love to spend the rest of this book discussing, but doubtless most readers would rather hear about the Mirage, which is the focal point of the company's success story.

One of the guiding principles of the founder, Marcel Dassault, is to try to avoid technical risk. But when he flew the first Ouragan jet fighter in February 1949 there had to be plenty of risks, though these were minimised by making the Ouragan as ordinary as possible – rather like an F–84, in fact. From it stemmed a splendid line of Mystère and Super Mystère jets that provided steady business for his company and whose classic lineage is now once more in full production with the Super Etendard. In 1952 the Armée de l'Air issued a requirement for a Light Interceptor, preferably to be powered by two small afterburning turbojets, possibly backed up by a rocket. It was an ill-conceived short-range idea, rather

Hardly recognisable as related to a modern Mirage, the baby MD.550 Mirage I was powered by two
British Viper turbojets ; later a rocket was added.
Dassault was right to scorn so low-powered a fighter.

Above: *One that came and went was the Mirage IIIC2, exhibited at the 1965 Paris Salon. It was an interceptor with the long body and large fin of the E and the more powerful Atar 9K engine.*
Below: *The prototype of the Mirage IIIR reconnaissance aircraft, similar to the IIIE attack fighter but with a slim, camera-filled nose*

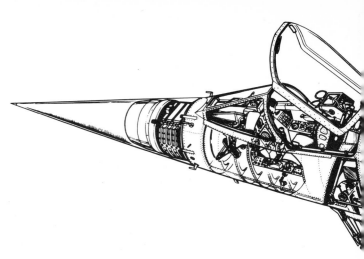

Two of the first Israeli Kfir fighters (Nos 726 and 731) seen in Heyl Ha' Avir service in the summer of 1976. By that time the aerodynamically more advanced Kfir–C2 was coming into operation.

like the British thinking that led to the P.1 and SR.53 short-range interceptors, but on 25 June 1955 Roland Glavany flew the trim little prototype. Dassault himself had no faith in the basic concept, but was faced with so many possibilities he tried to hedge his bets with a profusion of larger and more versatile machines. What suddenly decided the issue was the setting up of a world speed record by Peter Twiss, flying the Fairey FD.2 on 18 March 1956. Dassault and Fairey were collaborating on delta wings. Dassault let the British company use the French test base at Cazaux in return for information on the FD.2, and Dassault immediately authorized work to begin, round the clock, on a larger Mirage powered by the Atar engine. This, the Mirage III, promised outstanding flight performance, but would carry less fuel or weapons than a conventional non-delta fighter and would need a longer runway.

The first Mirage III flew on 17 November 1956 – an amazingly early date, confirming the company's exceptionally fast pace with prototypes. There followed earnest talks with the Armée de l'Air, prolonged redesign and eventually, in 1960, production IIIC fighters entered service with the Atar 9 turbojet engine, a booster rocket pack and a simple Cyrano radar in the nose. A primitive air-to-air missile, the R.511, could be slung under the centreline, and with the rocket pack removed, two 30 mm cannon could be installed. Back in October 1958 Mach 2 had been exceeded without rocket boost, and for speed and climb the dainty Mirage had few equals. Wisely, the Armée de l'Air sponsored development of a family of special-purpose versions for all-weather attack, reconnaissance and dual training. Israel, Dassault's first and most consistent export customer, was by a full two years the first non-French authority to evaluate the new fighter, and an order for 72 followed in 1960. This was the first of a list of export contracts running over a far

longer time and far more valuable than Dassault himself had expected in 1959, when he thought nobody would pay the necessary £450000 for a fighter. Today even Mirages cost almost ten times as much but 24 countries have bought them, some (like Australia) strenuously resisting offers of improved versions, and one (Switzerland) changing all the most complicated parts and almost suffering a collapse of their programme in consequence. Exact figures for sales are not easy to come by, and certainly cannot be obtained from Dassault, but the biggest customer is probably South Africa, which has bought several versions and now makes the latest available kind of Mirage under licence. Total sales of all versions must amount to about 1700, more than 1000 of these being for export. Few jets of any kind have notched up the 1000 mark in exports, and it would be unfair to suggest that the chief reason for the Mirage's success is lack of competition.

In fact, Dassault has plenty of competition, partly from the massive political and financial power of the United States, which beat the French company in the first NATO fighter deal in 1960 (which went to the F–104 Starfighter) and beat it again in 1975 with the F–16. The other serious contender in the export market is the Soviet Union, which can undercut rivals on price and can offer increasingly formidable weapon systems in large and attractive package deals. However, despite the superpowers, Dassault's Mirage sales overseas to 23 countries continue to grow.

To a considerable degree this is the result of brilliant French salesmanship, by Dassault and government organizations in partnership, rather than because of any special brilliance in the aircraft's design. The original best-sellers, the Mirage III and the simpler Mirage 5, in which electronics are replaced by fuel or bombs, are really very limited machines which are fine for

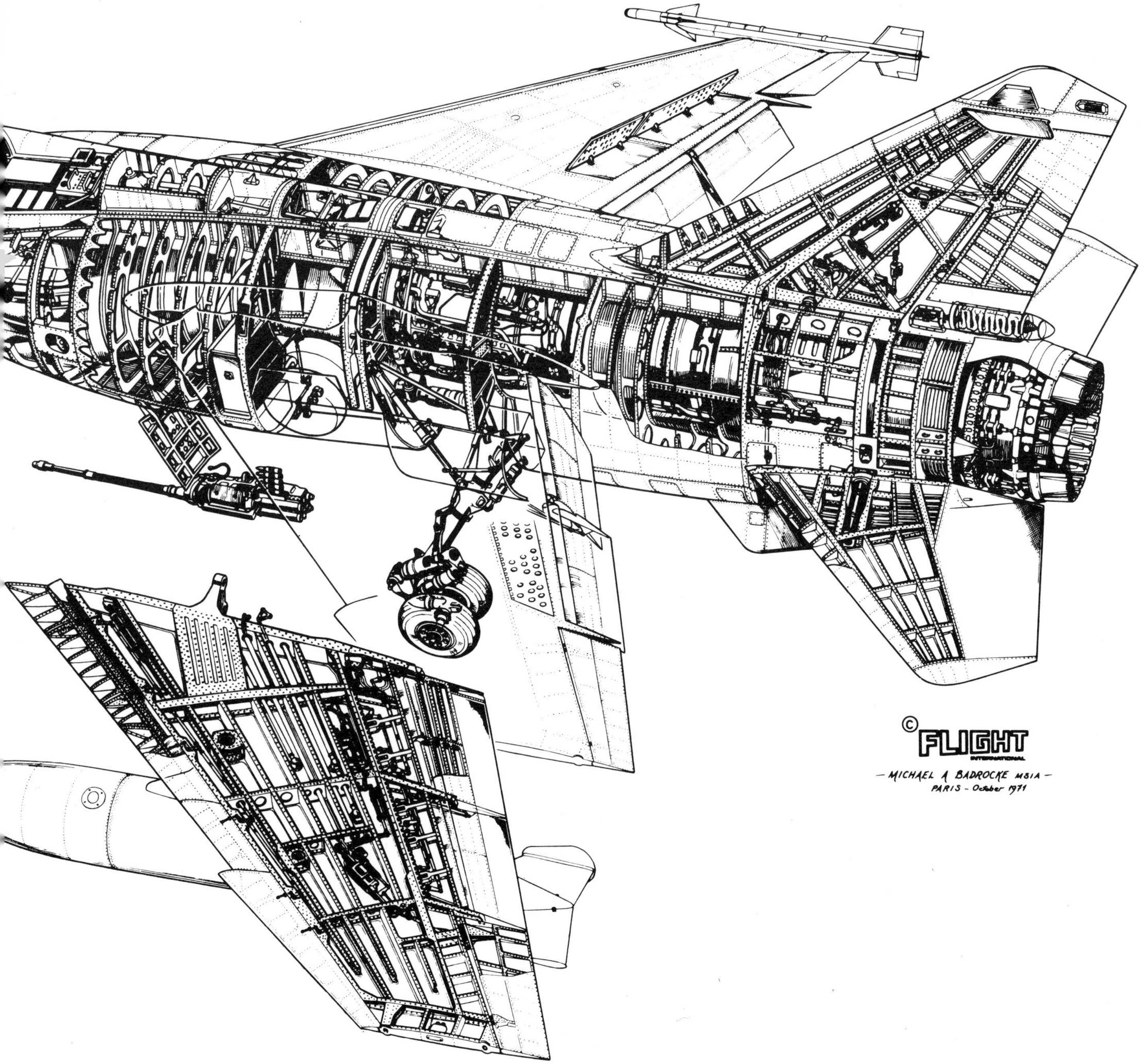
©FLIGHT
INTERNATIONAL
— MICHAEL A BADROCKE MSIA —
PARIS – October 1971

Quite unlike a delta Mirage III or 5, the trim Mirage F1 formed an ideal subject for this drawing by Mike Badrocke in 1971. Now a free-lance trading under the name of Aviagraphica, Badrocke is one of the top flight of contemporary technical artists.

SPECIFICATIONS

Mirage III and 5

Engine: (IIIC) 13 225 lb (6 000 kg) thrust (maximum afterburner) SNECMA Atar 9B single-shaft turbojet; all other versions – apart from IAI Kfir, 13 670 lb (6 200 kg) Atar 9C.

Dimensions: span 27 ft (8·22 m); length (IIIC) 50 ft 10$\frac{1}{4}$ in (15·5 m); (IIIB) 50 ft 6$\frac{1}{4}$ in (15·4 m), (5) 51 ft (15·55 m); height 13 ft 11$\frac{1}{2}$ in (4·25 m).

Weights: empty (IIIC) 13 570 lb (6 156 kg); (IIIE) 15 540 lb (7 050 kg); (IIIR) 14 550 lb (6 600 kg); (IIIB) 13 820 lb (6 270 kg); (5) 14 550 lb (6 600 kg); loaded (IIIC) 19 700 lb (8 936 kg); (IIIE, IIIR, 5) 29 760 lb (13 500 kg), (IIIB) 26 455 lb (12 000 kg).

Performance: maximum speed (all models, clean) 863 mph (1 390 km/h) (Mach 1·14) at sea level, 1 460 mph (2 350 km/h) (Mach 2·2) at altitude; initial climb, over 16 400 ft (5 000 m)/min (time to 36 090 ft, 11 000 m, 3 min); service ceiling (Mach 1·8) 55 775 ft (17 000 m); range (clean) at altitude about 1 000 miles (1 610 km); combat radius in attack mission with bombs and tanks (mix not specified) 745 miles (1 200 km); ferry range with three external tanks 2 485 miles (4 000 km).

A photograph taken in June 1970, showing a Mirage F1. Dassault spent years working on single- and twin-engined G-models, then developed the fixed-wing Super Mirage and finally switched to the small Mirage 2000 delta.

peacetime training but incapable of real effectiveness in any war involving sophisticated electronics, devastated runways, long distances or bad weather. To get over the problem of take-off from blasted runways Dassault devoted vast efforts, at government expense, to creating a jet-lift Mirage III-V which was eventually abandoned. Further prolonged work was hoped to lead to a bigger Mirage, the IIIT, and then on to an equally large machine with a high-mounted swept wing and tail, the F2. However, work then centred on the Mirage G series with variable-geometry swing-wings, which led to the G8 with two engines and thence to the Super Mirage with two new M53 engines and a fixed swept wing. This was abandoned in 1976 and replaced by a smaller and simpler machine, the Mirage 2000, which it is hoped will be built for the Armée de l'Air alongside yet another model, the excellent Mirage F1. The F1, first flown in 1966, is simply an F2 scaled down to accommodate a single Atar engine, and it is at present the most important production version. Of course it looks nothing like the original tail-less deltas, and though it has a much smaller wing, it carries far more fuel and a much heavier weapon load, and can use smaller airfields. It is this version that is being made in South Africa, and it is also selling fast to all the largest and most prosperous Arab nations. Predictably, several versions are on offer with one or two seats and different equipment ranges, as was done with the delta Mirages. Production is shared by Dassault with several other companies, especially the nationalized group Aérospatiale, the Belgian aircraft industry and the Spanish company CASA.

In 1976 Dassault set course yet again with the first of three prototypes of the Mirage 2000, which to the surprise of many is once more a tail-less delta. Such a machine cannot rival the lifting efficiency of a conventional aircraft, such as the Mirage F1, but the 2000 is far more advanced than the original Mirages. It has a radically different wing with high-lift, camber-changing leading edges which, with an American developed technology called CCV (control-configured vehicle), dramatically improve manoeuvrability. The engine is the more powerful M53, the control system is of the electrically signalled 'fly by wire' type, there are to be new navigation, instrumentation and weapon-aiming systems of the kind long since used in non-French fighters, and the airframe will also incorporate titanium and fibre-reinforced composite materials. It is hoped the Mirage 2000 will go into service in 1982, giving French industry a welcome shot in the arm. Dassault describe the 2000 as 'far superior' to the F-16 and other rivals, but do not explain how. Like the original Mirage III it would appear to be a nice little dogfighter but severely limited in other missions.

These limitations have prompted Dassault to fly a prototype of a much larger aircraft, the Delta Super Mirage. Not ordered by the Armée de l'Air, this twin-M53 engined machine would look like a bigger Mirage 2000, and its development is being paid for, we are told, by Dassault. As similar aircraft tax the resources of complete countries working in a partnership, with government orders to back them up, we can begin to see that there must be a special set of rules that apply only to Dassault. However, before making a judgement, we had better wait and see what happens to the proposed Delta Super Mirage.

McDonnell Douglas F-4 Phantom

The McDonnell Aircraft Company, abbreviated to MCAIR within the giant McDonnell Douglas Corporation but popularly known as MAC – a happy choice because James S. McDonnell's ancestors came from Scotland – is one of the younger companies among the world's combat aircraft builders. It really started only after the Second World War with the original FH–1 Phantom, the first jet designed from scratch to operate from carriers. Concentrating on the most advanced kinds of supersonic fighter, McDonnell built an unsurpassed reputation, with designs that were bold and at the very limits of technology yet which, with one exception, because of a total collapse of the engine programme, delivered the goods and put muscle into the US Navy and Air Force. Then in 1958 there took off from the company's home base at Lambert Field (St Louis Airport) the prototype XF4H–1 Phantom II. It was enormous for a fighter, and had a weird brutish appearance, with extraordinary up-sloping wings and down-sloping tailplanes that later made a major in the USAF say: 'When I first saw a Phantom, I thought it so ugly I wondered if it had been delivered upside-down'. It was a set-back for those who cling to the belief that successful aircraft, and especially, successful fighters, have to look lithe and graceful, for the Phantom has been unquestionably the world's No 1 combat aircraft during the 1960s and 1970s.

One of my favourite sayings (it was said by a Douglas Aircraft man when Eastern and TWA bought the TriStar in 1968, thereby seemingly putting an end to the DC–10) is: 'The game has not yet been fully played out.' Many times, when it looked as if all was lost, that statement has brought comfort and proved to be justified. It certainly applied to MAC's management when, in May 1953, the Navy picked its rival, Chance Vought, to build its first supersonic fighter. Most companies might have called it a day, but MAC went ahead instead and gradually put together a proposal for a larger missile-armed fighter which the Navy accepted in principle in July 1955. It was powered by two of General Electric's new J79 turbojets, with variable-incidence compressor stator blading and many other new features, boldly installed in between the first fully variable supersonic inlets and nozzle systems ever fitted to a fighter. The broad but thin wing had folding outer panels with extended leading

Splendid portrait of F4H–1 No 145 310 engaged in stores-separation trials, probably in the neighbourhood of China Lake in 1959. This was the 11th of 47 of this type, later re-styled F–4A.

edges but no trailing-edge controls, while the inner wings had drooping leading edges, inboard ailerons and broad flaps, across which was blown hot high-pressure air piped from the engines to give greatly increased lift at low speeds. The fuselage contained a powerful Westinghouse radar for all-weather interception, matched with four large Sparrow air/air missiles half-submerged in recesses in the broad flat underside. Flight development in 1958 showed exceptional performance, with greater promise than a rival XF8U–3 by Vought, which had only three missiles, one engine and one seat. The Phantom carried a radar intercept officer in the back seat.

The first Navy production order was placed for the F–4A model in December 1958. When the Navy did its own test-flying of the F–4A at Patuxent River it found that it exceeded guarantees by an unprecedented amount, the sum of all the percentage improvements adding up to 75 per cent on the plus side.

In 1959 the new fighter, which even then was simply called the Phantom without bothering about the suffix 'II', began to collect a series of world records that has never been equalled by any other type of aircraft. They included speed at height (1606 mph), speed at sea level (903 mph, in hot bumpy air), speed round various closed circuits, rates of climb to all chosen heights, absolute ceiling, coast-to-coast across the United States and, in 1966, the shortest time from New York to London. Nor was this all. Though the 1955 idea had been for a fighter pure and simple, the F–4 was so obviously capable that the inevitable happened and it soon appeared carrying 14000 lb of bombs. This was a much greater weight than could be carried by any of the attack aircraft of the USAF Tactical Air Command.

Another part of the USAF, now called Aerospace Defense Command, found that the F–4 had much better radar than any of its purpose-designed interceptors, and also higher performance and more armament. It was also obviously superior in every way to the latest tactical reconnaissance aircraft, and to cap it all it demonstrated better serviceability and lower maintenance man-hours per flight-hour than any of the latest USAF combat types. The margins were so significant that in March 1962, for the first time ever, a Navy aircraft was adopted as a standard type by the Air Force. It was a staggering achievement for a design that had never been asked for in the first place, and came about only because of the dogged persistence of MAC.

Since 1962 most of the Phantoms have gone to the USAF. The first model in volume production was the Navy/Marines F–4B, with much bigger

Frank Munger, a former colleague of Arthur Bowbeer and, like Bowbeer, ex-RAF in the Second World War, still works in the Flight *offices producing drawings as pleasing as this immensely detailed F–4M 'British Phantom'. Once such a drawing has been done, other artists find things much easier.*

SPECIFICATIONS

Types F–4A to F–4N, RF–4, QF–4
Engines: (B, G) two 17 000 lb (7711 kg) thrust General Electric J79–8 single-shaft turbojets with afterburner; (C, D) 17 000 lb J79–15; (E, EJ, F) 17 900 lb (8120 kg) J79–17; (J, N) 17 900 lb (8120 kg) J79–10; (K, M) 20 515 lb (9305 kg) Rolls-Royce Spey 202/203 two-shaft augmented turbofans.

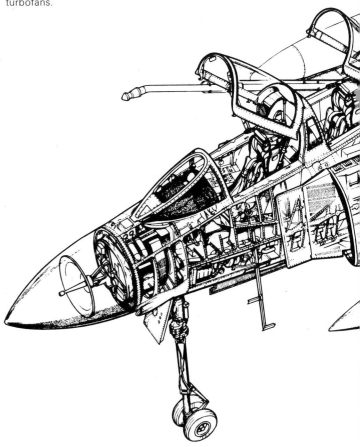

Dimensions: span 38 ft 5 in (11·7 m); length (B, C, D, G, J, N) 58 ft 3 in (17·76 m); (E, EJ, F and all RF versions) 62 ft 11 in or 63 ft (19·2 m); (K, M) 57 ft 7 in (17·55 m); height (all) 16 ft 3 in (4·96 m).
Weights: empty (B, C, D, G, J, N) 28 000 lb (12 700 kg); (E, EJ, F and RF) 29 000 lb (13 150 kg); (K, M) 31 000 lb (14 060 kg); maximum loaded (B) 54 600 lb; (C, D, G, J, K, M, N, RF) 58 000 lb (26 308 kg); (E, EJ, F) 60 630 lb (27 502 kg).
Performance: maximum speed with Sparrow missiles only (low) 910 mph (1464 km/h, Mach 1·19) with J79 engines, 920 mph with Spey, (high) 1 500 mph (2 414 km/h, Mach 2·27) with J79 engines, 1 386 mph with Spey; initial climb, typically 28 000 ft (8 534 m)/min with J79 engines, 32 000 ft/min with Spey; service ceiling, over 60 000 ft (19 685 m) with J79 engines, 60 000 ft with Spey; range on internal fuel (no weapons) about 1 750 miles (2 817 km); ferry range with external fuel, typically 2 300 miles (3 700 km) (E and variants, 2 600 miles (4 184 km).

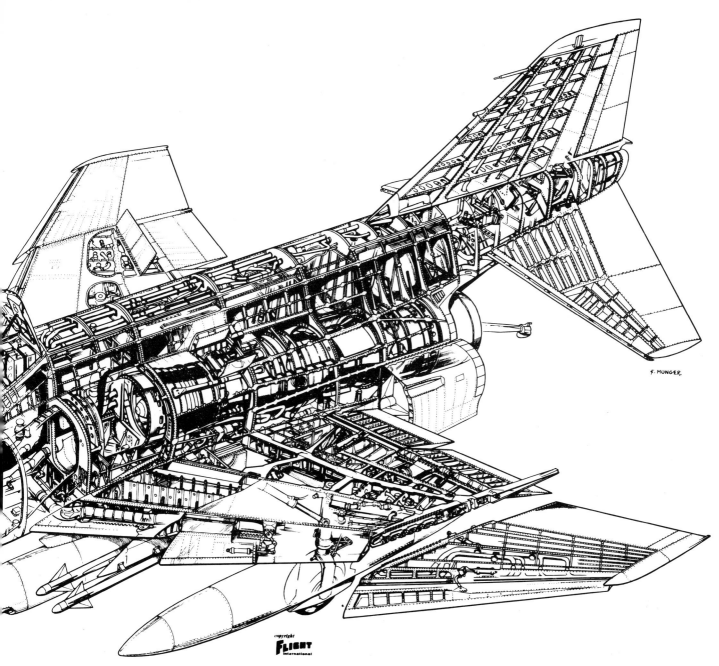

F. MUNGER.

copyright
FLIGHT
international

An F–4D of the US Air Force (serial 66–7591) seen landing at Shaw AFB, South Caroline, in October 1967.

Above: *Fairly bristling with sensors and defensive electronics, this F–4B (No 153 018) assigned to VF–114 aboard USS Kitty Hawk was photographed during a mission over North Vietnam in March 1968. It is armed with AIM–7E Sparrows and AIM–9C/D Sidewinders.*

Centre: *Grand-daddy of them all, the original XF4H–1 (serial 142 259), flying with a single test pilot and dummy Sparrows near the St Louis plant in 1958.*
Below: *An F–4J (155 825) of the second-generation type that replaced the F–4B in US Navy fighter squadrons. This*

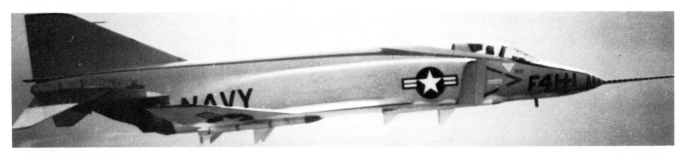

nose radar than the A and a raised canopy to give better view on the approach. The USAF bought the F–4C, a minimum-change model with a flight-refuelling boom receptacle instead of a probe, a rear cockpit equipped for a rated pilot, large wheels and more powerful anti-skid brakes and many other changes, including completely different inertial navigation and weapon-delivery systems. Soon the unarmed RF–4C reconnaissance aircraft appeared, packed with cameras, radars, infra-red linescan, ECM (electronic countermeasures) and electronic intelligence systems, and later the Marines bought the RF–4B. In 1964, when over 1 000 Phantoms had been delivered to the Air Force, permission was granted for a version tailored specially to Air Force needs, and the F–4D introduced completely new electronics for navigation, fire-control and weapon delivery. The Navy and Marines followed the B with the J, with a dramatically advanced AWG–10 pulse-doppler radar and many other new items in an improved airframe with more power and better high-lift systems. The Royal Navy bought the K (called Phantom FG.1 in Britain) with more powerful Rolls-Royce Spey engines and an ultra-high-lift airframe containing many British parts and equipment. The RAF chose the M (Phantom FGR.2), a multi-role development of the K with even greater capability.

In the mid-1960s the F–4B and C began to be drawn into the tragic conflict in south-east Asia. It soon became by far the most important of all the combat aircraft types trying to hold the Vietcong at bay, and until 1973 it was by far the best fighter, reconnaissance and interdiction aircraft in the whole theatre of the war. The hours flown and ordnance dropped by the USAF, Navy

and Marine units involved, in many cases exceed comparable statistics for the Second World War, and the opposition grew ever more intense. Techniques were developed for finding hidden jungle targets, pinpointing trucks or parking areas on dark nights, and working in close partnership with lightplane or 'fast mover' FACs (Forward Air Controllers) or the big night-interdiction gunships, such as the AC–130 Hercules and AC–119K Shadow. These often did the killing while the Phantom suppressed 'triple A' (anti-aircraft artillery) fire. New ordnance appeared under the Phantom's broad wings, including improved Sidewinder and Sparrow missiles for shooting down the MiG–17 and –21, Bullpup guided air/ground rockets, Walleye glide bombs with pinpoint TV guidance, Shrike and Standard ARM for homing on to hostile radars, and a great variety of Hobos (homing bomb system) and Paveway 'smart' weapons with electro-optical or laser guidance for hitting difficult targets. To help protect the Phantom against the defending radars, Triple A and SAMs (surface-to-air missiles), a wide variety of 'defensive electronics' appeared, including ECM jammers, deception systems, warning devices and even free-flight decoys, as well as the latest thinking in the long history of 'chaff' – millions of slivers of metal or metallized plastics which, when released as a cloud behind an aircraft, present a highly reflective target which causes primitive radars to become confused. Taken together, these developments represent the main recent history of tactical air operations, and the Phantom was at the centre of all of them; but the basic Phantom possessed two major deficiencies.

It had been designed to operate at relatively

The only Phantoms not assembled at St Louis are the 128 F–4EJ models of the Japan Air Self-Defence Force, nearly all of which were made in Japan and assembled by Mitsubishi at Nagoya. Japan's RF–4EJ reconnaissance aircraft were made and assembled at St Louis.

light weights, carrying just air-to-air missiles, intercept at high altitude and return afterwards to a carrier. Instead, it was now engaging in violent manoeuvres at just over treetop height whilst carrying many tons of ordnance. Dozens of aircraft were to reveal a shortcoming in their handling, which had not much bothered the Navy in the early days: pulling back on the control column at moderate speeds, especially when heavily loaded, produced a vicious stall and fatal spin. The other deficiency was lack of an internally mounted gun. True, most Phantoms could carry up to three of the deadly SUU–16A or –23A 'Gatling' gun pods, each firing up to 6000 cannon shells a minute, but pilots wanted a precision tool for air combat, a gun built-in on the centreline. According to the most distinguished pilot in the Vietnam war, Col (as he then was) Robin Olds, 'A fighter without a gun ... is like an airplane without a wing'. This was always true, but back in the 1950s it had been forgotten.

The result of this was the final basic model of the Phantom, the F–4E, with the APQ–120 solid-state miniaturised radar, extra fuel, more powerful, 17 900 lb-thrust J79–17 engines, an M61 gun and 640-round tank of ammunition in the underside of the nose, and, from 1972, a new wing (since retrofitted to earlier E-models) with extremely powerful leading-edge slats. Variants of the E include the RF–4E multi-sensor reconnaissance aircraft and the F–4F simplified fighter, both for the West German Luftwaffe, the F–4EJ made in Japan, and the EF–4E Wild Weasel specialised ECM version, which either protects other attack aircraft or penetrates hostile airspace on its own as a self-protecting hunter/killer. The F–4N and S are late Navy and Marines models resulting from structural rebuild and updating programmes.

Today I am waiting for the publicity picture from St Louis that will show a Phantom with '5 GRAND' painted on it, because No 5000 is about to go out of the assembly plant door. Though big and expensive, it is such a fine machine that it has sold to air forces all over the world, and I would be surprised if any fighter in the Western world which may follow the Phantom reaches half its production total. More than half the Phantoms built have seen action, many of them over Israel; and the British models daily roar off to inspect probing Soviet Zombies (electronic intelligence aircraft). Modern fighters work hard; many Phantoms have logged more than 3000 hours flight time, or as much as five typical squadrons of Spitfires in the Second World War, where 50 hours was an average lifetime. And to log 3000 hours in the old days without ever scratching the paint would have been incredible, whereas with the Phantom today it is routine.

Seen from the ground the Phantom looks sinister, makes sonorous organ-pipe noises and leaves a trail of black smoke. On board, it exudes strength and familiarity. Though no longer new, it is still impressive, and capable of doing a first-class military job. In the course of time fighter pilots will have to make the transition to other sorts of fighter, some of which may be long-range interceptors (such as MAC's own masterpiece, the F–15 Eagle) and others nimble dogfighters, such as the F–16. A few, notably Grumman's F–14 Tomcat, try to excel at everything, as did the Phantom. But for a while at least nearly all fighter pilots in the Western world will have learned their trade in the Phantom, and that highly durable ordnance platform has a special place in their affections.